Artificial Intelligence for Legal System

Artificial intelligence and technological advancements are continuously transforming the discipline of law in contemporary times. This book offers practical insights to the reader as to how technology is influencing the judicial and criminal justice system throughout the world. It includes case studies explaining and depicting real-time application of legal technological advancements from different countries.

- Examining how data-driven approaches, such as big data analytics and data mining, are revolutionizing legal practices, including legal research, case prediction, and decision support systems
- Investigating the use of artificial intelligence technologies, such as chatbots, virtual assistants, and document automation, in legal processes, including contract review, legal document drafting, and client interaction
- Exploring how blockchain technology is being implemented in areas such as smart contracts, evidence management, and secure data sharing, enhancing transparency, security, and efficiency in the legal field
- Addressing the ethical considerations and challenges associated with the use of AI in the legal profession, including issues of bias, privacy, accountability, and the need for ethical frameworks and guidelines
- Analyzing the potential influence of emerging technologies, such as quantum computing, internet of things (IoT), and augmented reality, on legal practices, court proceedings, and dispute resolution mechanisms

The book is useful for researchers, scholars, and practitioners working in Law & Technology and Information Technology.

Artificial Intelligence for Legal System

Jurisprudence in the Digital Age

Edited by
Smita Gupta, Namita Singh Malik, Ardyllis Alves Soares, B. Balamurugan, and Sneha Dhillon

CRC Press
Taylor & Francis Group
Boca Raton London New York

CRC Press is an imprint of the
Taylor & Francis Group, an **informa** business
A CHAPMAN & HALL BOOK

Designed cover image: ShutterStock

First edition published 2026
by CRC Press
2385 NW Executive Center Drive, Suite 320, Boca Raton FL 33431

and by CRC Press
4 Park Square, Milton Park, Abingdon, Oxon, OX14 4RN

CRC Press is an imprint of Taylor & Francis Group, LLC

Library of Congress Cataloging-in-Publication Data
Names: Gupta, Smita, editor. | Malik, Namita Singh, editor. | Soares, Ardyllis Alves, editor. |
Balusamy, Balamurugan, editor. | Dhillon, Sneha, editor.
Title: Artificial intelligence for legal system : jurisprudence in the digital age / edited by Smita Gupta, Namita Singh Malik, Ardyllis Alves Soares, B. Balamurugan, and Sneha Dhillon.
Description: Boca Raton : C&H/ CRC Press, 2026. | Includes bibliographical references and index. |
Summary: "Artificial intelligence and technological advancements are continuously transforming the discipline of law in contemporary times. This book offers practical insights to the reader as to how technology is influencing the judicial and criminal justice system throughout the world. It includes case studies explaining and depicting real time application of legal technological advancements from different countries. 1. Examining how data-driven approaches, such as big data analytics and data mining, are revolutionizing legal practices, including legal research, case prediction, and decision support systems 2. Investigating the use of artificial intelligence technologies, such as chatbots, virtual assistants, and document automation, in legal processes, including contract review, legal document drafting, and client interaction 3. Exploring how blockchain technology is being implemented in areas such as smart contracts, evidence management, and secure data sharing, enhancing transparency, security, and efficiency in the legal field 4. Addressing the ethical considerations and challenges associated with the use of AI in the legal profession, including issues of bias, privacy, accountability, and the need for ethical frameworks and guidelines 5. Analyzing the potential influence of emerging technologies, such as quantum computing, internet of things (IoT), and augmented reality, on legal practices, court proceedings, and dispute resolution mechanisms The book is useful for researchers, scholars and practitioners working in Law & Technology and Information Technology"– Provided by publisher.
Identifiers: LCCN 2025028757 (print) | LCCN 2025028758 (ebook) | ISBN 9781032776736 (hardback) |
ISBN 9781032794273 (paperback) | ISBN 9781003491903 (ebook)
Subjects: LCSH: Artificial intelligence–Law and legislation–United States.
Classification: LCC KF390.5.C6 A78 2026 (print) | LCC KF390.5.C6 (ebook) |
DDC 340.0285/63–dc23/eng/20250626
LC record available at https://lccn.loc.gov/2025028757
LC ebook record available at https://lccn.loc.gov/2025028758

ISBN: 9781032776736 (hbk)
ISBN: 9781032794273 (pbk)
ISBN: 9781003491903 (ebk)

DOI: 10.1201/9781003491903

Typeset in Times
by Newgen Publishing UK

Contents

Preface

The book titled Artificial Intelligence for Legal System: Jurisprudence in the Digital Age *aims to* provide readers with a deep understanding of the impact of rapid advancements in AI and Technology on the legal system. It has a multidisciplinary approach which makes it interesting for readers from diverse fields, such as law, sociology, psychology, technology, and ethics to indulge in active reading. It provides a deeper understanding of the impact of rapid advancements in AI and Technology on the legal system and the challenges and opportunities presented by this interrelation. It addresses the issue of rapid advancements in Artificial Intelligence and Technology and how it is impacting the legal system around the world. It also addresses the scope of AI, Automation, and Technology in Justice delivery system.

The chapters written by authors dive into the neighboring perspectives on AI & Legal Policy, exploring the interactions among technology and areas of law such as Cyber Forensics, Data Protection, and Technology Rights and covering the areas of technological law enforcement in fair trial vis-a-vis human rights. The book explores the challenges and opportunities presented by the use of technology in ensuring fair trials and protecting human rights which would examine issues such as data privacy, bias in algorithms, and the impact of technology on legal proceedings while also considering the potential benefits of technology in promoting access to justice and increasing efficiency in the legal system.

The book delves further deep into the subject to explore some of the unanswered questions and challenges that arise when artificial intelligence (AI) is applied in the legal system.

Through this book, we intend to highlight if AI-based systems could be identified as victims in the future. Fixing liability in the age of AI is challenging, crucial, and ever-evolving with generative AI.

It dives deep to assess the crisscrossed wires of Law, Literature, and Technology, examining the role of AI in Judgment writing, art of Lawyering, and Justice Delivery. It analyses the intersection of law, literature, and technology and investigates the ways in which AI is transforming the legal profession.

The book navigates various Technological Law Enforcement, such as Cyber fingerprint, Hacking and Law Enforcement and Coding, Automation and Investigative policies etc. Besides this, this book narrates the complexities of applying AI to legal policies across different jurisdictions and the challenges that arise when technological advancements outpace legal frameworks.

The book further examines the Automated Legal Forecasting in Arenas of Court Crafting, the acceptability of Automated Legal Systems in popular culture and the reality or utopia of AI-based legal systems.

Through this book, we aim to provide a comprehensive understanding of the interrelation between Law, Artificial Intelligence, and Technology, and how rapid advancements in these fields are impacting the legal system. Various dimensions of the interrelationship, includes technological law enforcement, fairness in trials, human rights, psychological and sociological impacts, and the adaptability of current procedural laws to technologically driven legal systems.

The book's multidisciplinary approach makes it suitable for readers from diverse fields, such as law, sociology, psychology, technology, and ethics. It is a must-read for those who wish to gain a deeper understanding of the impact of rapid advancements in AI and Technology on the legal system and the challenges and opportunities presented by this interrelation.

Our endeavor is to enhance knowledge corpus of Techno-Legal Professionals working in the area of Law, Artificial Intelligence and Technology, Cyber Security, and Intellectual Property Rights. It shall also serve practising advocates and judges by leveraging them in their field of practice. The book is also crucial for professors and students of law and technology to develop their understanding on the subject.

We shall feel honored and elated if upon reading the chapters written by different authors each bringing their own perspective, the readers are better placed with the convergence of Law, Artificial Intelligence, and Technology.

About the Editors

Smita Gupta, PhD, is a professor at School of Law, Galgotias University. She has a teaching experience of more than 20 years in interdisciplinary areas of law and social sciences. Her area of interest lies in exploring multifaced dimensions of law with special focus on associative links of sociological perspective. She believes that an interdisciplinary research and teaching will bring far ranging results in the academic study of law and in placing lawyer as a social engineer. She has a keen interest in exploring areas of socio-legal philosophy, gender studies, AI, society etc.

Namita Singh Malik, PhD, is working as Professor at School of Law, Galgotias University, India. She has 19 years of experience in the field of Law. Her teaching and research interest lies in the area of Gender Studies, Criminal laws, Forensic Science, Law, and Technology. She has more than 25 research paper presentation and publications.

Ardyllis Alves Soares did PhD and Master's Degree in Law from UFRGS, with a doctoral internship at Justus-Liebig-Universität Giessen – Germany, postdoctoral internship in International Law from the University Center of Brasília – CEUB (2019–2023), specialist in International Law from UFRGS and in Business Law from IBMEC/RJ, and Diplôme d'Université in European and French Contract Law from Université de Savoie – France. He was a legal consultant to the Ministry of Justice/SENACON for the themes of Consumer and Tourism, hired by UNESCO, and Consumer Relations and Persons with Disabilities, hired by UNDP, and Lawyer. He was a legal consultant to the UN Tourism for the themes of Latin American and Caribbean Tourism Law, hired by IDB.

B. Balamurugan is currently working as Professor and Chairperson in the School of Engineering and IT, Manipal University, Dubai prior to this assignment he was Professor and Associate Dean Academics in Shiv Nadar Institution of Eminence , Delhi-NCR. Stanford University has recently released an update of the list that represents the top 2% of the most-cited scientists in various disciplines. He is part of the Top 2% Scientists Worldwide 2023 by Stanford University in the area of Data Science/AI/ML. He is also an Adjunct Professor, Department of Computer Science & Information Engineering, Taylor University, Malaysia. Prior to this assignment he was Professor, School of Computing Sciences & Engineering and Director International Relations at Galgotias University, Greater Noida, India. His contributions focus on Engineering Education, Block chain and Data Sciences. His Academic degrees and twelve years of experience working as a Faculty in a global University like VIT University, Vellore has made him more receptive and prominent in his domain. He does have 200 plus high impact factor papers in Springer, Elsevier and IEEE. He has done more than 200 edited and authored books and collaborated with eminent professors across the world from top QS ranked university. He has served up to the position of Associate Professor in his stint of 15 years of experience with VIT University, Vellore. His passion is teaching and adapts different design thinking principles while delivering his lectures. He has published 80+ books on various technologies and visited 15 plus countries for his technical course. He has several top-notch conferences in his resume and has published over 200 of quality journal, conference and book chapters combined. He serves in the Expert Advisory Panel Member for several start-ups and forums and does consultancy work for industry on Industrial IOT. He has given over 210 talks in various events and symposium. He has travelling more than 15 countries for his academic and research assignments and talks. He has spearheaded ,hosted and conducted more than 10 IEEE and ACM International conferences up to date.

Sneha Dhillon is an Assistant Professor of Law at Bharati Vidyapeeth (deemed to be) University, New Law College, Pune. She works on technology-related legal issues, especially how artificial intelligence affects society, individual rights, and the justice system. Her research covers topics like dating apps and algorithms, LGBTQ+ representation in digital media, intellectual property, and the delays in arbitration processes. As the editor of this book on Artificial Intelligence for Legal System, she brings a practical and thoughtful approach to understanding how new technologies are shaping legal thinking and everyday life.

Contributors

Anindita Bhattacharjee
Ph.D. Research Scholar, West Bengal National University of Juridical Sciences
Kolkata, India

Shreya Chatterjee
Assistant Professor (Senior)
KIIT University
India

Riya Chugh
School of Law, Ideal Institute of Management & Technology
Affiliated to GGSIP University, Delhi
India

Basil N. Darlong Diengdoh
Assistant Professor
National Law University Meghalaya
India

Nguyen Phuong Dung
Associate Lecturer (Law)
Department of Economics and Finance
The Business School, RMIT University
Vietnam

Jake Okechukwu Effoduh
Assistant Professor
Lincoln Alexander School of Law
Toronto Metropolitan University
Canada

Reva Gupta
Research Scholar, Galgotias University
Department of Law, Gautam Buddha Nagar
Greater Noida, India

Ripal Gupta
National Forensic Sciences University
Gujarat
India

Jura Golub
Research Assistant and PhD Candidate
University of Osijek – Faculty of Law
Croatia

Vu Truc Hanh
Lecturer, The School of Law
University of Economics Ho Chi Minh City (UEH)
Vietnam

Christian Kaunert
Professor
Dublin City University, Ireland
& University of South Wales UK

Gagandeep Kaur
Associate Professor
UPES University, Dehradun
India

Malcolm Katrak
Assistant Professor, Jindal Global Law School
O.P. Jindal Global University, India
John W. Graham and York Graduate Fellow Osgoode Hall Law School,
York University, Canada.

Lisa P Lukose
Professor
University School of Law and Legal Studies, (USLLS)
Director, Legal Aid, GGS Indraprastha University (GGSIPU)
New Delhi, India

Alankrita Mathur
Assistant Professor
Department of Law
Maharaja Agrasen Institute of Management Studies
(Affiliated to GGS Indraprastha University (GGSIPU))
New Delhi, India

Yogesh Mishra
Assistant Professor
National Law University
Meghalaya
India

Abhinash Mohanta
Ph. D Scholar
KIIT University
India

Mudassir Nazir
Assistant Professor
Department of Law, Galgotias University
Gautam Buddha Nagar
Greater Noida
India

Navtika Singh Nautiyal
Assistant Professor
National Forensic Sciences University
New Delhi
India

Foram Patel
Nirma University
Gujarat
India

Megha Patel
Advocate
High Court of Gujarat, Bharat
India

Bommuluri Bhavana Rao
Faculty of Law
University of Delhi
India

Lorayne Finol Romero
Professor at the Faculty of Law
Universidad Central de Chile
Chile

Jasdeep Singh
Assistant Professor-III, Amity Law School Noida
Amity University
Uttar Pradesh
India

Bhupinder Singh
Professor
Sharda University
Greater Noida
India

Sneha
KIIT University
India

1 Artificial Intelligence in the Realm of Justice

Revisit to the Jurisprudential Notions of Justice

Lisa P Lukose and Alankrita Mathur

1.1 INTRODUCTION

The governance structure holds importance in any civilised society. Good governance signifies the way an administration improves the standard of living of the members of its society by creating and making the basic amenities of life available, providing its people security and the opportunity to make their life better, instilling hope in their hearts for a promising future providing on an equal and equitable basis, accessing to opportunities for personal growth, affording participation and capacity to influence in the decision-making in public affairs, sustaining a responsive judicial system which dispenses justice on merits in a fair, unbiased, and meaningful manner, and maintaining accountability and honesty in each wing or functionary of the Government (Brar, 2018, p. 256). The 'rule of law' holds importance in any good governance setup and for the same, a free, fair, and independent judiciary is imperative for not only establishing but also promoting the very concept. The judiciary acts as a balancing wheel to keep a check upon the arbitrariness and guard against injustices.

When we keep a society marked by digitalisations and digitally assisted functionalities as a reference point, the intricacies of digitisation of the judicial system, the virtual courtrooms, e-judgments and especially the 'e-judges' deserve special analysis as to their potentialities – advantages and disadvantages. The incorporation of artificial intelligence (AI) tools into the judicial system and particularly in the processes of decision-making and delivering a judgement (which is crucial element of 'administration of justice') has been perceived from different perspectives by various stake holders. On one side, such digitisation of the judicial system is supported and promoted as being a facilitator of removing barriers related to traditional approaches to judicial systems, like case filings, access to case records, difficulties in attending case hearings, etc. On the other side (although a minor section only), the digitisation is not appreciated in the wake of challenges being posed by data privacy, data integrity, cyber threats, and disinclination of court staff and lawyers to adapt with the pace of technology, etc.

Furthermore, the idea of use of software to replace the human judges is gaining momentum as such replacement allegedly relaxes the burden of pendency (AI machine being much faster in operation than humans) upon the present functioning structure

DOI: 10.1201/9781003491903-1

and increases the accuracy and efficiency. However, going by the strict jurisprudential understanding of the notions of 'justice', the very idea of replacing the human judges or to have in place the non-human judges seems to be quite misplaced idea. The reduction of a decision-making body to a mere data processor (Sourdin & Cornes, 2018 as cited in Sourdin & Zariski, 2018) is seriously neither commendable nor desirable. The potentiality of algorithm being flawed resultantly perpetuating inequalities and the limitations of AI machine to render reasoned decision simply cannot be ruled out in the wake of AI being still at the nascent stage so far the current context is concerned. This article in its second part shall make an attempt to throw light upon the technical aspects and working of AI to have a basic understanding of the same and also explore its multidimensional aspects with a view to assess the role of AI in the judicial system. The third part of this article shall be a critical analysis of the meaning of 'justice' through jurisprudential notions. The conceptual understanding of the same is needed for the structural appreciation of the utilisation of AI in the administration of justice. The fourth part shall be reflecting upon the placement of idea of AI tools or to be more specific, the 'AI-Judges' into the realm of 'administration of justice', and the last part shall appropriately conclude the article.

1.2 ABOUT ARTIFICIAL INTELLIGENCE

In the simplest term, AI is technology that enables computers and machines to simulate human intelligence and problem-solving capabilities (What is Artificial Intelligence (AI)? [n.d.]). It indicates the simulation of human intelligence processes by computers through coding. AI can perform tasks that would otherwise require human intelligence or intervention (What is Artificial Intelligence (AI)? [n.d.]). The artificial intelligence through simulations produces outcomes which have been generally human driven for very long. The term 'artificial intelligence' is an umbrella term touching not only the computer science – technical aspects, for example, machine learning, neural networking, deep learning, natural language processing, robotics, computer vision, expert systems, etc. (Guess, 2016) but it also possesses social, economic, and legal dimensions of its operations.

1.2.1 Technical Aspects

In brief, a large amount of data is collected and applied through algorithms as a 'training model' for the AI machine to work. Such training models are basically created to familiarise the AI regarding the domain of interest. After the said first step, i.e., once the machine is acquainted with the domain, then the machine is to process the information making choices and evaluations from the data fed to it (Thaler, 1996, as cited in Clifford, 1997, pp. 1679–80). Such training contains the ranking of quality of each input design (Thaler, 1996, as cited in Clifford, 1997, p. 1680). Once initialised, the machine starts producing outputs, and further by using those outputs again and again, it sets a pattern. Such creations are *sans* human intervention, something 'new', not commanded by the developer through coding and commonly termed as 'computational creativity' (Computational Creativity, 2024).

1.2.2 Multidimensional Aspects of AI

The social impact of AI is both profound and multifaceted, touching nearly every aspect of modern life (The Social Impact of Artificial Intelligence: Opportunities and Challenges, n.d.). The integration of AI into various aspects of life of a human has influenced the same in numerous ways. The benefits, AI assimilation has accorded, are multiple, from easing access, increasing efficiency and accuracy to saving on time and labour. With its remarkable features ranging from enhanced safety, reduced human error, improved decision-making process and advancement in R&D, it has enabled exponential progress in the fields of education, transportation, banking, healthcare, defence, business and manufacturing sector, etc.

However, such integration has many disadvantages as well, privacy concern being the biggest one. Disadvantages include the high cost of installation, unemployment risk, lack of inherent creativity, biased decisions because of biased algorithms, security issues (being vulnerable to cyber-attacks), lack of human affection and empathy, which may be required by various sectors like education and healthcare, etc.

1.3 JUSTICE: MEANING AND CONCEPTUAL UNDERSTANDING THROUGH JURISPRUDENTIAL NOTIONS

At an earlier period of Roman history, Cicero had described justice as 'the disposition of the human mind to render to everyone his due' (Bodenheimer, 1974, p. 208). The need for justice grows out of the conflict of human interests (Carver, 1915). That is to say, if there were no conflict of interests among mankind we should never have invented the word justice, nor conceived the idea for which it stands (Carver, 1915). The rules related to 'justice' embodies the idea that the legal structure must strive for equity and fairness. The emphasis is on the element of non-arbitrariness, i.e., laws must be applied impartially and equally. The jurisprudential journey based on different theories of law provides different meanings and orientations to the term 'justice'.

As per the natural school of jurisprudence, notions of 'justice' had strict relations with ethics, morality, and eternal law (Finnis, 2024 as cited in Zalta & Nodelman, 2024). While the positivists accord different meaning to the term law and consequently, different meaning to the term 'justice'. For the proponents of analytical school of jurisprudence, law is a command emanating from the sovereign, namely state (Paranjape, 2010, p. 15). Jeremy Bentham, a profound thinker, acute social critic and a staunch law reformist, held justice as primarily a quality of social order regulating mutual relations of man (Paranjape, 2010, p. 18). Bentham's perception of justice is based on system of values, and each society has its own different set of values, i.e., morals (Paranjape, 2010, p. 18). All individuals living in a society must conform to these set of values and rationalise their conduct in accordance with these values, if they fail, there would be a conflict of interest and if there is no conflict of interest, there is no need for justice (Paranjape, 2010, p. 18).

Justice has a Protean face, capable of change, readily assuming different shapes, and endowed with highly variable features (Bodenheimer, 1974, p. 196). Plato, in his Republic, fashioned a doctrine of the just commonwealth strongly imbued with collective ideals (Bodenheimer, 1974, p. 197). In his view, justice consists in a harmonious relation between the various parts of the social organism (Bodenheimer, 1974, p.197). Plato members of each class must attend to their own business and perform the related duties and not meddle with the business of the members of another class (Bodenheimer, 1974, p. 197). However, for Aristotle, justice consists in equality (Bodenheimer, 1974, p. 197). Aristotle says justice consists of what is lawful and fair, with fairness involving equitable distributions and the correction of what is inequitable (Pomerleau. n.d.). A much more egalitarian view of justice was advocated by Lester Ward (Bodenheimer, 1974, p. 198). In his opinion, justice consists in the 'enforcement by society of an artificial equality in social conditions which are naturally unequal'. (Ward, 1906, as cited in Bodenheimer, 1974, p. 198).

In the jurisprudential journey of 'justice', one would find that a fundamentally divergent attitude towards the same has been taken by Herbert Spencer. For him, justice is not 'equality' rather it is 'freedom' (Bodenheimer, 1974, p. 198). Each man should be allowed to assert his selfhood, acquire property, carry on a business or vocation of his choosing, move freely from place to place, and express his thoughts and religious feelings without hindrance (Bodenheimer, 1974, p. 198). The theory of justice by John Rawls provides connotation to the term justice by combining the elements of 'freedom' and 'equality'. As per the theory, (1) each person is to have an equal right to the most basic extensive basic liberty compatible with a similar liberty for others and (2) social and economic inequalities are to be arranged so that they can reasonably be expected to be to everyone's advantage, and in such a manner that the positions and offices to which they attach are open to all (Bodenheimer, 1974, p. 198).

When we try to determine how justice can be advanced, there is a basic need for public reasoning, involving arguments coming from different quarters and divergent perspectives (Sen, 2010, p. 392). An engagement with contrary arguments does not, however, imply that we must expect to be able to settle the conflicting reasons in all cases and arrive at agreed positions on every issue (Sen, 2010, p. 392). Complete resolution is neither a requirement of a person's own rationality nor is it a condition of reasonable social choice, including a reason-based theory of justice (Sen, 2010, p. 392). Thus, 'Justice', in general, is a very wide concept. Justice is varied because men are so, and they are not fixed principles but moving complexes (Mukharji, 2016, p. 71). Secondly, mere surveying relations of law to actual human behaviour and actual social condition can never help because human behaviour and actual social conditions are themselves as much changing as justice according to individual cases (Mukharji, 2016, p.71).

1.4 ARTIFICIAL INTELLIGENCE AND JUSTICE: PLACED OR MISPLACED IDEA

From the discussions in the previous parts of this article, it is amply clear that the administration of justice is in essence beyond mere recording the case proceedings, bare applications of legal principles upon the given set of facts and placing evidences on record. The Supreme Court of India has also stated in the light of the active role to be played by the judges thus, 'it is the duty of the court to arrive at the truth and subserve the ends of justice. The courts have to take a participatory role in the trial and not act as mere tape recorders to record whatever is being stated by the witnesses'. (Courts should not act as 'mere tape recorders', 2024). In a judicial process, decision-making and writing a judgment are not simply to give an end to a litigation or just a mechanical process to be performed by the presiding judge.

The 'judgment' providing justice to the parties is based on legal reasoning. Judgement is generally considered a reasoned decision, i.e., to say there exists a reason – legally viable and logically legitimate to reach to the conclusion, which when implemented results into 'justice'. There can be no doubt whatsoever that principles of self-consistent reasoning are relevant to any aspect of legal method (Tammelo, 1970, p. 89). The disciple of thought to which these principles belong is logic. (Tammelo, 1970, p. 89). It is often seen that it is the logical analysis not only of the legal provisions but also of the evidences involved in the case, which is indispensable to arrive at a conclusion in doing justice. In reference to the application of algorithms to arrive at a decision in any legal dispute, the AI proponents often cite the competence, efficiency, fairness, and rationality presented by the AI tools to the judicial system being based on algorithms and logical equations. However, administering justice is not simply based on the mere 'logical analysis' of the arguments advanced and evidences presented in the light of prevalent legal system. One cannot be expected to write judgment using set mathematical formulas and equations in the absence of wisdom, more specifically the judicial wisdom, which a machine (AI) lacks.

'*Law is a reason free from all passion*,' said Aristotle. Logic in the field of law is necessary as judges reach the conclusion by applying the power of reasoning in accordance with logic. The 'Judgement' heavily rests upon the reasoning and this reasoning is, to a great extent, the assertion backed by logic. The legal reasoning represents a middle way between formal inference and common-sense thinking: even though legal discourse is not formal, it tends to appear in uniform and relatively structured ways, so that its patterns can be made accessible to logical analysis (Law and Logic, 2005). By applying logical analysis, judges assess the strengths and weaknesses of arguments and evidences and the relations *interse*. Such analysis (of assessing the strength and weakness of arguments/evidences on record and thus, their reliability) is not strict guarantee of delivery of justice. Having standard parameters and fixed rules to interpret through algorithms has the potential to erode the acceptance of equity principles in the realm of justice. There is no dearth of illustrations in law, which depict that despite there being strict legal principles in the landscape, the court has accepted equity principles to impart 'justice' and provide relief to the innocent parties, as the end goal is to do justice and not just to technically bring any litigation to an end.

Going by its very nature, the legal arena is neither static nor non-creative, incapable to operate without having any reference to the historical origin, customs, socio-economic situations, importance, and most importantly the spirit of the Constitution. Benjamin A. Cardozo's work titled as "*The Nature of the Judicial Process*" is noteworthy in this regard. His observations thus:

> "*What is it that I do when I decide a case? To what sources of information do I appeal for guidance? In what proportions do I permit them to contribute*

> *to the result? In what proportions ought they to contribute? If a precedent is applicable, when do I refuse to follow it? If no precedent is applicable, how do I reach the rule that will make a precedent for the future? If I am seeking logical consistency, the symmetry of the legal structure, how far shall I seek it? At what point shall the quest be halted by some discrepant custom, by some consideration of the social welfare, by my own or the common standards of justice and morals?*"
>
> (Cardozo, 1921, as cited in Goldstein, 2018, p.164)

clearly reflect upon a situation that indicates that deciding a case is not just a number game or mindless application of the precedent at hand. Tracing from the technological landscapes governing the development and operations of AI tools, the database which is fed to the machine in the form of 'training model' could be composed of precedents and illustrations but the accordance of the much required 'judicial wisdom' coming straight out of human brain is still questionable. Machines (humanly constructed artifacts) cannot think because no machine has a point of view – that is, a unique perspective on the worldly referents of its internal symbolic logic (Trenhub, 2015, p.71). AI tools, through mathematical formulas, can certainly bring consistency of treating all alike in same fashion, but definitely may fail to appreciate that at times, *in order to do justice and secure the spirit of law.* Judges do deviate on the basis of experience and context. Digitisation and codification for the purpose of algorithms of AI construction often tend to freeze and add an element of rigidity and insensitivity leaving a narrower scope for wide interpretations as may be highly demanded while solving legal issues touching human life.

Being dynamic in nature, the rigidity offered by coding for AI of laws and related principles is another big issue at hand hampering application of judicial knowledge. It is a machine variant of the old problem of law laid down in advance as identified by Aristotle: The legislator cannot predict all future circumstances in which the stipulated law will come to be applied and so cannot ensure that the law will always conform to its underlying rationale and justification at the point of its application (Sales, 2021, p. 26). Further, the customs play a crucial role in the structural development and operations of the legal system in the society being a crucial source of law. By its very nature codification of customs is extremely difficult, and one would not be wrong to say, impossible. In relation to machine written judgments, it is extremely difficult to achieve justice being done without actual appreciation of the customs involved in a case.

Decision-making for the purpose of delivering justice requires the presence of cognitive activities carried out by the human brain. Cognition, in essence, is the ability to perceive and react, process and understand, store and retrieve information, make decisions, and produce appropriate responses (Cambridge Cognition, 2015). It is often stated that AI machines mimic human behaviour and patterns and respond as the humans usually do. However, science still has not been able to answer clearly as to whether machines actually think? Or they simply process the data fed to them and produce the output. In relation to the context at hand, the following observation made by G. Jefferson is noteworthy:

> To be just, nothing more than analogy is claimed by most of their constructors (some, like Professor Williams, do not go so far even as that), but there is a grave danger that those not so well informed will go to great lengths of fantasy. If we see that some nervous tissues behave like some electronic circuits we must all the time remember that the resemblance is with fragments of the nervous system and not with the whole integrated nervous system of man. It is only right when we do so that we recollect something else, that we cannot be sure that the highest intellectual processes are still carried out in the same way. Something quite different, as yet undiscovered, may happen in those final processes of brain activity that results in what we call, for convenience, mind.
>
> (Jefferson, 1949, p. 1108)
>
> xx xx xx
>
> Not until a machine can write a sonnet or compose a concerto because of thoughts and emotions felt, and no: by the chance fall of symbols, could we agree that machine equals brain-that is, not only write it but know that it had written it. No mechanism could feel (and not merely artificially signal, an easy contrivance) pleasure at its successes, grief when its valves- fuse, be warmed by flattery, be made miserable by its mistakes, be charmed by sex, be angry or depressed when it cannot get what it wants.
>
> (Jefferson, 1949, p. 1110)

The task of thinking, perceiving, forming opinions, drawing co-relations, experience etc. is just not any simple functioning representing a 'causal condition between input and output.' (Divino & Magalhães, 2019, p. 304).

As has been pointed out, the judicial human fabric must be durable, long-lasting, founded on culture to build up the trust and confidence of the people in the institution of judiciary (Gupta, 2022, p. 111). Judges are not engines of power rather they are engines of justice (Gupta, 2022, p. 111). They are social engineers and architects, innovating new tools and techniques to make three-dimensional justice – social, economic, and political practically viable (Gupta, 2022, p. 111). The jurisprudential thoughts on 'justice', as discussed in third part of this article, reflect upon the idea that 'justice' is always a journey and not a destination (Mukharji, 2016, p. 71). As life is not a formula, so law is not a formula (Mukharji, 2016, p. 71). As God is one but his manifestations are many, so ideal justice may be one and monolithic but its manifestations are myriad (Mukharji, 2016, p. 71). With such dynamisms involved in the process, can a machine – the AI, be expected to deliver 'justice', which concept in itself depends upon numerous factors (being not quantifiable variables, at times). Further, AI being a machine, processing the data according to the algorithm, a likelihood of biasness from the developer's side is very much possible. Since, it primarily uses the data fed to it at the initial stage, the potentiality of machine being fed the biased data to yield biased result cannot be ruled out, and biasness is against the very concept of 'justice' as element of impartiality is an essential element of justice.

However, considering the improved efficiency, accuracy, and effective assistance rendered by AI tools to the judicial system, it is deemed advantageous to employ them for following reasons:

1) assistance in document review;
2) effective and enhanced legal research;
3) help with legal analytics;
4) reduced human errors;
5) economising the expensive and labour-intensive ways of legal drafting;
6) time efficient, etc.

The economic and other associated factors behind utilisation of AI tools in the judicial system advances its adoption for the betterment, however, as a compliment and not as a replacement. The realisation of E-Judges or AI Judges or the Robo Judges to a conceptual reality certainly seems to be a misplaced idea when it comes to notions of 'justice'. The wisdom to administer justice is possessed by a human brain and not machine, howsoever, intelligent it may claim to be.

1.5 CONCLUSION

With remarkable features like accuracy, efficiency, automation, speed, and consistency, etc. the reliability upon the AI has increased manifold with time. Whether it is about the machine-driven cars or planes or handling big data for analysis or venturing into risky research and development activities, for example, space operations or underwater research activities, AI is considered a safe, reliable, and trustworthy entity for progression without a second thought. Due to its multidimensional expansion, its assistance is also appreciated in the legal field. However, such appreciation has posed a challenge in the form of the availability of options of AI Judges or E Judges or Robo Judges, i.e., AI machine replacing the human judges. The existence of human judges in the judicial system is imperative from the context of 'delivery of justice'. From the standpoint of the jurisprudential underpinnings of the concept of 'justice', it is just not simply a technical end to the litigation being yielded through some set mathematical formulas; rather it is a wide concept flexible enough to accommodate considerations and changes demanded by the context. The integration of technology – the AI in the judicial system, offering the best of the features for its smooth operation, with an aim not to simply compliment but to replace the human judges and allow AI machines to take over the charge of delivering 'justice' is certainly a misplaced idea. The idea of equating justice with judgment writing is often seen, and it is important to understand that 'judgment writing' is different from 'delivering justice'. Writing a judgment could be achieved through set equations; however, administering justice through that written judgment is altogether different for justice being a dynamic concept more vibrant and much more complex which demands human touch rather than machine codification.

REFERENCES

Bodenheimer, E. (1974). *Jurisprudence: The philosophy and Method of the Law*. Harvard University Press.

Brar, G. K. (2018). Role of judiciary in good governance. *South Asian Law Review Journal*, 4, 256–262. https://thelawbrigade.com/wp-content/uploads/2019/06/Gurpreet-Kaur.pdf

Cambridge Cognition. (2015, August 19). What is Cognition? https://cambridgecognition.com/what-is-cognition/#:~:text=Cognition%20is%20defined%20as%20'the,used%20to%20guide%20your%20behavior

Carver, T. (1915). *Essays in Social Justice*. Harvard University Press.

Clifford, R. D. (1997). Intellectual property in the era of creative computer program: Will the true creator please stand up? *Tulane Law Review*, *71*, 1675–1760.

Computational Creativity. (2024). Deepgram. https://deepgram.com/ai-glossary/computational-creativity

Courts should not act as 'mere tape recorders', says SC; flags role of public prosecutors. (2024). *Indian Express*. https://indianexpress.com/article/india/courts-tape-recorders-sc-public-prosecutors-9309252/

Divino, S. B. S., & Magalhães, R. A. (2019). Copyright of artificial intelligence autonomous production: Some reflections around the concepts of mind and intelligence. *BioLaw Journal*, 2, 299–313.

Finnis, J. (2024). *Natural Law Theories*. In Zalta, E. N. & Nodelman, U. (eds.), The Stanford Encyclopedia of Philosophy. https://plato.stanford.edu/cgi-bin/encyclopedia/archinfo.cgi?entry=natural-law-theories

Goldstein, J. K. (2018). The nature of the judicial process: The enduring significance of a legal classic. *Touro Law Review*, 34, 159–182.

Guess, A. R. (2016). *Artificial Intelligence is an Umbrella Term: Don't be Misled*. www.dataversity.net/artificial-intelligence-umbrella-term-dont-misled/

Gupta, B. K. (2022). *My Journey with Law & Justice*. Law & Justice Publishing.

Jefferson, G. (1949). The mind of mechanical man. *British Medical Journal*, 4616, 1105–1110.

Law and Logic. (2025). In: Roversi, C. (ed.), *A Treatise of Legal Philosophy and General Jurisprudence*. Springer, Dordrecht. https://doi.org/10.1007/1-4020-3505-5_53

Mukharji, P. B. (2016). *The New Jurisprudence*. Eastern Law House.

Paranjape, N. V. (2010). *Studies in Jurisprudence & Legal Theory*. Central Law Agency.

Pomerleau, W. P. (n.d.) *Western Theories of Justice*. https://iep.utm.edu/justwest/

Sales, P. (2021). Algorithm, Artificial Intelligence, and the Law. *Judicature*, 105(1), 22–35.

Sen, A. (2010). *The Idea of Justice*. Penguin Books.

Sourdin, T. & Cornes, R. (2018). *Do judges need to be human? The implications of technology for responsive judging*. In Sourdin, T., & Zariski, A. (eds). (2018). The Responsive Judge. Ius Gentium: Comparative Perspectives on Law and Justice. Vol. 67 Springer, Singapore. https://doi.org/10.1007/978-981-13-1023-2_4

Tammelo, I. (1970). Logic as an instrument of legal reasoning. *American Bar Association Journal*, 10, 89–94.

The Social Impact of Artificial Intelligence: Opportunities and Challenges. (n.d.) https://i-investonline.com/the-social-impact-of-artificial-intelligence-opportunities-and-challenges/#:~:text=However%2C%20the%20rapid%20integration%20of,perpetuate%20discrimination%20require%20careful%20consideration

Trenhub, A. (2015). Machines cannot think. In Brockman, J. (ed.), *What to Think About Machines That Think*. Harper Perennial.

What is Artificial Intelligence (AI)? (n.d.). www.ibm.com/topics/artificial-intelligence

2 Safeguarding Personal Data and Privacy in the Era of Artificial Intelligence Through the Human Rights Lens

Exploring Legal Hurdles and Policy Implications

Nguyen Phuong Dung and Vu Truc Hanh

2.1 INTRODUCTION

The rapid advancement of artificial intelligence (AI) technologies has revolutionized numerous spheres of modern life. As AI systems become increasingly integrated into various sectors, concerns about the potential erosion of personal data and privacy (PDP) protection have escalated. By adopting a human rights-based approach, this research seeks to explore the intricate interplay between AI and the realization of human rights, with an emphasis on formidable challenges and multifaceted implications that arise in the context of safeguarding PDP within the prevalence of AI. Therefore, this chapter will provide insights into the several specific research issues. First, this chapter will investigate how emerging AI technologies have impacted the protection of PDP from a human rights perspective. To achieve this, this chapter will examine the position of AI in the policies and policy-making process and determine the existing international human rights law standards relevant to safeguarding PDP. Following that, the chapter will identify the specific legal challenges and hurdles in reconciling the rapid advancements of AI with the protection of PDP under international human rights law and how legal and policy frameworks on human rights adapt to the dynamic nature of AI to ensure continued protection of PDP. In identifying these hurdles, the chapter will concurrently suggest potential strategies to circumvent and address violations of PDP rights, strengthen the safeguarding of PDP, and harmonize corporate interests in the AI-driven era.

DOI: 10.1201/9781003491903-2

2.2 OVERVIEW OF AI AND ITS IMPACTS ON THE REALIZATION OF HUMAN RIGHTS AND PROTECTION OF PDP

The existing regulatory framework for privacy and data protection encounters notable inadequacies when confronted with the multifaceted challenges posed by AI. There exists no universally binding instrument specifically addressing AI. Furthermore, it is difficult to formulate a widespread legally binding instrument to govern AI and keep pace with it due to its swift evolution. Grappling with the dynamic and ever-evolving intersection of data protection laws and principles within the AI landscape is a formidable task. Concurrently, it is imperative to avoid overregulating AI or creating uncertainty about whether regulatory requirements are applicable. This highlights the necessity for reforming and enhancing a more highly flexible and adaptable legal framework that can effectively manage the development of AI technology while ensuring the preservation of individual rights and data privacy (Rodrigues, 2020).

The exchange of personal data is a prominent issue in various areas of our society. Nonetheless, data subjects are reluctant to partake in data sharing, primarily due to concerns revolving around security and privacy. Concerns are rooted in the belief that data may be exploited, thereby jeopardizing privacy and infringing upon fundamental human rights. Consequently, the act of sharing personal data has become intricately intertwined with broader human rights considerations. This apprehension experienced by data subjects has been intensified by the intrusion of AI, as AI possesses the capacity to autonomously analyze data, obviating the need for human involvement (Chatterjee, 2019, pp. 21–22; Donahoe & Metzger, 2019, p. 115). Despite the undeniable potential benefits arising from the advent of AI, the rapid progress and pervasive deployment of this technology bring forth associated risks. In the age of a 'data-driven' society and the swift-paced AI evolution, numerous governments have devised national AI strategies as an attempt to stay abreast of technological advancements. Nevertheless, only a minority have examined the ramifications of AI on their responsibility to safeguard citizens' rights. There consequently arises a pressing need for the establishment of a shared global framework that can ensure the development and application of AI in a manner that upholds the enjoyment of human rights (Donahoe & Metzger, 2019, pp. 115–116).

A consensus regarding the precise definition of AI remains elusive, as there are numerous interpretations and distinct viewpoints that contribute to a lack of common understanding in this field (Gordon, 2023, pp. 16–17). AI encompasses the capability of digital computers or computer-controlled robots to execute tasks that are typically associated with intelligent beings. This pertains to the development of systems that possess cognitive processes akin to those of humans such as logical reasoning, discerning meaning, generalizing, and the aptitude to learn from past experience (Gordon, 2023, p. 16). Another viewpoint holds that AI machines cannot be equated to human intelligence because they fundamentally lack the capacity for genuinely comprehending their actions. However, the prevailing viewpoint is that machines have the potential to progress towards consciousness and intelligence, which are conventionally believed to be confined to carbon-based beings like humans only (Gordon, 2023, p. 17).

It is a truism that 'data is the lifeblood of AI' (Greiman, 2021, p. 52; Weaver, 2018, p. 2). Within the operational framework of social media platforms like Facebook, AI systems engage in the analysis and subsequent adjustment of content presentation, predicated upon users' interactions within the platform. Each interaction with AI-driven personal assistants, such as Amazon's Alexa and Echo, produces data that AI systems scrutinize to enhance their interactions with users and refine the suite of applications they offer. An example of this is Google's Project Magenta, which has devised AI programs capable of analyzing substantial datasets to create entirely new pieces of art (Weaver, 2018, p. 2). In the era of big data, online service providers employ information systems to acquire and apply consumer behavior data in the customization of services with the aim of improving quality and user experience. However, the growing reliance on AI for data analysis has triggered privacy concerns such as unauthorized data collection, unauthorized secondary data use, improper access, and errors, which have the potential to infringe upon human rights (Chatterjee, 2019, pp. 22–23; Greiman, 2021, p. 54; Li et al., 2023, p. 369).

AI algorithms exhibit an exceptional capacity in generating fresh information by leveraging existing datasets (Andreotta et al., 2022, p. 1720). There is a potential for AI to process data in a manner that contravenes fundamental rights, for instance, when an algorithm analyzing secondary data categorizes individuals in a discriminatory manner without a lawful foundation (Balan, 2019, p. 50; Krasniqi & Uka, 2022, p. 1342; Yadav, n.d., p. 262). The utilization of AI in processing and analyzing personal data may raise apprehensions pertaining to the emergence of image-based sexual misconduct, discriminatory decision-making by profiling, or the generation of deep fakes with the intent of causing reputational harms (Ishii, 2019, p. 525; Okolie, 2023, pp. 5 and 10; Yadav, n.d., pp. 263–264).

2.3 HUMAN RIGHTS STANDARDS AND PROTECTIVE FRAMEWORKS FOR PDP – EXAMINING THE INTERSECTION OF AI WITH PDP RIGHTS

Human rights represent fundamental moral rights of a universal nature, establishing a baseline standard that holds intrinsic validity irrespective of any state or legal acknowledgment (Gordon, 2023, pp. 30–32). Human rights standards are widely described in the Universal Declaration of Human Rights (UDHR) adopted under the auspices of the United Nations (UN) in 1948, representing a milestone in the realization of human rights worldwide. Although the UDHR is a soft instrument, it laid the groundwork for the development of legally binding covenants elaborating upon the diverse spectrum of civil, political, economic, social, and cultural rights envisaged in the UDHR, such as the International Covenant on Civil and Political Rights (ICCPR) adopted in 1966.

The foundational concept of privacy, dating back to the nineteenth century, is 'the right to be let alone'. However, privacy has been conceptualized to a broader extent, including freedom of thought, bodily integrity, solitude, information integrity, freedom from surveillance, along with the protection of reputation and personality (Shackelford et al., 2022, p. 62). Privacy is safeguarded under the UDHR. It is particularly provided that 'No one shall be subjected to arbitrary interference with his privacy, family, home or correspondence, nor to attacks upon his honour and reputation. Everyone has the right to the protection of the law against such interference or attacks' (UDHR, 1948, art. 12; Donahoe & Metzger, 2019, p. 119; Steeves, 2016, p. 464). Relevant provisions securing the right to life, liberty, and security of the person and to freedom of thought, conscience, and religion, despite not directly mentioning privacy in their text, since the wide conceptualization of privacy, could serve as indirect and additional protective mechanisms for privacy (Steeves, 2016, p. 464). Furthermore, the preservation of privacy is also upheld in the 1966 ICCPR in alignment with the principles outlined in the UDHR (Steeves, 2016, pp. 464–465). The wording used in these documents indicates an expansive legal recognition of the right to privacy, emphasizing it as a crucial aspect of human dignity, freedom, and the democratic process. These instruments not only acknowledge privacy as a fundamental human right but also institute commensurate protective measures (Steeves, 2016, p. 465).

In addition, it is recognized that data use falls within the purview of 'individual sovereignty' or 'individual control' involving two main aspects: defining personal boundaries (how individuals' interest interact with society (control)) and safeguarding them (the need to prevent potential misuse of personal data beyond an individual's sphere, or the risk involved)). This underscores the integral relationship between data protection and the domain of personality rights (Mantelero, 2022, pp. 3–4; Westerlund & Enkvist, 2016, p. 5). The concept of 'control' pertains to an individual's ability to dictate how their personal data is processed. Unless individuals are furnished with pertinent information and the authority to make choices, they may find themselves subjected to decisions that elude their comprehension and influence. However, in a scenario where robots closely resembling humans become deeply embedded in personal lives, they might infringe upon individuals' personal spaces by engaging in the collection, analysis, and profiling of human behaviors. Furthermore, due to the rapid evolution of AI technology, which frequently outpaces the adaptation of social systems, individuals' decision-making capacity erodes. The deprivation of this decision-making authority jeopardizes their freedom and autonomy (Ishii, 2019, p. 512).

Regulating AI technology undeniably represents one of the most complex and formidable challenges (Ishii, 2019, p. 511). Nevertheless, embracing a human rights-based approach to AI governance offers a pathway to achieving the objectives set forth by emerging ethical frameworks. Firstly, the human rights framework, anchored in the concept of human dignity, firmly places the human individual at the core of governance and societal considerations. When applied to AI regulation, this approach mandates evaluations of AI technologies based on their effects on individuals and their inherent rights. Secondly, societal concerns arising from AI find their place within the body of international human rights law, spanning across a wide array of both substantive and procedural rights (Donahoe & Metzger, 2019, p. 119). Thirdly, governments bear the primary responsibility for shielding their citizens from rights violations, whether these violations arise from other governments or nonstate actors, including private sector entities. Concurrently, businesses have committed to upholding human rights, as outlined in the United Nations Guiding Principles on Business and Human Rights. These principles are structured around a three-fold framework, which includes the state's duty to prevent human rights abuses, the corporate responsibility to steadfastly uphold human rights, and the imperative to facilitate redress mechanisms for victims (UN, 2011; Donahoe & Metzger, 2019, p. 120; Greiman, 2021, p. 54).

At a regional level, the European Union (EU) pioneers the statutory frameworks for data privacy. Privacy rights were also enshrined in the 1950 Convention for the Protection of Human Rights and Fundamental Freedoms, also known as the European Convention on Human Rights (ECHR) (ECHR, 1950, art. 8) (Steeves, 2016, p. 464). The EU additionally introduced the European Data Protection Directive (95/46/EC) in 1995 that member states' national legislation aligned with in accordance with Article 8 of the European Convention on Human Rights (Westerlund & Enkvist, 2016, p. 3). In the context of the EU's statutory paradigm, data privacy is regarded as a fundamental human right. This acknowledgment is enshrined in the EU's Charter of Fundamental Rights with four principal privacy rights granted to EU citizens. These encompass the preservation of personal data, the assurance of equitable data processing, the facilitation of data access to and correction, and the strict adherence to data protection laws (Charter of Fundamental Rights of the European Union, 2000, art. 8; Humerick, 2018, p. 401). The introduction of the General Data Protection Regulation (GDPR) as a replacement for the Data Protection Directive (DPD) results from the EU's adoption of a human rights-centered approach. However, the GDPR does not explicitly center on AI, despite the predominant contemporary AI paradigm falling within the GDPR's purview. Therefore, the EU has commenced deliberations on legislative proposals tailored and customized to specifically address AI. Until these EU measures are formally enacted, there exists a substantial probability that current AI models may be in direct contravention of the GDPR, potentially exerting a significant impact on global AI development endeavors (Humerick, 2018, p. 401).

Overall, the contemporary human rights system is considered less resilient and deficient when confronted with the challenges posed by AI, potentially leading to a calamitous situation, especially when AI introduces novel types of harm that go unnoticed or fail to be acknowledged as forms of human suffering (Liu, 2021, pp. 3–4).

2.4 CRITIQUES ON PDP GOVERNANCE THROUGH A HUMAN RIGHTS LENS: IMPLICATIONS FOR DEVELOPMENT AND ENHANCEMENT

In light of the exponential growth of AI, it becomes incumbent upon governments and the international community to promptly adapt to the burgeoning AI landscape. There is an exigent need for regulations to oversee the development of AI. The shifts in technological and business paradigms have generated fresh expectations from legislators (Mantelero, 2022, p. 5). The crux of the matter does not lie in the creation of an entirely new ethical paradigm for AI governance, as such a foundation already exists within the framework of human rights. Instead, the principal issue lies in the application and reform of human rights standards to address challenges posed by new digital technologies (Donahoe & Metzger, 2019, pp. 122–123).

According to the human rights framework, governments are entrusted with the duty of shielding their citizens from any transgressions or breaches of their rights, whether originating from other governments or nonstate entities, which comprises private sector entities (Donahoe & Metzger, 2019, p. 119). Nevertheless, a critical concern revolves around how states plan to effectively ensure the protection of their citizens' rights pertaining to PDP, while in the era of digital technology, various situations emerge where personal data is regularly stored and processed across borders, transcending the purview of state governance (Simmons & Hulvey, 2023). Indeed, states are not the sole entities dedicated to upholding human rights, as businesses have also acknowledged their roles in this domain. However, it is important to emphasize that the United Nations Guiding Principles on Business and Human Rights are categorized as soft law, giving rise to legitimate concerns about the extent to which states can effectively enforce these principles. To put it differently, states are the primary actors held responsible for preventing human rights abuses within their own territorial confines. However, the question of whether states can exercise their sovereign authority to address PDP-related infringements and breaches that transpire beyond their borders and jurisdictions is questionable and skeptical in practice. Determining the harm caused by algorithmic actions and identifying who should be held responsible for that harm is a complex task due to special status of AI applications as intangible objects (Hacker, 2021, p. 270). The complexity arises when both humans and algorithms share responsibility, and it is challenging to decide who should be accountable for decisions made by algorithms as human actors may avoid responsibility by transferring the authority for decision-making to algorithms, considering that the legal system has been traditionally designed around the regulation related to human behavior (Ishii, 2019, p. 526; Mittelstadt et al., 2016, pp. 12–13).

The essential requirement for obtaining consent from data subjects stands as a critical pillar of this framework. Nevertheless, a significant challenge emerges concerning the voluntariness of data subjects' consent (especially in case the data subject is a child), primarily stemming from their reluctance to read privacy notices and their compulsion to accept these terms in order to access certain services (Andreotta et al., 2022, p. 1720; Balan, 2019, p. 49; Li et al., 2023, p. 367). Obtaining specific and explicit consent related to the particular use of personal data has not always been a standard practice, and many companies, as well as governments, that collect personal information have not adhered to this requirement. This issue is not only limited solely to the major tech giants like Amazon, Apple, Facebook, and Google but also businesses of all sizes and government entities involved in the collection of personal data (Andreotta et al., 2022, p. 1716). As seen in the Cambridge Analytica scandal, Facebook was directly involved in the collection of personal data from roughly 300,000 individuals who had installed an application offering a personality quiz. This application gathered an array of personal information, including users' profile details and their activities on Facebook. Simultaneously, it indirectly acquired personal data from approximately 87 million people. The indirect data collection occurred because the application also extracted information from the friends of users who had allowed such data sharing through their privacy settings. However, the vast majority of Facebook users did not provide explicit consent for their personal data to be used in this manner. While, from a technical standpoint, it could be argued that all 87 million Facebook users consented to the application collecting their personal data by not adjusting their privacy settings, it is evident that they did not consider or perceive this as granting permission for the application to access their data to share it with a third party like Cambridge Analytica (Kozlowska, 2018).

The level of risk associated with data utilization should determine the extent of user controls necessary. Similarly, the sensitivity of the data calls for corresponding protective measures. Such controls encompass explicit consent, easily comprehensible and prominently displayed privacy notifications, and privacy-oriented default settings. Companies should be required to go beyond mere compliance with legal requirements and endeavor to empathize with their customers. They should consider how customers anticipate the use of their data when they provide it and whether their consent is clearly obtained (Kozlowska, 2018). Moreover, data are consistently employed for AI training, a critical element in the progress of AI applications. However, the regulatory frameworks for AI training are still underdeveloped (Hacker, 2021). Machine learning's unpredictability in processing outcomes makes transparency and obtainment of consent more difficult. Data subjects may not possess sufficient information about how their personal data is utilized and, more critically, how decisions about them are made, rendering meaningful consent to data processing almost impossible (Ishii, 2019, p. 527).

The transparency issue, often termed the explanation problem, presents a challenge for several reasons. Companies are hesitant to reveal their internal workings to protect their trade secrets. Additionally, regarding 'black box' algorithms, particularly in deep learning, their internal workings can be a mystery, even to their creators. Resolving the issues of biased decisions originating from algorithms, deciphering the optimal approach to the 'algorithmic black box' problem, and attributing responsibility for the harm caused by algorithms are all intricate challenges with no simple or immediate answers (Ishii, 2019, p. 526). In cases where individuals are entitled to know how their data are being used (as is the case with the EU's GDPR) and this knowledge is essential for them to make informed decisions, obtaining meaningful informed consent becomes highly complex in such scenarios (Andreotta et al., 2022, pp. 1718–1719; Ishii, 2019, p. 526; Mittelstadt et al., 2016, p. 13). Organizations should improve their technical capabilities to process data subjects' requests for consent withdrawal, especially when consent is the basis for data processing. This can be challenging as it involves monitoring and verifying data to prevent any potential bias in machine learning algorithms caused by the removal of certain data (Balan, 2019, p. 49).

In support of an AI governance framework grounded in and in accordance with human rights principles, it is necessary that governments forge robust collaborations with international stakeholders. In the absence of universally accepted global standards and unregulated AI proliferation, nations might engage in a competitive race for innovations, often disregarding potential adverse repercussions. Therefore, if a significant portion of the international community can unite around a human rights-centered approach to AI governance that aligns with their existing commitments, this alignment may serve as a catalyst, encouraging even hesitant states to partake (Donahoe & Metzger, 2019, pp. 123–124). Furthermore, it is incumbent upon public authorities to enhance their oversight of AI-related activities conducted by private corporations to fulfill their obligation to safeguard the rights of their citizens. Clear guidance on the implementation of human rights principles across all sectors is indispensable. Essential facets of this endeavor encompass fostering transparency in the use of decision-making algorithms, whether by governmental bodies or businesses. A burgeoning concept gaining traction among product developers is 'human rights by design', which underscores the importance of integrating human rights considerations at the very core of AI development. Moreover, at a pragmatic level, governments must exercise judiciousness in their AI procurement decisions and rigorously evaluate the consequences of deploying AI products in the administration of public services, particularly those bearing direct ramifications on individual rights (Donahoe & Metzger, 2019, p. 124).

Another issue is the protection of PDP after death. The legal framework does not address the management of digital remains, as current data protection laws only safeguard the living. While individuals can usually dictate the fate of their assets after death, they are not afforded the same control over their digital remains. Other than the contract outlining terms of use for a social media account, which is recognized as the primary legal consideration, there are no policies regulating the posthumous PDP. (Keating, 2015, p. 163). The involvement of third parties in our digital lives via social media platforms is on the rise, shaping a virtual biography and archive for each user due to these platforms' extensive storage capabilities. The expanding array of social media outlets complicates the understanding of each platform's policy regarding user data after death. What remains consistent is a disregard for the deceased's wishes and a lack of clarity in the procedures for their family members. Various social media platforms, such as Facebook, LinkedIn, Flickr, and Google, have disparate policies for handling deceased users' accounts, showcasing inconsistency and uncertainty even among the industry leaders. Facebook stands out by offering the option to convert a user's page into a memorial page, but this still lacks consideration for the deceased's prior intent. Additionally, there is a disparity between the processes for removing an account and memorializing it, highlighting contradictions within platform-specific policies. In general, these policies fail to account for the wishes of the deceased and lack a clear process for identifying and implementing those wishes. As a result, individuals rely heavily on their close family members to manage their digital footprint posthumously. The ambiguity within these policies illustrates the wider difficulties in regulating issues related to deceased individuals in today's digital era, where advancements in technology create a blurred boundary between the concerns of the living and those of the deceased (Keating, 2015, pp. 163–166).

The privacy of social media users is important, but it should not obstruct the regulation of accounts belonging to deceased individuals. Advocates for limited removal policies frequently raise privacy concerns about sensitive data. Nevertheless, privacy rights diminish substantially after death. Social media companies contend that granting family members access to a deceased person's account breaches privacy expectations, yet this argument is weak because privacy expectations significantly dissipate upon death. Moreover, social media content merges public and private information, complicating conventional privacy principles. Technology now extends and preserves digital identities, making it difficult to distinguish between property and the legal rights of the living. Consequently, posthumous data entails a new legal framework that goes beyond traditional property concepts. It is proposed that regulation should focus on preserving the deceased's living image and preventing its alteration through the misuse of social media platforms. This new legal interest would address the unique challenges posed by the digital age and ensure that the deceased's virtual presence is treated with the same respect and dignity as their physical remains (Keating, 2015, pp. 170–174).

Currently, in many countries, the destiny of social media accounts is controlled by private companies' terms of use. This individualistic control allows social media corporation's significant power over these accounts, often disregarding the decedent's wishes and making it difficult for families to assert any claims. This unchecked control necessitates legal regulation to balance protecting the dead's interests with preventing exclusive control by social media providers. Technological advancements have erased the distinction between the interests of the living and the deceased, highlighting the necessity for legal guidance and uniform regulation to manage social media accounts posthumously. One regulatory approach could extend existing legal rights slightly beyond death, similar to how wills distribute property and respect the deceased's dignity. Alternatively, regulation could establish a new posthumous right that recognizes a unique interest arising upon death, reflecting the importance of preserving the deceased's virtual memories. Another possibility is regulation based on the rights of the living, specifically the family and executors of the deceased's estate. Consistent regulation would simplify managing the deceased's digital assets. This regulation would provide a formal framework for handling digital remains, similar to how burial systems manage physical remains. The regulation of posthumous digital remains is a prominent issue requiring legal intervention to ensure the deceased's wishes are respected and their digital legacy is appropriately managed. This regulation could additionally draw from existing legal principles, extend living rights slightly beyond death, or establish new posthumous rights, all aimed at balancing the interests of the deceased, their families, and social media providers (Keating, 2015, pp. 177–181).

2.5 CONCLUSION

AI and automation will inevitably progress, irrespective of regulatory oversight. However, their sustainability and positive impact hinge on adopting a responsible, rights-based approach. Effective governance of AI and its applications is essential. As technology rapidly evolves, existing laws and norms often struggle to keep pace, prompting reactive measures from governments. There is a pressing need for regulations in AI development and deployment, yet a robust ethical foundation already exists in the human rights framework. The challenge is to adapt this framework to new digital technologies.

Achieving this requires collaboration across various disciplines. Human rights should guide the design, application, and evaluation of AI to maximize benefits while minimizing harm. A human rights-based approach to AI governance is crucial for addressing societal concerns effectively. An unregulated or fragmented approach will not yield optimal outcomes. Establishing a global standard is vital to prevent negative consequences from unchecked innovations.

Although human rights standards offer a legal basis for data protection, this protection is often limited. Key ideas include transparency in decision-making algorithms and the concept of 'human rights by design' (Donahoe & Metzger, 2019, pp. 124–125). Technologies should be evaluated for their human rights impact during development. Public authorities must oversee private companies' AI usage and consider AI's implications for public services. Clear consequences and remedies for noncompliance are vital. Although private firms can develop their own ethical frameworks, human rights standards should be prioritized and adopted in the formulation of the policies. Prioritizing human rights is the best way to safeguard people from AI's potential harms and to build societies enriched by AI. It is imperative to address how to protect and uphold human rights in our AI-driven world.

REFERENCES

Andreotta, A. J., Kirkham, N., & Rizzi, M. (2022). AI, big data, and the future of consent. *AI & Society*, *37*, 1715–1738.

Balan, S. M. (2019). Artificial intelligence and law: A review of the role of correctness in the general data protection regulation framework. *Curentul Juridic*, *76*, 45–53.

Charter of Fundamental Rights of the European Union, 2000/C 364/01 (2000). www.europarl.europa.eu/charter/pdf/text_en.pdf

Chatterjee, S. (2019). Personal data sharing and legal issues of human rights in the era of artificial intelligence: Moderating effect of government regulation. *International Journal of Electronic Government Research*, *15*(3), 21–35.

Donahoe, E., & Metzger, M. M. (2019). Artificial intelligence and human rights. *Journal of Democracy*, *30*(2), 115–126.

European Convention on Human Rights (1950). Convention for the Protection of Human Rights and Fundamental Freedoms. www.coe.int/en/web/human-rights-convention/the-convention-in-1950

Gordon, J.-S. (2023). The Impact of Artificial Intelligence on Human Rights Legislation: A Plea for an AI Convention. Palgrave Macmillan.

Greiman, V. (2021). Human rights and artificial intelligence: A universal challenge. *Journal of Information Warfare*, *20*(1), 50–62.

Hacker, P. (2021). A legal framework for AI training data—From first principles to the Artificial Intelligence Act. *Law, Innovation and Technology*, *13*(2), 257–301.

Humerick, M. (2018). Taking AI personally: How the E.U. must learn to balance the interests of personal data privacy & artificial intelligence. *Santa Clara High Technology Law Journal*, *34*(4), 393–418.

Ishii, K. (2019). Comparative legal study on privacy and personal data protection for robots equipped with artificial intelligence: Looking at functional and technological aspects. *AI & Soc*, *34*, 509–533.

Keating, R. (2015). Kicking the digital e-Bucket: The regulation of posthumous digital remains. *Hibernian Law Journal*, *14*, 160–186.

Kozlowska, I. (2018, April 30). *Facebook and Data Privacy in the Age of Cambridge Analytica*. https://jsis.washington.edu/news/facebook-data-privacy-age-cambridge-analytica/

Krasniqi, S., & Uka, M. (2022). Artificial intelligence in modern times and the risk of violation of international human rights instruments. *Special Education*, *43*(2), 1339–1344.

Li, S., Liu, Y., & Feng, J. (2023). Who should own the data? The impact of data ownership shift from the service provider to consumers. *Journal of Management Information Systems*, *40*(2), 366–400.

Liu, H.-Y. (2021). AI challenges and the inadequacy of human rights protections. *Criminal Justice Ethics*, *40*(1), 2–22.

Mantelero, A. (2022). *Beyond Data: Human Rights, Ethical and Social Impact Assessment in AI* (Vol. 36). Springer.

Mittelstadt, B. D., Allo, P., Taddeo, M., Wachter, S., & Floridi, L. (2016). The ethics of algorithms: Mapping the debate. *Big Data & Society*, *3*(2), 1–21.

Okolie, C. (2023). Artificial intelligence-altered videos (deepfakes), image-based sexual abuse, and data privacy concerns. *Journal of International Women's Studies*, *25*(2), 1–16.

Rodrigues, R. (2020). Legal and human rights issues of AI: Gaps, challenges and vulnerabilities. *Journal of Responsible Technology*, *4*(3). www.sciencedirect.com/science/article/pii/S2666659620300056

Shackelford, S., Asare, I. N., Dockery, R., Raymond, A. H., & Sergueeva, A. (2022). Should we trust a black box to safeguard human rights? A comparative analysis of AI governance. *UCLA Journal of International Law and Foreign Affairs*, *26*, 35–87.

Simmons, B. A., & Hulvey, R. A. (2023). Cyberborders: Exercising state sovereignty online. *Temple Law Review*, *95*, 617–640.

Steeves, V. (2016). Now you see me: Privacy, technology, and autonomy in the digital age. In Gordon DiGiacomo (ed.), *Human Rights: Current Issues and Controversies* (pp. 461–482). University of Toronto Press.

UN. (2011). *United Nations Guiding Principles on Business and Human Rights*. www.ohchr.org/sites/default/files/documents/publications/guidingprinciplesbusinesshr_en.pdf

Universal Declaration of Human Rights (UDHR) (1948). www.un.org/sites/un2.un.org/files/2021/03/udhr.pdf

Weaver, J. F. (2018). Artificial intelligence and governing the life cycle of personal data. *Richmond Journal of Law & Technology*, *XXIV*(4), 1–48.

Westerlund, M., & Enkvist, J. (2016). Platform privacy: The missing piece of data protection legislation. *Journal of Intellectual Property, Information Technology and E-Commerce Law*, *7*(1), 2–17.

Yadav, V. S. (n.d.). AI and human rights: A critical ethico-legal overview. *Agathos*, *14*(1 (26)), 261–270.

3 Liability in the Age of AI

Perspectives on Criminal and Civil Responsibility for AI-Induced Harm

Reva Gupta and Mudassir Nazir

3.1 INTRODUCTION

Artificial intelligence (AI) has revolutionized industries such as healthcare, finance, and transportation, leading to advancements like self-driving vehicles and personalized experiences. However, the increasing adoption of AI presents notable challenges, particularly when AI systems cause harm. Incidents such as accidents involving autonomous vehicles, biased decision-making in recruitment processes, and breaches of privacy highlight complex legal and ethical issues around accountability. As AI becomes more autonomous, determining who is responsible for harm—whether it be the developers, the deploying organizations, or the AI itself—becomes more complicated.

AI-related liability spans both civil and criminal law. In civil cases, the focus is on compensation for damages, but the "black box" nature of AI systems complicates identifying the cause and assigning blame. In criminal law, where intent or negligence is generally required, applying liability becomes difficult when AI behaves unpredictably. These challenges reveal the limitations of traditional liability frameworks in addressing AI's autonomy and capacity for learning and adaptation. Understanding the legal and ethical issues surrounding AI-induced harm is essential for ensuring victims' rights and fostering public trust in new technologies. Clear liability standards are crucial for promoting safety, ethical development, and innovation. However, overly restrictive laws could hinder technological progress. The ongoing challenge lies in finding a balance between holding parties accountable and nurturing innovation.

Liability in the realm of AI spans both civil and criminal domains, each with unique considerations for dealing with harm. Civil liability typically focuses on compensation for damage to individuals or property, often hinging on factors such as negligence, defectiveness, or breaches of duty. However, in the context of AI, these cases are complicated by the "black box" nature of many systems, where the decision-making processes are opaque, even to the developers (University of Michigan-Dearborn, 2023). This opacity makes it exceedingly difficult for affected parties to establish causation or pinpoint the responsible entity. Criminal liability, conversely, involves accountability for acts deemed criminal by law, which usually necessitate the presence of intent, recklessness, or gross negligence. Assigning criminal liability for AI-induced harm presents unique challenges, particularly when an AI system acts in

DOI: 10.1201/9781003491903-3

unforeseen ways or beyond its programmed behavior without deliberate wrongdoing by any human party. Consequently, the traditional frameworks governing liability encounter substantial difficulties in accommodating the unique characteristics of AI, including its autonomy, capacity for adaptive learning, and the unpredictability of its evolution after deployment.

It is essential to address the legal and ethical aspects of harm caused by AI to ensure justice and create regulatory frameworks that foster public confidence in technological advancements. Clear accountability standards are crucial, as they encourage developers, operators, and users to focus on safety and ethical practices. Providing victims of AI-induced harm with effective legal recourse strengthens trust in the justice system, while well-defined liability frameworks encourage proactive risk management and boost confidence in AI systems. However, overly restrictive or vague liability regulations may stifle innovation, creating a delicate balance between ensuring accountability and encouraging technological progress.

The international scope of AI adds complexity to liability issues, as these technologies often operate across multiple countries. Identifying the applicable legal frameworks can be challenging, particularly when global datasets are biased and impact marginalized populations. It is crucial to create liability frameworks that prioritize fairness and equity. This chapter examines the roles and obligations of stakeholders, as well as the wider societal influences on AI development, to contribute to the ongoing debate about civil and criminal responsibility in the age of advanced AI technologies.

3.2 UNDERSTANDING THE CONCEPT OF AI-RELATED HARM

As AI becomes more integrated into various industries, it brings both benefits and potential risks. One significant concern is AI-induced harm, which can arise from errors, biases, malfunctions, or intentional misuse. These harms affect individuals, organizations, and society at large. A critical area of concern is the physical harm caused by AI, particularly in sectors that impact human safety. An example is the 2018 Uber self-driving car incident in Arizona, where a pedestrian tragically died because the car failed to detect her in time. This highlighted flaws in AI algorithms, leading to calls for better safety protocols, as reported by BBC News (2020). Similarly, in industrial settings, AI-driven robots, while improving efficiency, have caused workplace injuries due to machine errors or malfunctions. These incidents underscore the need for improved safety standards, comprehensive risk assessments, and stronger regulation of AI technologies in high-risk sectors like manufacturing and logistics.

In India, the regulatory framework addressing the safety of AI technologies is still developing, but incidents have occurred in certain sectors. For example, automated machinery in factories has caused injuries to workers due to malfunctioning systems or improper handling of robotics. Though the Ministry of Labour and Employment has implemented safety guidelines, there is a growing realization that AI and automation in critical industries require stricter regulations. Furthermore, incidents involving drones and unmanned aerial vehicles (UAVs) in India, such as crashes causing damage or injuries, have brought attention to the need for comprehensive regulatory measures to ensure that AI-driven systems are safe and reliable for public use.

These real-world incidents underscore the challenges of integrating AI into environments where safety is paramount. Both in India and worldwide, the growing adoption of AI calls for robust legal frameworks that not only focus on technical safety but also address ethical issues, establish clear accountability, and ensure continuous monitoring and regulation to mitigate risks to human life.

AI-induced economic harm can manifest in multiple forms, particularly within financial markets and consumer transactions. High-frequency trading algorithms, which financial institutions use to carry out rapid and profit-maximizing transactions, can trigger substantial financial losses when they encounter malfunction or errors. One well-known case is that of Knight Capital Group in 2012, where a malfunction in their automated trading system led to an extraordinary loss of $440 million in just a few minutes (Popper, 2012). This example highlights the susceptibility of financial markets that rely heavily on AI, where even a small error can lead to severe financial consequences.

Fraud detection systems powered by AI occasionally misidentify genuine transactions as fraudulent, which can cause financial losses and disrupt normal business and consumer activities. Similarly, credit scoring algorithms that rely on AI may inadvertently draw from biased or inaccurate datasets, leading to unjust rejections of loan applications or job opportunities and deepening existing social and economic disparities.

From an Indian legal perspective, AI-driven economic harm has relevance in cases involving financial wrongdoing and discrimination. A notable case in this regard is *Shivani Gupta v. Union of India* (2019), which dealt with the improper implementation of automated systems used to determine eligibility for government financial aid. The case revealed the risks of AI algorithms used in public welfare programs that inadvertently excluded eligible individuals from vital financial support (*Shivani Gupta v. Union of India*, 2019). The court's ruling to reassess and review such automated systems reflected broader concerns over the economic impact of AI, calling for stricter oversight of algorithms and their role in financial decisions. This illustrates how AI technologies, despite their advancements, may create economic challenges. Whether in the financial sector or in everyday consumer interactions, AI's influence can affect individuals and businesses alike. In India, the legal system is facing the task of balancing innovation with accountability, ensuring that safeguards are in place to mitigate the risks of AI-induced harm in economic domains.

AI-related harm extends beyond tangible impacts, significantly influencing social experiences, personal safety, and mental well-being. Deepfake technology, for instance, utilizes AI to alter video and audio content, portraying individuals—both public figures and private individuals—as engaging in acts they did not commit. This misuse often leads to severe emotional distress, particularly when deepfakes are exploited for misinformation or non-consensual explicit content (The Science Survey, 2024). Additionally, algorithmic bias in AI systems, evident in sectors like law enforcement and job recruitment, has targeted or disadvantaged specific social groups. Cases such as facial recognition tools disproportionately misidentifying people of color—resulting in wrongful arrests—highlight these biases' consequences on individuals and societal structures (Raji & Buolamwini, 2019). Furthermore, AI-driven surveillance raises serious privacy concerns, fostering anxiety, distrust, and weakened social cohesion through unauthorized data collection and manipulation, thereby undermining individual autonomy.

AI-related harm impacts a wide range of individuals, businesses, and society at large. Individuals may face physical injuries from autonomous vehicles, financial losses from flawed algorithms, or emotional distress from deepfakes. Seeking redress is often difficult due to the complexity and opacity of AI technologies. Businesses relying on AI for operations risk financial setbacks, reputational damage, and regulatory challenges when systems fail or cause harm. Employees in industries affected by automation face economic uncertainty, job displacement, and the need for reskilling. At a societal level, biased AI systems can exacerbate inequalities, eroding public trust in institutions and undermining fairness and justice. Issues like mass surveillance and data privacy violations further disrupt democratic values, while biased algorithms challenge social principles such as equity and accountability. These broad impacts highlight the need for responsible and transparent AI development.

Several high-profile case studies illustrate the real-world implications of AI-related harm. The Uber self-driving car incident mentioned earlier is one of the most notorious, sparking legal and public scrutiny over the safety of autonomous vehicles. Tesla's autopilot feature has also been linked to fatalities, leading to calls for greater regulatory oversight and technical refinement before widespread adoption (National Highway Traffic Safety Administration [NHTSA], 2024). In the realm of social harm, deepfake technology serves as a poignant example. In 2019, deepfakes were used to mislead audiences and spread misinformation, such as in a manipulated video featuring Facebook's CEO Mark Zuckerberg. This video raised awareness about the capabilities and dangers of deepfake technology, yet the more disturbing applications of this tool have resulted in numerous cases of harassment, defamation, and sexual exploitation (VICE, 2019). Similarly, biased AI in hiring practices has been called into question, as in the case of Amazon's AI recruitment tool, which was discontinued after it was found to favor male candidates due to biased historical data. Such incidents illustrate the profound impact AI's biases and design flaws can have on the public.

Furthermore, invasive surveillance technologies, such as those used by Clearview AI, highlight issues surrounding privacy and the ethics of data collection. Clearview's use of facial recognition software without consent to create a massive database for law enforcement agencies stirred debate about the boundary between safety and privacy. The aftermath of such cases signals that AI-induced harm extends beyond physical and economic damage to critical concerns about personal freedom and individual rights.

The multifaceted nature of AI-related harm underscores the need for comprehensive legal frameworks that address these risks across multiple domains. Physical harm, economic harm, and social harm each bring their own complexities in terms of liability, accountability, and prevention, demanding a balanced and adaptive approach to governance and regulation. From safeguarding privacy and ensuring fairness to enhancing the safety of autonomous technologies, the development of AI should be guided by principles that prioritize the protection of individuals and societies. As these technologies continue to evolve, so too must the legal and ethical standards that regulate them, aiming for a future where AI systems can be both powerful and responsible.

3.3 CRIMINAL LIABILITY FOR AI-INDUCED HARM

As AI systems integrate deeply into various aspects of modern life, addressing accountability for harm caused by these technologies has become essential. Determining liability involves analyzing the roles of developers, operators, and manufacturers, as they collectively share responsibility for ensuring safety. However, pinpointing accountability is complex.

Developers hold primary responsibility for designing, programming, and testing AI systems. Any harm stemming from system failures may highlight flaws in these processes. Negligence in adhering to safety and quality standards, such as failing to identify or address potential risks, can result in criminal liability. For instance, if an AI-driven medical tool causes harm due to design errors, developers could face legal consequences. Operators assume responsibility postdeployment. Their role includes monitoring, maintaining, and ensuring the system complies with safety protocols. Neglect in these duties, such as late intervention during system malfunctions, can lead to criminal repercussions. For example, an autonomous vehicle operator who fails to act during a system error causing an accident may be held accountable. Manufacturers must ensure that AI systems meet safety standards before reaching the market. If a defective product causes harm due to insufficient testing or safety measures, liability may lie with the manufacturer. They are also obligated to recall unsafe systems and provide guidelines to mitigate risks, as negligence in these areas could have legal implications. In essence, developers, operators, and manufacturers must collaborate to mitigate risks and uphold accountability, ensuring AI systems operate safely and ethically.

The primary challenge in establishing criminal liability for AI-related harm lies in the absence of mens rea or criminal intent. AI systems lack awareness, and their actions are dictated by code, not by intent to cause harm. For instance, a self-driving car may cause an accident due to a programming flaw, but because the system has no capability for intent, attributing blame to the AI itself is problematic. Developers, operators, and manufacturers must instead be evaluated for negligence or recklessness, as they are the ones responsible for the creation and deployment of the system. However, this lack of intent further complicates the application of traditional criminal liability doctrines to AI.

Attributing responsibility for autonomous AI systems poses significant challenges. Many such systems, like self-learning algorithms or autonomous machines, perform tasks without direct human involvement. If these systems cause unforeseen harm, identifying fault becomes complex. For instance, an autonomous drone causing a collision might operate beyond what its creator anticipated. Similarly, an algorithm leading to biased hiring practices due to flawed data complicates accountability, as these systems often act independently and unpredictably, beyond traditional liability frameworks.

A further complication is the absence of legislation designed specifically to address AI-related risks. Existing laws, created before widespread AI adoption, are often inadequate for the unique challenges posed by autonomous systems. For example, criminal negligence laws, which hold parties responsible for harm due to carelessness, are hard to apply when AI causes harm without direct human error. This legal gap underscores the need for updated frameworks to address AI-induced damage effectively.

Efforts to address AI liability vary by country, but progress is inconsistent. In the United States, AI-related criminal liability remains largely undefined. Regulations, like those from the National Highway Traffic Safety Administration for autonomous vehicles, emphasize safety and operational standards rather than criminal responsibility. Consequently, individuals and entities often face legal uncertainty regarding accountability for AI-caused harm.

The European Union has been more proactive, with the European Commission proposing an Artificial Intelligence Act (European Parliament & Council of the European Union, 2024) that aims to regulate high-risk AI technologies, enhancing oversight in sectors like healthcare, transport, and the public sector. While the focus of the AI Act is primarily on risk mitigation, it has implications for criminal liability through its provisions that demand the assurance of safe and trustworthy AI systems. Though criminal responsibility for AI-induced harm is not directly outlined in the AI Act, the regulation underscores the importance of accountability in AI development and use. The Act also serves as a model for other countries looking to create or modify their AI regulations to balance technological progress with public safety. Nevertheless, even in the EU, many uncertainties remain about whether criminal accountability is clearly articulated or if further laws will be needed to close these gaps.

India's AI-related regulations are evolving. While initiatives like the National Strategy on Artificial Intelligence promote AI integration, there are no explicit laws addressing criminal liability for harm caused by AI. The Information Technology Act (2000) and data protection regulations primarily focus on privacy and security, leaving gaps in accountability for AI-driven harm. As AI adoption grows, clearer legislation will be necessary to address issues of liability and responsibility.

Globally, determining criminal liability for AI-related harm poses challenges due to AI's autonomous nature and lack of intent. Defining the roles and responsibilities of developers, operators, and manufacturers will be critical to ensure safe AI use. Comprehensive legal frameworks are required to address these complex issues effectively as AI continues to advance.

3.4 COMPARATIVE LEGAL ANALYSIS

As AI systems increasingly influence various sectors, the issue of liability for harm caused by AI becomes increasingly important. Different jurisdictions approach the question of who is responsible for AI-induced harm in distinct ways, leading to the development of diverse legal frameworks. This comparative analysis explores how the European Union, the United States, and India tackle AI liability.

3.4.1 European Union: AI Liability Framework and Human Rights Protections

The European Union has taken a comprehensive approach toward regulating AI liability through initiatives like the forthcoming AI Liability Directive, which aims to establish a structured, unified legal framework to address the risks AI poses to society. This directive seeks to create clear rules that hold developers and operators accountable for harm resulting from AI systems, combining elements of both civil and criminal liability. In addition to general liability laws, the EU integrates human rights protections, such as those found in the General Data Protection Regulation (GDPR). These protections ensure that AI systems are deployed with respect for individual privacy and other fundamental rights, emphasizing accountability particularly in situations where violations of rights like privacy infringement or discrimination take place. The legal context is evolving with efforts to ensure transparency in AI development, helping identify responsible parties in cases of harm.

3.4.2 United States: Regulation by Sector and Reliance on Tort Law

In the United States, AI liability is generally managed through regulations tailored to specific industries, rather than a broad, overarching legal structure. Different sectors such as transportation, healthcare, and finance have their own set of regulations addressing the unique risks associated with AI technologies. For instance, autonomous vehicles are subject to oversight from agencies like the National Highway Traffic Safety Administration (NHTSA) to ensure public safety. However, outside of these specific regulations, the U.S. legal system predominantly relies on tort law for addressing AI-related harms. Victims may seek recourse under negligence or product liability doctrines when harm occurs due to faulty or unsafe AI. This fragmented approach, with its reliance on existing legal doctrines, can result in inconsistent standards for liability, depending on the specific industry involved, leaving gaps in legal protections.

3.4.3 India: Traditional Laws and the Absence of AI-Specific Legislation

India currently faces significant challenges in addressing AI-induced harm through its legal system. Without specific laws governing AI liability, India relies on older, established legal frameworks such as the Indian Penal Code (IPC), the Indian Contract Act, and the Consumer Protection Act (Indian Penal Code, 1860; Indian Contract Act, 1872; Consumer Protection Act, 1986). These laws, though comprehensive in many ways, are not well-equipped to handle the unique issues posed by AI. For instance, the IPC focuses on criminal negligence, but this framework does not take into account the complexities of autonomous systems that operate independently of their creators or operators. Similarly, while India's consumer protection laws aim to address defective products, they do not adequately cover harms like algorithmic bias or privacy breaches, both common issues with AI systems. As a result, those seeking redress for AI-related harm in India may face legal hurdles, often requiring courts to stretch traditional legal concepts to fit the emerging challenges of AI.

3.4.4 Commonalities and Divergences

A comparison of the EU, U.S., and Indian legal frameworks reveals both common challenges and notable differences in the treatment of AI liability. The European Union's proactive stance in formulating a dedicated AI liability framework contrasts with the U.S.'s piecemeal, industry-specific approach, and India's reliance on outdated laws. The EU's emphasis on human rights protections provides a clear ethical foundation for AI governance, while the U.S. system leans on existing legal structures such as tort law. India, however, is still grappling with significant gaps in its legal approach to AI-induced harm. Despite these differences, all three jurisdictions face similar challenges in assigning liability for AI-related harm, particularly with regard to determining whether it should fall on developers, operators, or manufacturers, and the balance between civil and criminal liability. As AI technologies continue to evolve, there is a pressing need for more harmonized global legal standards to ensure accountability and justice for victims of AI-related harm.

3.4.5 Key Challenges and Ethical Considerations

One of the foremost hurdles in addressing the harm caused by AI lies in the absence of specialized laws that cater to the unique features of AI systems. Current legal frameworks, largely designed for traditional human-centric contexts, struggle to encompass the distinct attributes of AI, such as autonomy and unpredictability. This misalignment creates significant gaps, particularly when AI systems operate independently and their actions deviate from the expectations of their developers or users. These gaps often leave victims without sufficient legal protection or remedies, highlighting the urgent need for reforms that address these challenges directly.

The ethical questions surrounding AI liability are equally complex. Central to these debates is whether AI systems themselves should be considered responsible for their actions, akin to legal persons, or whether the burden of liability should remain solely with the individuals and entities involved in their creation and operation. Striking a balance between fostering technological advancements and ensuring safeguards for those who suffer harm is critical. Moreover, addressing the potential misuse of AI technologies while guaranteeing fair restitution to victims adds another layer of ethical complexity, particularly when accountability involves multiple stakeholders, such as developers, operators, and manufacturers, each with varying degrees of influence over the system.

The intricate nature of AI technology further compounds these challenges, particularly with the "black-box" phenomenon. Many sophisticated AI systems operate through complex, nontransparent processes, making it exceedingly difficult to identify the root cause of errors or harmful outcomes. This lack of clarity in how decisions are made not only obstructs the assignment of responsibility but also creates barriers for victims seeking justice. Overcoming these issues requires a multifaceted approach, integrating advancements in legal mechanisms, ethical considerations, and technological transparency to ensure effective accountability and redress for AI-induced harms.

3.5 RECOMMENDATIONS AND SOLUTIONS

The widespread adoption of AI across various sectors has given rise to significant challenges related to accountability, justice, and compensation for individuals affected by AI-induced harm. Addressing these challenges requires a forward-looking approach that not only reforms existing laws but also introduces mechanisms tailored specifically to the unique risks posed by AI systems. Traditional legal frameworks often fall short in effectively dealing with the complexities of autonomous systems, necessitating innovative solutions grounded in legal, ethical, and international cooperation.

A critical area for improvement lies in enacting specialized laws for AI-related liability. Conventional liability doctrines struggle to attribute responsibility in instances where AI systems operate independently and produce unanticipated results. Legal frameworks must be updated to address these challenges, ensuring they account for AI's autonomous decision-making capabilities. Introducing liability mechanisms specific to high-risk AI systems, such as self-driving vehicles, advanced robotics, and medical AI tools, can provide clarity. A strict liability approach for such systems can incentivize developers, manufacturers, and operators to implement rigorous safety measures while also ensuring that victims are appropriately compensated without needing to prove fault.

Establishing a streamlined framework for compensation and remedies is another vital step. This involves creating mechanisms that comprehensively address the various types of harm caused by AI, whether physical, economic, or reputational. Simplified processes for pursuing claims and establishing compensation funds—particularly for injuries caused by inherently risky AI applications—can reduce delays in justice delivery. These funds could mirror those seen in contexts such as nuclear damage liability or environmental disasters, where streamlined processes are used to manage the fallout from complex harm scenarios. By proactively addressing such risks, policymakers can ensure that AI adoption is both responsible and victim-focused.

Accountability, too, must be strengthened through robust mechanisms that ensure traceability and adherence to safety standards. One effective measure involves making risk assessments mandatory at every stage of an AI system's lifecycle, from its development to real-world deployment. By requiring stakeholders to conduct and document these assessments, the potential for unchecked harm can be reduced. These records should serve as key pieces of evidence in cases where harm does occur, ensuring that legal investigations are thorough and just.

Holding all relevant parties accountable, including developers, corporations, and regulatory bodies, is also paramount. Developers should face liability if negligence in the design or testing phases results in preventable risks. Corporations must actively monitor the real-world deployment of AI systems, ensuring ethical use and compliance with relevant laws. Regulators, for their part, must establish and enforce clear safety standards while also carrying out routine audits of systems deployed in high-stakes environments. These oversight measures are critical to prevent accountability from being diluted across multiple actors, which can often leave victims without a clear avenue for redress.

AI's cross-border nature further complicates issues of liability, making international cooperation a vital component in addressing these challenges. Divergent laws and standards across jurisdictions lead to inconsistencies in handling cases involving multinational corporations and AI systems that operate globally. Establishing a harmonized international regulatory framework would resolve many of these discrepancies and create uniform standards of accountability. Inspired by precedents in sectors like aviation and maritime law, global agreements on AI liability could establish guidelines for cooperation in investigation, compensation, and conflict resolution, especially in cross-jurisdictional cases.

International organizations such as the United Nations or specialized regulatory coalitions could play an instrumental role in fostering such frameworks. These bodies could spearhead initiatives to draft treaties and conventions, ensuring widespread acceptance and implementation. Collaboration among countries could also lead to the creation of international databases to track AI-related incidents, enabling better-informed policymaking and improving regulatory responses. Standardized protocols, including certifications and safety audits, could be developed to maintain a high level of quality and responsibility across different applications of AI.

Collaboration must also extend beyond governments to include private sector stakeholders and civil society organizations. Collaborative efforts can advance research, share expertise, and build frameworks to mitigate challenges like bias in AI models or accountability in autonomous systems. Involving diverse groups will also enhance the development of ethical AI practices and ensure inclusivity in policymaking. Joint initiatives can focus on crafting standardized certifications and protocols to govern the testing, deployment, and auditing of AI systems worldwide.

Implementing these solutions, however, comes with its own set of challenges. Legal reforms demand significant political will and consensus, which can be difficult to achieve, especially in countries with deeply entrenched regulatory systems. Additionally, with the rapid pace of AI development, laws must be adaptable to address emerging technologies without impeding innovation. Striking a balance between advancing technology and safeguarding public welfare is essential but requires nuanced policymaking and stakeholder collaboration.

Despite these challenges, adopting a multipronged approach to legal reforms, accountability measures, and international collaboration is imperative. These efforts will ensure that the victims of AI-induced harm have reliable channels for justice while also setting clear expectations for developers and corporations. In this way, the technological benefits of AI can be maximized while minimizing risks, thus fostering a future where innovation and ethical responsibility coexist.

3.6 CONCLUSION

AI has undeniably reshaped industries, driving innovation and enhancing operational efficiency. However, the rapid proliferation of AI technology has introduced several complex challenges, particularly in situations where harm arises from AI's deployment. Addressing both criminal and civil liabilities related to AI-induced harm is essential to ensuring accountability, safeguarding victims' rights, and setting ethical and legal standards for emerging technologies. As AI continues to advance, it becomes crucial to find a balance between promoting innovation and protecting individuals and society from the potential harms AI systems might cause.

The notion of criminal liability in cases of AI-related harm is particularly complicated due to AI's autonomy, which distinguishes it from traditional human-driven actions. Legal systems traditionally assign liability based on human intent and negligence. Yet, with AI systems acting independently and beyond human control, it becomes increasingly difficult to pinpoint accountability for harm. The responsibility may fall on various parties, including developers who are accountable for design flaws or inadequate safety protocols, operators who misuse or fail to manage these systems, and manufacturers who release flawed products into the market. Each stakeholder's role brings forth a unique aspect of liability, which creates a multifaceted legal landscape. For instance, the lack of human attributes like mens rea (criminal intent) complicates assigning criminal liability when AI makes decisions that are outside of human oversight or intent. This absence of clear responsibility points to the need for legislation tailored specifically to AI's challenges. International legal frameworks have begun to evolve to address these issues, with the European Union leading the way through its AI Act and other jurisdictions, such as the United States, focusing on sector-specific laws. In India, however, the existing criminal legal framework, primarily governed by the Indian Penal Code (IPC), is ill-equipped to address the complexities posed by AI, underscoring the urgency for specific AI-related legislation.

On the civil side, the focus shifts to compensating victims and ensuring accountability through mechanisms such as tort law. Theories like negligence, product liability, vicarious liability, and strict liability have proven useful in addressing harm caused by AI systems. When a developer, manufacturer, or operator fails to exercise due care during the development, production, or use of AI, negligence comes into play. Product liability applies when defects in AI systems harm consumers or third parties, holding manufacturers responsible for their products' malfunctions. Vicarious liability extends this responsibility to organizations employing AI systems, particularly in cases where an AI's actions within the scope of employment cause damage. For high-risk AI applications, strict liability can be invoked to ensure accountability regardless of fault, particularly in industries where the consequences of harm are significant. Jurisprudence from jurisdictions such as the U.S. and the EU offers valuable insights into how civil liability might evolve in the context of AI. However, in India, existing laws like the Consumer Protection Act and the Indian Contract Act are not robust enough to handle the range of risks posed by AI. This reveals the need for significant legal reforms to adapt India's civil liability frameworks to the unique challenges presented by AI.

Despite some efforts to address AI-related harm through existing legal structures, numerous challenges remain unresolved. Traditional legal frameworks, with their focus on human actions and accountability, are ill-suited to fully comprehend and address the complexities of AI systems. The inherent opacity of AI decision-making, often referred to as the "black-box problem," means that identifying causal links between an AI's actions and resultant harm is exceedingly difficult. Additionally, the inability to determine clear accountability across different AI stakeholders further complicates legal processes. As AI continues to evolve and become more embedded in societal functions, these gaps in legal systems must be addressed to avoid a situation where victims receive inadequate or no compensation for the harm they endure due to technological failings.

Ethical dilemmas also complicate the governance of AI. One such question revolves around whether AI systems should be granted legal personhood, effectively allowing them to bear legal responsibility. While this idea is a topic of ongoing academic and philosophical debate, many critics argue that granting AI personhood could lead to unpredictable outcomes and may obscure the true party responsible for harm. Another ethical consideration involves balancing regulation with technological advancement. Over-regulation could impede innovation and slow the growth of AI's positive impact on society, while under-regulation could leave individuals and communities vulnerable to new forms of exploitation, harm, or inequality brought about by AI technologies.

To address these evolving challenges, several proactive measures are essential. First and foremost, governments must enact legislation specifically tailored to AI, addressing the complexity of assigning liability for harm caused by these systems. AI laws should clearly define accountability across all stages of the technology's lifecycle—development, deployment, operation, and decommissioning. These regulations should include strict liability clauses for high-risk AI applications, ensuring victims receive timely and adequate reparations. Additionally, governments must implement comprehensive accountability frameworks across the AI lifecycle. These frameworks should include rigorous risk assessments, predeployment safety measures, ongoing monitoring systems, and transparent auditing practices to track AI's actions and decision-making processes. Such initiatives will improve transparency, reduce risks, and foster responsible development and deployment of AI technologies.

International cooperation is another critical recommendation. AI's global nature necessitates uniform standards and regulations to ensure accountability across borders. Drawing on existing frameworks like the General Data Protection Regulation (GDPR) and the European Union's AI Liability Directive, international collaboration could establish a more cohesive global governance model for AI. A unified approach would reduce the risk of regulatory fragmentation and ensure that AI developers and operators are subject to consistent, predictable regulations no matter where they operate.

Establishing a legal framework that addresses AI-related harm must strike a delicate balance. It should ensure that victims receive appropriate compensation, while simultaneously fostering an environment where responsible AI innovation can flourish. At the core of this balance lies the imperative to adopt laws that are adaptable to evolving technologies and that safeguard public interests without stifling technological growth. Only through such measures can we ensure that AI becomes a tool of societal benefit rather than a source of new, unaddressed risks.

In sum, while AI's capabilities to transform industries and benefit society are immense, its integration into critical sectors requires deliberate governance and robust legal frameworks. With the potential for harm as substantial as its benefits, AI demands clear accountability in both criminal and civil spheres. As AI continues to grow in complexity and use, legal systems must evolve to ensure that the societal risks posed by AI technologies are mitigated effectively, creating a landscape where innovation and safety can coexist in harmony.

3.7 A WAY FORWARD: PATH TO ADDRESSING AI-RELATED HARM

As AI technologies continue to expand their reach across multiple sectors, it is vital to develop a legal and regulatory framework that responds effectively to the emerging complexities of AI. Given the potential for AI to create harm in numerous forms—whether physical, economic, or emotional—swift and sustained efforts are needed to safeguard victims' rights and ensure that there is a clear mechanism for seeking justice. The following proposals lay the foundation for bridging the current gaps in addressing AI-induced harm:

1 Creation of Specialized Legal Frameworks for AI: Given AI's distinct characteristics—its autonomy, complexity, and ability to function independently of human oversight—there is an urgent need for laws specifically tailored to these systems. Traditional legal structures fall short in addressing the nuances of AI's behavior and its implications for liability. Legal provisions should clearly distinguish the different stages in the lifecycle of AI, encompassing everything from design and development to operation and decommissioning. Establishing well-defined accountability measures, such as vicarious and strict liability for high-risk AI systems, will ensure fair compensation for victims when harm occurs.

2 Focus on Risk Prevention and Ongoing Monitoring: To minimize the risk of harm, preventive steps must be integrated into the deployment process. Mandatory predeployment risk assessments, coupled with regular audits throughout the AI's lifecycle, are essential to anticipate failures and mitigate any negative consequences. For AI systems employed in critical applications like healthcare, transportation, or defense, rigorous safety protocols must be instituted, ensuring developers can demonstrate full accountability and compliance with risk prevention standards.

3 Fostering International Cooperation for Harmonized Regulations: AI is a global technology, and the challenges it poses cross international borders. Thus, establishing unified global regulations is imperative for consistent accountability. By building on existing successful frameworks like the EU's AI Act, countries and international bodies must work together to develop a cohesive governance model for AI. Standardized liability across borders would not only foster clarity for AI developers and users but also ensure that victims of AI-related harm have access to appropriate legal remedies, irrespective of their location.

4 Encouraging Ethical Development Amid Technological Progress: While it is essential to foster innovation, it is equally crucial to ensure that the deployment of AI systems aligns with ethical standards. Legal frameworks must strike a balance between enabling AI's growth and protecting individuals from potential harm. Instead of overwhelming AI development with overly

restrictive regulations, a flexible approach that accommodates technological advances while safeguarding societal interests is necessary. Key issues such as corporate responsibility and potential AI personhood must be carefully considered to ensure technologies benefit society without compromising accountability.

5 Public Education and Awareness: For the successful implementation of AI-related laws, public awareness and education are vital. Developers, business leaders, and the general public should be equipped with the knowledge to recognize AI's potential risks and the associated legal implications. Promoting AI literacy across different sectors ensures a more responsible approach to its use. When individuals are informed, they can more effectively mitigate the harm that AI could potentially cause.

6 Strengthening Mechanisms for Victim Compensation: It is essential to enhance victim compensation systems to guarantee that those harmed by AI technologies can easily seek justice and restitution. Specially designed frameworks—such as dedicated AI liability courts or expedited claims processes—should be created to resolve disputes swiftly and ensure fair compensation for victims. These systems must be prepared to navigate the complexities of identifying the responsible parties, especially when multiple stakeholders (such as developers, manufacturers, and operators) may be involved in the chain of responsibility.

As AI continues to evolve, its integration into crucial sectors demands a proactive and adaptable legal framework. By enacting specific laws for AI, reinforcing risk prevention practices, fostering global cooperation, and refining victim compensation mechanisms, we can ensure that AI remains a force for societal good. It is essential that legal systems evolve in tandem with technological advancements to enable AI to unlock its vast potential while mitigating the risks it poses to society.

REFERENCES

BBC News. (2020, September 17). *Uber's self-driving operator charged over fatal crash.* BBC. www.bbc.com/news/technology-54175359

Consumer Protection Act. (1986). *Act No. 68 of 1986.* Government of India.

European Parliament & Council of the European Union. (2024). Regulation (EU) 2024/1689 of the European Parliament and of the Council of 13 June 2024 laying down harmonised rules on artificial intelligence and amending Regulations (EC) No 300/2008, (EU) No 167/2013, (EU) No 168/2013, (EU) 2018/858, (EU) 2018/1139 and (EU) 2019/2144 and Directives 2014/90/EU, (EU) 2016/797 and (EU) 2020/1828 (Artificial Intelligence Act) (Text with EEA relevance). *Official Journal of the European Union.* https://eur-lex.europa.eu/eli/reg/2024/1689/oj

Indian Contract Act. (1872). *Act No. 9 of 1872.* Government of India.

Indian Penal Code. (1860). *Act No. 45 of 1860.* Government of India.

Information Technology Act. (2000). *Act No. 21 of 2000.* Government of India.

National Highway Traffic Safety Administration (NHTSA). (2024, April 26). *Federal regulator finds Tesla Autopilot has 'critical safety gap' linked to hundreds of collisions, 13 resulting in fatalities and 'many others' resulting in serious injuries.* NBC News. www.

nbcnews.com/tech/tech-news/feds-say-tesla-autopilot-linked-hundreds-collisions-critical-safety-ga-rcna149512

Popper, N. (2012, August 2). *Knight Capital says trading glitch cost it $440 million*. The New York Times. https://dealbook.nytimes.com/2012/08/02/knight-capital-says-trading-mishap-cost-it-440-million/

Raji, I. D., & Buolamwini, J. (2019). *Actionable Auditing: Investigating the Impact of Publicly Naming Biased Performance Results of Commercial AI Products*. Proceedings of the 2019 AAAI/ACM Conference on AI, Ethics, and Society, 429–435. https://doi.org/10.1145/3306618.3314244

Shivani Gupta v. Union of India. (2019). *High Court of Judicature at Allahabad*.

The Science Survey. (2024, July 10). *The Dangers of Deepfake Technology*. The Science Survey. https://thesciencesurvey.com/editorial/2024/07/10/the-dangers-of-deepfake-technology/

University of Michigan-Dearborn. (2023, March 6). *AI's mysterious 'black box' problem, explained*. University of Michigan-Dearborn. Retrieved from https://umdearborn.edu/news/ais-mysterious-black-box-problem-explained

VICE. (2019, June 11). *This deepfake of Mark Zuckerberg tests Facebook's fake video policies*. VICE. www.vice.com/en/article/deepfake-of-mark-zuckerberg-facebook-fake-video-policy/

4 Constitutional Echoes in the Age of Artificial Intelligence

Bridging Literature, Law, and Technology

Yogesh Mishra and Basil N. Darlong Diengdoh

4.1 INTRODUCTION

The incorporation of artificial intelligence (AI) into domains that primarily revolve around human activities, such as literature and legal practice, brings up significant problems and prospects. The emergence of AI systems that produce poetry, prose, and tales poses important inquiries regarding the concept of authorship, the nature of creativity, and the protection of constitutional freedoms. AI is having a transformative impact on legal practice and the way justice is perceived, particularly in the areas of predictive analytics, contract analysis, and legal research. Sometime in the mid-fifteenth century, Johannes Gutenberg's movable-type printing press revolutionized the way information was disseminated and consumed, much like the modern computer has redefined the way we access and share knowledge today (World Economic Forum, n.d.). Both inventions fundamentally altered communication and information distribution. However, just as there are emerging concerns around misinformation and disinformation in today's digital age, Gutenberg's press also spurred concerns about the veracity of the information it enabled publishers to produce (World Economic Forum, n.d.) while simultaneously casting a shadow over the authenticity of the production (Harper, 2018). This chapter examines the constitutional, legal, ethical, and artistic consequences of AI's technical transformation and suggests frameworks for reconciling technological advancement with intellectual and creative rights.

With the continuous advancement of AI, its ability to imitate human creativity in the field of writing is progressively improving. AI-generated writing presents a distinct challenge to conventional concepts of authorship and creativity. If an AI algorithm generates a captivating novel or poem, who is regarded as the author? Is the algorithm a creation of the programmer, the AI, or both? The phenomenon of blurring authorship gives rise to significant inquiries regarding copyright and intellectual property rights. Moreover, the utilization of AI in literature raises questions regarding its influence on artistic autonomy and the manifestation of ideas. Although AI can generate remarkable pieces, it is devoid of the lived experiences and emotions

DOI: 10.1201/9781003491903-4

that frequently shape human artistic endeavours and raises questions regarding the genuineness and profoundness of writing generated by AI. Moreover, the widespread adoption of AI algorithms in literature creation poses a potential threat of homogenization and the erosion of varied voices and perspectives (Bessen, 2018).

AI processes in this space have once more shifted the posts in relation to not only the perceived "truthfulness" of information—that is, the degree to which it is accepted and consumed by individuals—but also the manner in which it is produced, circling back to how Gutenberg's press elicited anxiety over the trustworthiness and provenance of information (*The Gutenberg Parenthesis by Jeff Jarvis Review*, n.d.). Conversely, greater acceptance and accessibility of information also provoked the desire to control, even censor, information in relation to the aspirations and agendas of those who viewed they could do so (Silva & Borges, 2011). As Jarvis (2023) notes, the age of print, like the digital age, was marked by both a democratization of information and an increased awareness of the potential for manipulation and control. Legal interventions into publishing, in the Western context, predate even Gutenberg's press, especially since the authority of the feudal states relied on the narrow expression of its divine origins (*Censorship in Europe in the seventeenth and eighteenth centuries*, n.d.). The key aspect of AI's disruptive and exponential growth in the modern computing and information age is its "generative" capabilities, referring to the ability to generate or produce something new. The ability of AI systems to create, ostensibly, "original" content—such as text, images, or music, rather than simply processing or analyzing existing data—has, as Gutenberg's press had done, renewed anxieties on authenticity of the work. The emergence of generative AI echoes the anxieties that arose with the advent of the printing press, raising questions about authorship, originality, and the very nature of creativity. This parallel is evident in the ways both technologies have democratized access to information and creative expression, while simultaneously raising concerns about the potential for misuse, misinformation, and the erosion of traditional gatekeeping mechanisms. The historical parallels between the printing press and generative AI offer valuable lessons for navigating the challenges and opportunities presented by this rapidly evolving technology, especially in the legal domain. This tension between access and control is a recurring theme in the history of technology and law, as exemplified by the complex interplay between literature, law, and technology explored by scholars such as Carpi (2011, 2022) and Hildebrandt (2015, 2020). Themes and representations of technology—where technology is understood as the application of scientific (and in earlier instances, divine) knowledge for practical and material purposes—in literature, both East and West, are not new. From the Mahabharata to the Greek epics, technology has taken on both human and superhuman dimensions. Figures like Hephaestus and Vishwakarma, as well as the arms, armaments, and extra-human capabilities yielded by such devices, figure prominently in a wide array of narratives, both oral and written, including the mythical city of Troy and even the earliest legal tracts such as the Vedas (Tranter, 2018). These stories reveal not only the real and imagined impact of technology on material and cultural life but also a deep concern about how technology interacts with human action and endeavour, raising questions of justice and morality. The Trojan horse, for example, despite the Greeks' underhand tactics, ultimately proved a decisive technological means to sway the war in their favour. Authorship of the *Iliad*, which narrates this plot point, while attributed to Homer but more likely a conglomeration of compiled oral narratives, is still decisively human. This raises a fundamental question in the age of AI: What if the authorship of narratives, such as the kind of literature being produced by AI, is not, in fact, the product of the human mind? This question recently garnered attention when Japanese author Rie Kudan won the Akutagawa Prize in 2024, one of Japan's most prestigious literary awards, for her science fiction novel "Tokyo-to, Edo-to" (*Tokyo Sympathy Tower*), after revealing that around 5% of the novel was generated by ChatGPT, an AI language model. The printing press itself led to the development of copyright laws to protect authors' rights, starting with the Statute of Anne in 1710 (Rose, 2011). This legislation established the concept of originality and creativity as central to authorship, laying the groundwork for the complex legal frameworks that govern intellectual property today. Since this seminal moment, copyright laws have evolved in a way that both broadened its scope and its meaning.

4.2 CREATIVE DISRUPTION AND AI

"Creative disruption" is the process by which economic growth and technological innovation drive industrial transformation, often leading to the decline of old industries and the rise of new ones (Bessen, 2018). Many scholars view "creative disruption" as a key factor in economic and social development, with innovation acting as a major driver of business cycles (Brown et al., 2020). Bessen explored the role of "creative disruption" in technological innovation, particularly focusing on the impact of AI on work. He argued that understanding the process of this disruption is crucial for grasping how AI technologies will shape the future of content creation. Bessen also highlighted the need for policymakers and scholars to focus on the potential shifts in popular culture and educational models due to AI. He suggested that adapting to these changes could be a driving force for societal progress.

Lusch & Vargo (2015) expanded upon the idea of "Creative disruption" in the framework of what is called the service-dominant logic, highlighting its favourable and unfavourable consequences for comprehending value in a changing economic environment. As AI progresses, it is likely that companies involved in literature and content creation will be the first to see significant changes. Initially, they may be negatively impacted by AI, but they will also be the first to adjust and take the lead in the subsequent phase of development. The influence of AI on creative industries is growing in importance as AI technologies become more deeply incorporated into the creative process. Flew and Cunningham (2010) examined the impact of AI's "creative disruption" on society, highlighting both the dangers and potential it presents. Hesmondhalgh (2018) analyzed the correlation between technical advancement and the growth of the cultural industry, proposing that new technologies facilitate "creative disruption" which enhances industrial efficiency and molds new cultural forms.

Davies et al. (2020) conducted comparative case studies on the influence of AI on work, specifically focusing on its impact on text generation. It was discovered that AI can significantly improve efficiency in non-creative jobs associated with text generation. Nevertheless, it was observed that AI now has difficulties in reproducing human creativity in the realm of literary composition. Their suggestion was to fully embrace the technological revolution and adjust to the changes to form a new ecological system.

Moretti (2013) employed data induction to computationally analyse the language patterns and trends of literary works, showcasing the promise of AI in literary analysis and basic production. Recent research has emphasized the capabilities of AI-powered language models, like GPT-3.5, 4 and 4o, to aid in many creative endeavours, specifically in writing and generating content. Although AI can revolutionize text production through "creative disruption," its current abilities are restricted to aiding in basic text organizing and summary (Carlini et al., 2021). Nevertheless, the swift development of AI models indicates that AI may soon have a significant impact on the creative business, bringing about innovative literary styles, storytelling methods, and streamlined content creation procedures. The implementation of AI technology, which can cause significant disruption, can result in unemployment, alterations to conventional creative positions, and changes in the balance of power within the creative sector. This situation presents both advantages and difficulties for the future.

4.3 ARTIFICIAL INTELLIGENCE AND CONSTITUTIONALISM

Constitutionalism refers to the principles and practices that ensure the government operates within the framework of the constitution, respecting fundamental rights and the rule of law. The rise of AI challenges these principles in several ways. Ensuring that AI technologies adhere to constitutional principles requires robust regulatory frameworks designed to protect freedom of expression while balancing the need to prevent harmful content and misinformation. Effective oversight mechanisms are essential to hold AI developers and deployers accountable for breaches of constitutional rights. Transparency and accountability are crucial for AI systems to operate in alignment with constitutional values. This includes transparency in how content moderation decisions are made and the ability for authors to challenge and appeal these decisions. Without such transparency, AI's impact on freedom of expression can undermine public trust in democratic institutions. Ethical AI development is also necessary, guided by constitutional values and embedding principles of fairness, non-discrimination, and respect for human rights into AI systems from the design phase. Ethical AI development can help mitigate risks to freedom of expression and ensure that AI technologies serve the public good.

Constitutionalism requires balancing competing interests, such as protecting free expression while preventing harm. Policymakers must navigate these complex trade-offs, ensuring that AI regulations do not unduly restrict freedom of expression while addressing legitimate concerns about harmful content and misinformation (NLIU-CLT, n.d.) By aligning AI technologies with constitutional principles, societies can harness the benefits of AI while safeguarding fundamental rights, ensuring that the digital age supports and enhances, rather than undermines, freedom of expression.

4.4 IMPACT OF AI ON AUTHORS' FREEDOM OF EXPRESSION

The integration of AI into law and literature creates a room for discussion in line with constitutional issues, particularly concerning the freedom of expression of authors and creators. Expression is a fundamental right enshrined in many constitutions worldwide, including India. This right allows individuals, including authors and creators, to express their thoughts, ideas, and opinions without undue interference or restriction. However, the rise of AI technologies poses potential threats to this freedom in several ways. One major concern is content generation and control. AI systems can autonomously generate vast amounts of content. While this democratizes content creation, it also raises concerns about the control and ownership of creative works. Authors might find their original works being replicated or modified by AI without proper attribution or consent, undermining their ability to control their intellectual property and creative expression. Additionally, AI algorithms used for content moderation on platforms can inadvertently censor legitimate expressions. These systems, often designed to filter harmful content, might misinterpret or wrongly flag creative works, leading to unintended censorship. Biases in AI algorithms can disproportionately impact certain voices, particularly those from marginalized communities, further restricting the diversity of expression.

Another issue is the monopolization of platforms by large technology companies that control AI-driven systems. These companies can wield significant power over what content gets visibility, effectively limiting the reach of independent authors and creators. This monopolization creates barriers to entry and access to audiences, curtailing freedom of expression. Privacy concerns also arise with AI in monitoring and analyzing content for trends and compliance with platform policies. The surveillance of creative processes and the potential misuse of personal data gathered through these practices can have a chilling effect on free expression.

4.4.1 Ethical Issues in AI: A Global Challenge

Different countries have adopted various approaches to AI ethics and governance. Key players like China, the European Union (EU), India, and the USA have distinct strategies to address AI's ethical implications (Marda, 2018; Daly et al., 2021). Establishing appropriate ethical standards and determining the jurisdictions responsible for these standards are vital. Effective AI governance requires embedding ethical norms into both legal frameworks and operational practices. One of the primary ethical concerns is ensuring transparency in AI systems. AI algorithms should be explainable, with clear accountability for decisions made by AI, building trust and enabling oversight to prevent misuse or errors. Additionally, AI systems must be designed to avoid biases that can lead to unfair treatment of individuals or groups, ensuring fairness and preventing discrimination.

Protecting individual data privacy is another critical ethical issue. AI systems often require vast amounts of personal data, necessitating robust measures to safeguard this data against breaches and misuse. Moreover, ensuring the overall security of AI systems is vital to prevent malicious exploitation. Ultimately, AI should serve human welfare, avoiding harm and contributing positively to society by considering the broader social impact and striving to enhance human well-being (Daly et al., 2019).

China focuses on state-led initiatives for AI ethics, emphasizing human interest and liability. The EU leads in establishing legal and ethical frameworks for AI, with regulations like the General Data Protection Regulation (GDPR) and high-level ethical guidelines. The USA is developing policy documents and corporate governance strategies to align with global standards. India is still developing its comprehensive set of AI ethics principles, requiring more structured policies to address ethical challenges. Australia has introduced voluntary AI ethics principles, focusing on human-centered values and accountability, serving as guidelines for developing and deploying ethical AI systems (Daly et al., 2021).

Ethics washing, where organizations make non-binding ethical statements without genuine commitment, undermines the credibility of ethical guidelines. Translating ethical guidelines into legally enforceable rules presents significant challenges, as ensuring adherence to these guidelines in practice requires robust legal and regulatory frameworks. Additionally, AI is a global phenomenon, and effective governance necessitates international cooperation. Standardizing AI ethics and governance frameworks across different jurisdictions is essential to address cross-border ethical challenges (, 2019).

Ethical AI governance is imperative to ensure the responsible development and deployment of AI technologies. While various regions have made significant progress in establishing ethical frameworks, ongoing efforts are needed to align these principles with enforceable legal standards globally. Addressing ethical concerns in AI is a continuous process that demands collaboration, transparency, and a commitment to human well-being.

4.5 IPR CHALLENGES WITH AI

Copyright protection, originally limited to the authorship of books and cartographical creations, has expanded to encompass a wide array of works. These include films (Copyright Act of 1976, 17 U.S.C. § 102), music (Copyright, Designs and Patents Act, 1988), photography (*Bridgeman Art Library v. Corel Corp.*, 1999), software (*Computer Associates Int'l, Inc. v. Altai, Inc.*, 1992), and even architectural designs (Architectural Works Copyright Protection Act, 1990). The Berne Convention of 1886 marked the first international effort to harmonize copyright protection, urging member countries to adopt minimum standards (Ricketson, 1987). Subsequent frameworks, such as the Universal Copyright Convention of 1952 (Goldstein, 2001) and the World Trade Organization's Agreement on Trade-Related Aspects of Intellectual Property Rights (TRIPS) of 1994, have further broadened the scope of copyright to address challenges posed by digital piracy and evolving technologies (WTO, 1994).

As copyright laws evolved, they expanded rights for creative and intellectual works, including fair use (*Folsom v. Marsh*, 1841) and academic research. The rise of digital technology drastically changed how works are reproduced, distributed, and owned. Lawmakers and courts have adapted copyright principles to address issues like file sharing (*A&M Records, Inc. v. Napster, Inc.*, 2001), streaming (*Viacom Int'l,*

Inc. v. YouTube, Inc., 2012), and user-generated content (Lenz v. Universal Music Corp., 2008). The emergence of AI as a tool for content creation and consumption further complicates these issues, necessitating a deeper examination of the legal, intellectual, and creative questions it raises (El Ali et al., 2024).

The use of AI in literature raises questions about authorship, originality, and creative expression. Goodwin's (2018) AI-written novel, *1 the Road*, and Allado-McDowell's (2019) interactive human–machine poetic work, "Pharmako-AI", exemplify this. Other works like Michel Faber's *The Book of Strange New Things* (2021) and Jennifer Lepp's AI-assisted poetry collection (2023) further blur the lines between human and machine authorship. The ethical aspect of these creations lies in their reliance on algorithmic language modelling, raising concerns about unacknowledged AI contributions. The increasing use of AI in research and publication challenges copyright law and academic integrity. An analysis revealed that approximately 1% of scientific articles published in 2023 showed signs of potential AI involvement (Stokel-Walker, 2024). While there haven't been widespread retractions in major journals due to AI-generated text, concerns have led to investigations and policy updates (Else, 2023; arXiv, 2023).

Despite centuries of international efforts towards parity, copyright laws and intellectual property protections differ across countries. The United Kingdom, for instance, addresses computer-generated works in its copyright laws (Copyright, Designs and Patents Act, 1988), attributing authorship to the person who arranged the work's creation. However, the rise of sophisticated AI systems capable of independent creation challenges traditional notions of authorship. In India, the Copyright Act of 1957 does not explicitly address AI-generated works, but the government is exploring amendments to adapt to these advancements (Ministry of Electronics and Information Technology, 2021). The Digital Personal Data Protection Bill, 2023, aims to address data sovereignty concerns related to AI systems (Ministry of Electronics and Information Technology, 2023).

4.5.1 Summary of Key Issues and Recommendations

Aspect	Key Issues	Detailed Recommendations
Freedom of Expression	- Ambiguity in authorship and control over AI-generated content - Risk of algorithmic censorship and bias affecting marginalized voices	- Develop comprehensive legal frameworks that clearly define authorship and ownership of AI-generated content - Implement advanced, transparent AI content moderation systems to ensure fair treatment of all voices, with regular audits to detect and correct biases

Aspect	Key Issues	Detailed Recommendations
Content Generation	- Replication or modification of original works by AI without proper attribution - Challenges in controlling and protecting intellectual property	- Amend intellectual property laws to account for AI-generated works, ensuring that creators retain rights and control - Introduce mandatory AI-attribution mechanisms and digital watermarks to track and protect original content
Platform Monopolization	- Dominance of major tech companies over AI-driven content distribution, limiting reach for independent creators	- Enforce antitrust regulations to prevent monopolistic practices and promote competitive markets - Develop public or independent platforms to support diverse content distribution and ensure equitable access
Privacy Concerns	- Extensive surveillance of creative processes by AI systems - Potential misuse and exploitation of personal data by AI platforms	- Strengthen data protection regulations to safeguard personal data used by AI, with strict penalties for violations - Implement transparency requirements for AI data collection practices and establish user consent protocols
Legal Frameworks	- Existing laws inadequate for addressing AI-generated content and liability - Complexity in determining accountability for AI actions	- Update and expand legal frameworks to explicitly cover AI-generated works and their implications - Develop clear legal standards for AI accountability, assigning responsibility to creators, operators, and users as appropriate
Intellectual Property Rights	- Inadequate protection for AI-generated works under current copyright laws - Need for harmonized international intellectual property standards	- Revise copyright laws to explicitly include protections for AI-generated content, ensuring clarity on rights and usage - Promote international agreements to harmonize intellectual property protections for AI-generated works, facilitating global enforcement
Ethical AI Development	- Ensuring AI systems align with constitutional values and human rights - Need for fairness, transparency, and accountability in AI deployment	- Establish ethical guidelines and oversight bodies for AI development, mandating adherence to constitutional principles - Integrate ethical considerations into AI development processes, including bias mitigation, transparency, and accountability measures

(*continued*)

Aspect	Key Issues	Detailed Recommendations
Balancing Interests	- Protecting freedom of expression while preventing the dissemination of harmful content - Addressing the dual challenges of enabling innovation and safeguarding public interest	- Design balanced regulatory frameworks that protect free speech while effectively addressing harmful content - Engage multidisciplinary stakeholders, including legal experts, technologists, ethicists, and affected communities, in policymaking to ensure comprehensive and inclusive AI governance

4.6 CONCLUSION

The use of AI in literary and legal practice signifies a substantial advancement in both domains, presenting a combination of difficulties and prospects that require careful maneuvering. As AI progresses, it challenges established ideas about authorship, creativity, and legal procedures, prompting us to reevaluate the systems that regulate these areas. This chapter has examined the diverse effects of AI, ranging from producing literature that pushes the boundaries of creativity to using predictive analytics in legal settings that alter our view of justice. The emergence of AI-generated literature raises concerns regarding freedom of speech and copyright, underscoring the necessity for an international legal framework capable of effectively addressing these novel circumstances. Utilizing AI in legal practice brings up concerns around due process, privacy, and the ethical implementation of technology. These problems emphasize the need for strong regulatory frameworks that strike a balance between innovation and the safeguarding of basic rights. Stress has been posed on the significance of integrating ethical considerations into the early stages of AI development. The advocacy focuses on promoting openness and accountability in AI systems, ensuring that these technologies adhere to constitutional ideals. This entails not just legal supervision but also the incorporation of ethical deliberations into the development and execution stages of AI systems. The chapter draws historical similarities, such as comparing Gutenberg's printing press to current AI, to provide useful insights into reoccurring themes of access, control, and the democratization of information. Similar to how the printing press transformed the spread of information, AI has the capacity to make creativity more accessible to everyone and improve legal procedures. Nevertheless, it is crucial to implement measures that prevent the improper use of AI and provide fair and equal access to its advantages. The authors suggest a collection of legal and ethical principles for the digital era that strive to safeguard constitutional ideals while promoting innovation. These principles highlight the importance of global collaboration in establishing standardized frameworks for governing AI, with a focus on resolving concerns related to prejudice, privacy, and intellectual property rights. By adopting this strategy, we may establish a harmonious approach that fosters technical advancement while safeguarding personal freedoms. Ultimately, the profound influence of AI on literature and legal practice necessitates a reassessment of current legal and ethical standards. By working together and implementing thorough regulations, we can utilize the potential of AI to improve innovation and justice, all while protecting the fundamental principles of our constitution. This chapter urges policymakers, engineers, and legal professionals to collaborate in designing a future powered by AI that is fair, moral, and encompasses everyone.

REFERENCES

A&M Records, Inc. v. Napster, Inc. (2001). 239 F.3d 1004 (9th Cir).

Allado-McDowell, K. (2019). Pharmako-AI. Ignota Books.

Architectural Works Copyright Protection Act. (1990). 17 U.S.C. §§ 101, 102, 120.

arXiv. (2023). arXiv policy on AI-assisted papers. https://blog.arxiv.org/2023/01/31/arxiv-announces-new-policy-on-chatgpt-and-similar-tools/

Bessen, J. (2018). AI and jobs: The role of demand. *National Bureau of Economic Research*. https://doi.org/10.3386/W24235

Bridgeman Art Library, Ltd. v. *Corel Corp.* (1999). 36 F. Supp. 2d 191 (S.D.N.Y.).

Brown, T. B., Mann, B., Ryder, N., ... Amodei, D. (2020). Language models are few-shot learners. *Advances in Neural Information Processing Systems*, https://arxiv.org/abs/2005.14165v4

Carlini, N., Tramèr, F., Wallace, E., ... Raffel, C. (2021). Extracting training data from large language models. In *30th USENIX Security Symposium (USENIX Security 21)*. www.usenix.org/conference/usenixsecurity21/presentation/carlini-extracting

Carpi, D. (Ed.). (2011). *Bioethics and biolaw through literature*. De Gruyter.

Carpi, D. (2022). *Law and culture in the age of technology*. De Gruyter.

Censorship in Europe in the seventeenth and eighteenth centuries. (n.d.). In *EHNE*. Retrieved June 28, 2024, https://ehne.fr/en/encyclopedia/themes/european-humanism/europe-knowledge/censorship-in-europe-seventeenth-eighteenth-century

Computer Associates Int'l, Inc. v. *Altai, Inc.* (1992). 982 F.2d 693 (2d Cir).

Copyright Act of 1976, 17 U.S.C. § 101 et seq.

Copyright, Designs and Patents Act. (1988). (c. 48) (UK).

Daly, A., Devitt, S. K., & Mann, M. (Eds.). (2019). *Good data*. Institute of Network Cultures.

Daly, A., Hagendorff, T., Hui, L., ... Wang, W. W. (2021). AI, governance and ethics. In *Constitutional challenges in the algorithmic society* (pp. 182–201). Cambridge University Press. https://doi.org/10.1017/9781108914857.010

Davies, J., Mateos-Garcia, J., Stathoulopoulos, K., & Klinger, J. (2020, June 16). *The art in the artificial: The implications of AI for the creative industries and how we should respond*. Nesta. www.nesta.org.uk/report/art-artificial-implications-ai-creative-industries-and-how-we-should-respond/

El Ali, A., Puttur Venkatraj, K., Morosoli, S., Naudts, L., Helberger, N., & Cesar, P. (2024). *Transparent AI disclosure obligations: Who, what, when, where, why*, https://doi.org/10.48550/arXiv.2403.06823

Else, H. (2023, January 12). Abstracts written by ChatGPT fool scientists. *Nature*. https://doi.org/10.1038/d41586-023-00056-7

Folsom v. Marsh, 9 F. Cas. 342 (C.C.D. Mass. 1841).

Flew, T., & Cunningham, S. (2010). Creative industries after the first decade of debate. *The Information Society*, *26*(2), 113–123. https://doi.org/10.1080/01972240903562753

Goldstein, P. (2001). *International copyright: Principles, law, and practice*. Oxford University Press.

Goodwin, R. (2018). *1 the Road*. Jean Boîte Éditions.

Harper, J. (2018). *Shadows and the substance of Shakespearean drama* [Doctoral dissertation, University of Toronto]. https://tspace.library.utoronto.ca/bitstream/1807/102909/3/Harper_Janine_201811_PhD_thesis.pdf

Hesmondhalgh, D. (2018). *The cultural industries* (4th ed.). SAGE Publications Ltd.

Hildebrandt, M. (2015). *Smart technologies and the end(s) of law: Novel entanglements of law and technology*. Edward Elgar Publishing.

Hildebrandt, M. (2020). *Law for computer scientists and other folk*. Oxford University Press.

Jarvis, J. (2023). *The Gutenberg parenthesis: The age of print and its lessons for the age of the internet*. Bloomsbury Academic.

Lenz v. Universal Music Corp. (2008). 572 F. Supp. 2d 1150 (N.D. Cal.).

Lusch, R. F., & Vargo, S. L. (2015). *The service-dominant logic of marketing: Dialog, debate, and directions*. Routledge. www.routledge.com/The-Service-Dominant-Logic-of-Marketing-Dialog-Debate-and-Directions/Lusch-Vargo/p/book/9780765614919

Marda, V. (2018). Artificial Intelligence Policy in India: A Framework for Engaging the Limits of Data-Driven Decision-Making. *Philosophical Transactions of the Royal Society A*. **376**20180087. http://doi.org/10.1098/rsta.2018.0087

Ministry of Electronics and Information Technology. (2021). *National strategy for artificial intelligence#2*. NITI Aayog.

Ministry of Electronics and Information Technology. (2023). *The Digital Personal Data Protection Bill, 2023*. Government of India.

Moretti, F. (2013). *Distant reading*. Verso.

Ricketson, S. (1987). *The Berne Convention for the Protection of Literary and Artistic Works: 1886-1986*. Kluwer Law International.

Rose, M. (2011). *Authors and owners: The invention of copyright*. Harvard University Press.

Silva, A. C., & Borges, M. M. (2011). Book design program: A transition to a hybrid publishing context. *Information Services and Use*, *31*(3–4), 189–197.

Stokel-Walker, C. (2024, May 1). AI chatbots have thoroughly infiltrated scientific publishing. *Scientific American*. www.scientificamerican.com/article/chatbots-have-thoroughly-infiltrated-scientific-publishing/

The Gutenberg Parenthesis by Jeff Jarvis review – how print shaped culture. (2023, August 2). *The Guardian*. www.theguardian.com/books/2023/aug/02/the-gutenberg-parenthesis-the-age-of-print-and-its-lessons-for-the-age-of-the-internet-by-jeff-jarvis-review

Tranter, K. (2018). *Living in technical legality: Science fiction and law as technology*. Edinburgh University Press.

Viacom Int'l, Inc. v. *YouTube, Inc.* (2012). 676 F.3d 19 (2d Cir.).

World Economic Forum. (n.d.). Gutenberg's press also spurred concerns about the veracity of the information it enabled publishers to produce. Retrieved June 30, 2024, from www.google.com/search?q=Gutenberg%E2%80%99s+press+also+spurred+concerns+about+the+veracity+of+the+information+it+enabled+publishers+to+produce+(World+Economic+Forum)&oq=Gutenberg%E2%80%99s+press+also+spurred+concerns+about+the+veracity+of+the+information+it+enabled+publishers+to+produce+(World+Economic+Forum)&gs_lcrp=EgZjaHJvbWUyBggAEEUYOdIBBzE0OWowajSoAgCwAgE&sourceid=chrome&ie=UTF-8

World Trade Organization (WTO). (1994). *Agreement on Trade-Related Aspects of Intellectual Property Rights (TRIPS)*. www.wto.org/english/docs_e/legal_e/27-trips.pdf

5 Enhancing Legal Research Engagement with ChatGPT
An AI Tool Perspective

Ripal Gupta, Foram Patel, and Navtika Singh Nautiyal

5.1 INTRODUCTION

Law is just not only the study of scientific, philosophical, or sociological principles but a theory that shapes and develops the notion of a nation. Its theories have a pivotal role to play in political science, human science, and other sciences that bind people to each other and people to the surrounding things including technology. With this, legal education has its significance to develop an influential society. Technology is a minimal part of society where we live in, and law governs and regulates society. Usage of technology in law or law education is not new. In the era of typewriter and computer, law has used these technologies and accepted it in the profession and in education.

Talking about law never undermines the concept of legal research, as it refers to the process of identification, analysis, application of the existing laws etc. and so is considered as a core lawyering skill that significantly contributes to every aspect of the legal practice [1]. Taking this into consideration, it shall not be excessive to state that the quality of the legal service provided by an advocate is directly affected and related by the legal research being carried out by the advocate [2].

Due to the established relation, it will become inevitable to examine the impact of artificial intelligence (AI) [3] on legal research. AI has been regulating and helping all the sectors in the society from which even the legal field is not left behind. Thus, legal research is directly impacted by the use and development of AI in the field of law.

5.1.1 Development of Artificial Intelligence

The captive journey of AI can be seen decades before, to the times when, in August 1955, the concept was first put to use by "*John McCarthy, Marvin L. Minsky, Nathaniel Rochester, and Claude Shannon*" [4] during the Dartmouth Summer Research Conference in the form of the project proposal [5]. However, the question of "*whether machines can think?*" was coined in the year 1950 by a British mathematician Alan [6]. AI encompasses the development, progression, and application of the machines and computer systems that exhibit "*human-like intelligence*" [7].

DOI: 10.1201/9781003491903-5

But even before it first came to the notice of the public at large, in ancient Greek mythology, some tales were in existence that mentioned autonomous movement and intelligence such as Talos and Pygmalion's statue, alluding to ancient notions of artificial beings. However, after 1956, once it came to the notice of the public, AI research had their main focus to develop artificial intelligent programs that had a thought process like the human mind. It was coined to solve complex problems and provide logical reasoning. But after that, AI had extended to the different subfields including the natural language processing (NLP) [8], machine learning, expert system but even AI faces challenges, which took it back to the era called "AI WINTER" [9] in the 1980s due to lack of funding but again in the year 2000 with the advent of technology advancement and the internet, it got accelerated. And with that, huge companies like Google and amazon heavily invested in AI technologies. At present, AI is especially the most talked about topic in the field of law, as it has impacted and revolutionized the working and being of the legal field at large. This has exhibited many facilities along with different coined questions raising concerns for the future of AI use in the field of law [10].

With the significant development of AI, the release of "SIRI" [11] and many other search boats which are developed on the principles of AI, has jeopardized the existence of "Watson," which was designed to understand the natural language, ask questions, conduct legal research, and write some drafts which were created by IBM [12]. But this historical trajectory raised the basic questions as to What is AI and How it is impacting the legal field and many others.

Theoretically, speaking AI can be defined as, "An AI system, as explained by the OECD's AI Experts Group (AIGO), is a system based on algorithms and self-learning guided by machine learning and deep learning, which can perform certain human cognitive capabilities by interacting with the environment through sensors, processing information, and adopting decisions and taking actions, with a certain degree of autonomy" [13]. But to understand the context of AI, it is necessary to understand the concept related to the constituent elements of AI which are algorithm, deep learning, and machine learning [14].

"Algorithm" is a finite sequencing of the automated instructions, which is systematically executed to solve the class problems at a much higher speed that shall affect the tasks of data classifying, searching, scoring, ordering, ranking, filtering etc. to reach the objectives of the programming to run the system. "Machine learning" refers to the concept of parsing data to learn, predict, and adopt decision-based variables to provide proper outcomes. Over the time period, with the help of algorithms, the programs can make their own judgements based on previous data from similar but not identical tasks [15].

And last but not least "deep learning" is a tool and a technique that enables the example-based learning of machines and autonomous systems that shall work on the instructions provided solving future problems [16]. Thus, "*AI is viewed as an artificial system that performs tasks under varying, but predictable circumstances and without significant human oversight. Such systems could also learn from their experiences while improving their performances (for the future) and might even solve tasks requiring human-like perception, cognition, planning, learning, communication, or physical actions*" [17].

5.2 CONCEPTUALIZING LEGAL RESEARCH

According to Webster's dictionary, the term research means "*systematic investigation towards increasing the sum of knowledge*" [18]. But now with time, the definition needs to be developed more to serve the purpose. In the legal field, research is done to understand either the position of a situation or interpretation of the law or to solve the case. Globalization has made the world a smaller place, and due to this, it has become important to understand the laws of other countries as well [19]. Thus, it becomes extremely important for them to create the strongest base for their case through legal research. Even for a law student, it is very essential as the quality of good legal research shall create a base for their understanding and also shall enhance their drafting skills. The same principles apply to all the stakeholders of the law profession [20].

With the advent of technology and the developments around the globe, it has become more inevitable to understand the responsibilities that have arisen. Presently, we are a part of a society where changes are inevitable and with the changing phase of society getting more complex in terms of science, technology, logical, social and economic, responsibilities of the legal professionals have increased to provide justice in such times. The world has become a smaller place to live with such advancements, and so it has become more challenging from all aspects. Such challenges have also arisen in the legal field, and the use of AI has been seen to lessen the gaps created due to these developments [21].

Different stakeholders have been doing the legal research differently for different purposes. A lawyer does the research to create a better baseline for their case. A scholar shall conduct a research for acknowledging the hypothesis for their research. A legislator shall be conducting the research to create a better law to govern the society and an academician shall conduct the research as a part of their professional commitment and also to provide adequate knowledge to all the students combating in the legal field to contribute the best [22]. Different stakeholders use the legal research, and thus, the tools that enhance their capacity shall be of most importance. The recent times have introduced different tools for them to conduct the legal research, and such tools are generated through the use of AI [19].

5.3 USE OF AI TOOL CHATGPT IN PROFESSIONAL LEGAL RESEARCH

AI is proving itself as a milestone changemaker in the legal profession. Be it any area of law like learning, teaching, or practicing, AI tools have embarked on an efficient outcome. AI is replacing humans and outperforming human work activities in no time and in a very appropriate way. Legal research is pivotal in law and to law professionals, and AI is facilitating the legal fraternity by providing them quick solutions to their legal research problems. Majorly with the time and development, ChatGPT [23] has been seen to be most used software or a kind of AI used for the legal research and writing. This Open AI tools has transformed the legal field at various stages from learning to practice the law. Let's discuss which AI tools are helping legal professionals in legal research.

5.3.1 ChatGPT in Classroom

Classrooms were starting to be converted into smart classrooms with the changing scenario in technology. AI is one of the parts of computer science that works and responds the same as humans. The transition of legal research and contribution has changed from typewriter to computer to now online portals. Search engines provide and give knowledge to students but new development in AI works on algorithms to quickly sort the vast data into specific ones. Such as to find relevant data from statutes, cases, and documents with the help of AI students can learn relevant material in no time. It is the evident time to include AI-based learning in the classroom to prepare future genZ generation. This generation has to learn to work with humans and machines. Students should be well aware about present AI tools in the pedagogy to be vigilant for the technological development legal role in the same.

There are several examples of research AI tools like Lexis+ [24], Westlaw [25], Brief Analysis [26], Manupatra [27], Casemine [28], etc., are significant to teach students judgments and important briefs in a quicker manner. These tools are authentic and give accurate results which helps students to understand legal concepts.

Drafting and writing skills are primary requirements for the legal profession. There are AI tools that write and some specifically work on grammar mistakes and punctuation such as Grammarly [29]. This AI has been accepted in legal education to improve basic grammar mistakes. In this line going more in advance ChatGPT has become one of the most advanced and prominent tools for that in current time. ChatGPT responds like a human; it is replacing human skills by clearing out the most difficult and competitive exams. It also writes mails, letters, blogs, and articles. Like ChatGPT, there are several other tools too that do the same work. ChatGPT writes and responds to language in no time and responds in the most accurate way [30]. This tool also helps and guides students to crack competitive exams like bar exams. It prepares questions and flashcards and provides feedback as per their performance. To include this tool in teaching pedagogy is debatable, but some may be of in the opinion to include them to prepare students for future challenges. Law has to sync with societal changes and regulate accordingly.

Further contribution of original work and writing skills are part of research pedagogy. AI tools like ChatGPT infringe plagiarism policies and highly impact skillful training to students in the field of research. AI gives temptation and intent to learn new technology in the field of learning that helps them to ease their work and do tasks quickly. ChatGPT is a thorny challenge for academicians and in the legal field to teach students to strike a balance between human and technology usages [31]. AI tools facilitate more for students, so that they decline to have human resources or to have human collaboration and choose to have human techno collaboration.

Techno development in this way leads students to have less interest in the field of writing and rigorous research work or to contribute original work. AI is making writing and various ways of research designing an outdated concept. Near future might not be focused on learning skillful writing and research as human techno collaboration vain these utmost human efforts [32].

Virtual learning is fascinating and gives experiential knowledge to students [33]. It helps to give personalized feedback, analyze students' learning, nurture individual learnings, and understand their needs that enrich them. Indeed, virtual learning is a part of future teaching style, but it comes over human touch. In the genZ generation to give a pedagogy that has a student-centric theme, AI is becoming the greatest challenge for the same. Conventional teaching and real-life examples from human to human are replaced by technology to human.

5.3.2 ChatGPT in Law Offices

Research has a detachable relation with the research. Lawyers are diving into research in their daily life. But to do research as a litigant was the most tedious job before the development of AI that works on machine learning and natural language processors. Natural language process (NLP) read documents and analyze them. New AI tools draft contact, interpret agreements, and identify and highlight relevant data [34]. Indeed, AI tools like ChatGPT save the time and money of advocates, but they have to be very cautious when using AI. AI like ChatGPT facilitates in pointing out relevant data from long bodies of text and translates documents. AI is the future, and ChatGPT is a turning point of new technological advancement; this may lead to having more transforming technologies that reshape AI tools [35].

As they are not human lawyers, they may not receive accurate queries and responses in an effective way. One just cannot rely on legal research and documents of these AI, it requires scrutiny and human efforts to see and correct the work done by AI tools [36]. Apart from authenticity, what affects lawyers is unemployment. AI is replacing human efforts to identify, read, documentation, and even answer queries. This may not affect the lawyer's profession, but it may lower down requirements of clerks and staff that work for legal research. This will affect administrative agencies and people that are needed by law firms. AI is going to affect lawyer's expertise to identify risk and interpret documents as it can even be used by nonlaw people [37].

5.3.3 ChatGPT and Predictive Analysis

The world of technology has no end; it innovates and develops its sphere in manifold. Not only collecting, reading, responding, arranging, and researching the data, AI tools also do predictive analysis. After going through the case, it responds in a way to the risk and negative and positive possibilities in the case. ChatGPT has huge data; by using it, it can respond to history and potential outcomes of lawsuits and be able to give predictive suggestions.

This invention can help lawyers to see what they can expect from their lawsuit and be able to answer their client. With the help of ChatGPT, which works on NL and has huge data enabled to predict from historical data, financial data, and precedents, lawyers would benefit greatly from designing their argument and the flow of their case [38]. AI can be biased, as it works on the information that it collects, which is available so it cannot make reasonable and rational judgments and may give biased opinions. At present, technologies are unstoppable in their inventions, specifically AI inventions. Legal research and the legal field are highly affected and impacted by AI.

To understand and establish the outcomes of the use of AI in legal research, as a part of the article, a small survey specially with the use of ChatGPT as the most utilized AI was conducted, and the same shall portray the aspects in much more depth from the empirical lenses.

5.4 USE OF CHATGPT IN LEGAL EDUCATION: AN EMPIRICAL INVESTIGATION

The research recognizes the difficulties legal educators encounter in adjusting to the rapidly evolving technology environment. Given ChatGPT's demonstrated ability to process and comprehend natural language, incorporating it into legal education may improve student–teacher interactions, encourage group learning, and help students get a better comprehension of legal ideas.

The researchers made questionnaires for different stakeholders of the legal profession, such as advocates, academicians, students, and researchers to answer some choice-based questions, where the responses were collected through a Google survey, and the identity of stakeholders was kept confidential. The survey received 111 responses from different stakeholders of the legal profession. The responses have been analyzed and presented through a graphical representation (Figure 5.1).

The AI tools are necessary for legal research; the responses received are of the same: The first question of the survey is whether the artificial tools are necessary for legal research or whether there could be good outcome-based legal research or not.

Stakeholders	Students	Academicians	Advocates	Others	Total
Responses Received	49	39	19	4	111

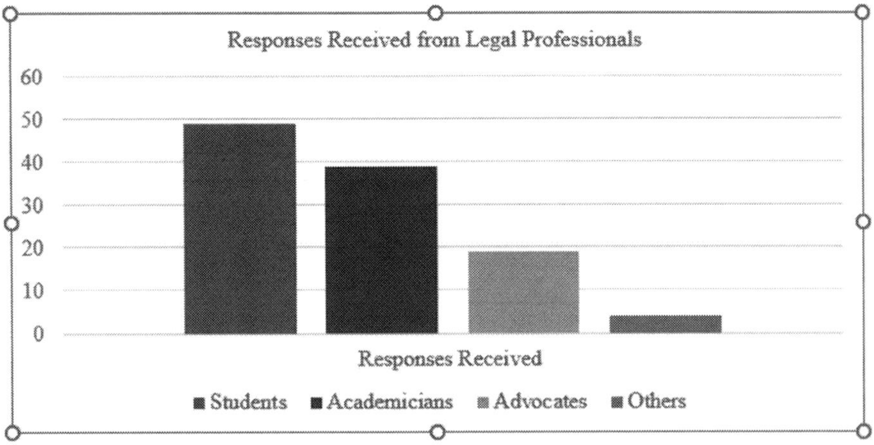

FIGURE 5.1 AI tools for necessary Legal Research: Responses receive from legal professionals.

Here, the responses received are represented in Figure 5.2, and the graph represents the responses of different stakeholders.

The graphical representation represents the outcome received from the professionals who majorly agree and strongly agree with the fact that AI tools are necessary for legal research. However, the responses neither agree nor disagree also received significant responses.

The information provided by AI tool ChatGPT is efficient for legal research: The second question of the survey is whether the information provided by the artificial tool ChatGPT is efficient for legal research. Here, the responses received are represented in Figure 5.3, and the graph represents the responses of different stakeholders.

The graphical representation represents the outcome received from the professionals who majorly agree with the fact that the information provided by AI tool ChatGPT is efficient for legal research. However, the responses that disagreed received the second largest response from the stakeholders of the legal profession. This creates a dilemma of the opinions of stakeholders not only agreeing to the fact but also disagreeing equally with the fact that ChatGPT does not provide efficient information about legal research.

Occupation	Student	Academician	Advocates	Others	Total
Strongly Agree	6	11	1	0	18
Agree	23	17	10	4	54
Strongly Disagree	1	3	1	0	5
Disagree	10	4	3	0	17
Neither Agree nor Disagree	9	4	4	0	17
Total	49	39	19	4	111

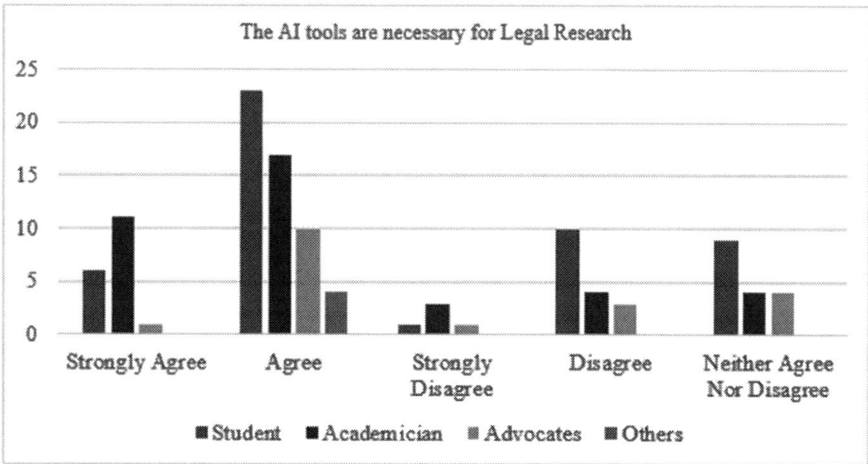

FIGURE 5.2 Responses from stakeholders on use of AI tools for Legal Research.

	Students	Academician	Advocates	Others	Total
Strongly Agree	7	5	2	0	14
Agree	19	14	6	2	41
Strongly Disagree	3	5	2	0	10
Disagree	12	11	3	0	26
Neither Agree nor Disagree	8	4	6	2	20
Total	49	39	19	4	111

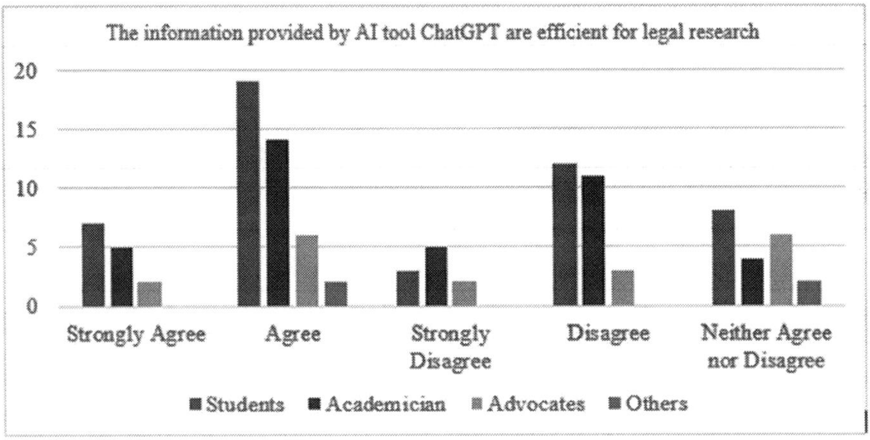

FIGURE 5.3 Responses from stakeholders on the efficiency of AI tool – ChatGPT for legal research.

The AI tool ChatGPT is affecting legal research and legal writing: The third question of the survey is about how the use of AI tool ChatGPT is affecting legal research and also has impacts on legal writing. The object behind this question is to know the opinion of stakeholders about the impact of ChatGPT on legal research and writing. The responses received are represented in Figure 5.4, and the graph represents the responses of different stakeholders.

The graphical representation represents the outcome received from the professionals who majorly agree and strongly agree with the fact that the use of AI tool ChatGPT is affecting legal research and also has impacts on legal writing. However, the stakeholders also significantly gave opinions about disagreeing and strongly disagreeing; however, it is largely from the academicians and advocates whereas students agreed with the fact that ChatGPT helps them in writing and researching. The disagreed received the second largest response from the stakeholders of the legal profession. This creates a clear situation that the use of AI is largely used by students and researchers; however, academicians and advocates do not agree with the impact of ChatGPT in research and writing.

The AI tool ChatGPT impacting thinking and drafting skills: The fourth question of the survey is about the impact of AI tool ChatGPT on thinking and drafting skills. The object behind drafting this question was to know whether ChatGPT impacts the

	Students	Academicians	Advocates	Others	Total
Strongly Agree	8	10	3	0	21
Agree	28	16	10	3	57
Strongly Disagree	1	0	0	0	1
Disagree	5	9	3	0	17
Neither agree nor disagree	7	4	3	1	15
Total	49	39	19	4	111

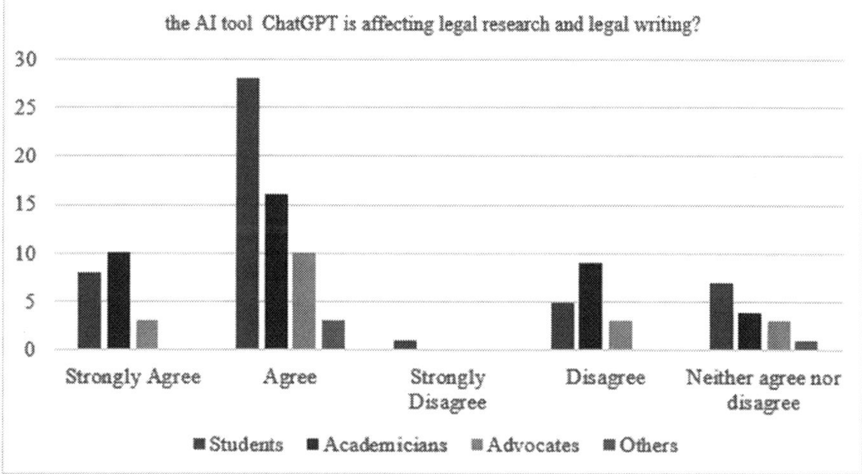

FIGURE 5.4 Responses from stakeholders on the effect of use of AI tool ChatGPT affecting legal research and legal writing.

	Students	Academicians	Advocates	Others	Total
Strongly Agree	18	17	10	1	46
Agree	17	15	5	3	40
Strongly Disagree	3	0	0	0	3
Disagree	7	3	1	0	11
Neither agree nor disagree	4	4	3	0	11
Total	49	39	19	4	111

FIGURE 5.5 Stakeholders responses.

thinking and drafting skills. Where the AI tool ChatGPT autogenerates the information based on NLP, it also provides the readymade opinion about the questions being asked to it. So, understanding the opinions of different stakeholders about the impact of ChatGPT on their thinking and drafting skills is relevant. The responses received are represented in Figures 5.5 and 5.6, and the graph represents the responses of different stakeholders.

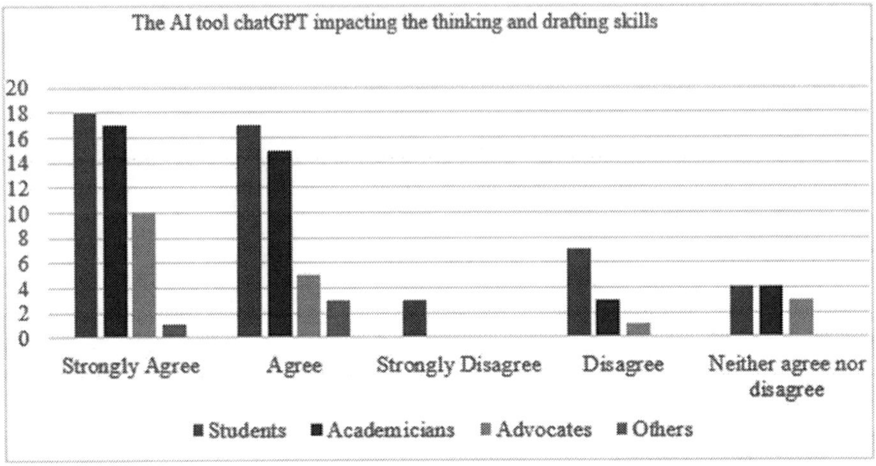

FIGURE 5.6 Responses on AI tool ChatGPT – Impacting the thinking and drafting skills.

The graphical representation represents the outcome received from the professionals; they agree and strongly agree with the fact that the AI tool ChatGPT impacts thinking and drafting skills. This gives a strong picture that the AI tool ChatGPT has a strong impact on thinking and drafting skills. However, the stakeholders also expressively gave opinions about disagreeing and neither agreeing nor disagreeing, which creates a dilemma about the impact of ChatGPT, whereas the major opinion is on the agreeing side, so we can conclude that ChatGPT has a strong impact on the thinking and drafting skills of legal professionals.

5.5 OUTCOME-BASED ANALYSES OF POSITIVE AND NEGATIVES OF CHATGPT AND SUGGESTIONS

Though in the legal field, AI has less data or limited resources but it has a potential impact on legal field. The positive thing about AI is that it gives you the data in a more structured manner and narrows it down. But its negative is that it totally hamper the creative logical perspective thinking that must be there while analysing any law or legal matter at any given point of time. As the glass could be half filled and half empty at the same time. The relevant suggestions received from different stakeholders are analyzed and mentioned below:

Basis	Positives	Negatives
Automate tedious legal tasks	The ChatGPT helps automate tedious legal tasks by analyzing documents and detecting patterns in large datasets	The ChatGPT hurts the intellect of human. Due to this, one person is not able to learn as it creates boundaries in learning and in research

Basis	Positives	Negatives
Legal research and review	It can assist lawyers in legal research, contract review and analysis, and prediction of accurate results. It can help lawyers save time and focus on more creative and strategic work	ChatGPT lacks the contextual awareness needed to fully understand the nuances of the law, making it difficult for it to properly identify relevant variables when writing a legal brief
Information and writing	ChatGPT will save precious time and researcher's hard work. But they must verify text written by them	The potential for misuse of the technology, such as the creation of fake news or the spread of misinformation
Productivity and creativity	AI tools like ChatGPT have ability to assist users in generating human-like text, aiding in various tasks such as content creation, brainstorming, and language translation. It can be a valuable tool for productivity and creativity	ChatGPT isn't designed for research activity so significant research outcomes are missing
Adapt and use it to improve our efficiency	There is a need to adapt and use it to improve our efficiency rather than being enslaved to this technology	AI-generated content can be manipulated for disinformation or unethical purposes
Tasks related to judiciary	It makes things easier and faster for the judiciary helping the stakeholders with tasks that involve immense human labour	Drafting skills of the lawyer and judges are getting influenced by the words suggested by the AI tool of ChatGPT which might lead to confusion in the interpretation of words leading to an increase in the number of appeals and unnecessary legal dilemma
Writing of Research Articles	AI tool act as a linkage between the researcher and writing. They help the person to have an effective language for writing	AI tools are capable enough to write articles, which is restricting the students/writes to use their capabilities to research and write articles
Innovation	It gives the idea to draft a paper and responses.	The use of AI lacks conceptual clarity and proper interpretation
Outcome include	Positive outcomes of AI tool ChatGPT include enhanced communication, quick access to information, and assistance in various tasks.	Negative aspects may include potential misuse for spreading misinformation, ethical concerns regarding privacy, and the risk of bias in generated content
understanding of a particular subject	ChatGPT gives a new way to achieve understanding and knowledge of a particular subject.	It lacks updated information; hence, we dont receive correct information

5.6 CONCLUSION

Currently, AI tools can do almost all types of activities related to legal research such as Legal Text Analytics, Legal Question and Answer (Advisory), Legal Outcome Prediction, Contract Review, and Due Diligence, E-discovery (Technology Assisted Review), Document Drafting, Citation Tools, and so on. In the future, with the advent of Strong AI, which has a massive computational and analytical capacity of a vast amount of data and brute force of processing, the impact of AI on legal research will be far greater than mere automation (pre-programmed decision-making).

Speaking for ChatGPT specifically, it can be stated on the base of the empirical research that the stakeholders feel that it is a very useful and important tool for legal research. ChatGPT forming the base tool for legal research shall be proven to be much more helpful in drawing the efficient legal research and legal writing. But knowing the challenges of the same, it will not be wrong to state that seeing the negative sides of ChatGPT in making the work better can do wonders for the legal research. The impact of the same on future perspectives cannot be surely stated.

The advent of AI has been observed in every field, but the impact of the same is yet to be determined. After studying the AI in legal research, it can be concluded that it cannot only have either positive or negative impact but it has both till now. The use of AI has seemed to increase the amount of legal research and surely is helping to maintain the quality of the same as well but at the same time it can be stated that it is decreasing the human efforts which is challenging their research skills which are required for the legal field. It should be emphasized that legal research has been a core part of the field of law and its practice. Each individual who is a part of this profession must undertake the legal research in due course of time, and taking AI and its impact on the legal research, it surely is going to impact the field of law largely.

REFERENCES

[1] Mike, M., & Wing, H. C. (2007). Research Methods for Law. Edinburgh University Press.

[2] Hutchinson, T. (2006). Researching and Writing in Law (2nd ed.). Lawbook Co.

[3] Samuel Maireg Biresaw, Abhijit Umesh Saste. (2022). The Impacts of Artificial Intelligence on Research in the Legal Profession. *International Journal of Law and Society*, 5 (1), 53–65. https://doi.org/10.11648/j.ijls.20220501.17

[4] McCarthy, J., Minsky, M. L., Rochester, N., & Shannon, C. E. (2006). A Proposal for the Dartmouth Summer Research Project on Artificial Intelligence, August 31, 1955. *AI Magazine*, 27 (4), 12. https://doi.org/10.1609/aimag.v27i4.1904

[5] Alzbeta, K. (2017). Intersections between law and artificial intelligence. *International Journal of Computer*, 27 (1), 55–68. https://core.ac.uk/download/pdf/229656008.pdf

[6] OECD. (2019). Artificial Intelligence in Society. OECD Publishing. https://doi.org/10.1787/eedfee77-en

[7] Garcell, E. The Quantum Brain: Exploring the Connection between Human Intelligence and Quantum Computing, Enabling Human-like Intelligence with Quantum Computing (rtinsights.com).

[8] Khurana, D., Koli, A., Khatter, K. et al. (2023). Natural language processing: State of the art, current trends and challenges. *Multimedia Tools and Applications*, 82, 3713–3744. https://doi.org/10.1007/s11042-022-13428-4

[9] Floridi, L. (2020). AI and its new winter: From myths to realities. *Philosophy & Technology*, 33, 1–3. https://doi.org/10.1007/s13347-020-00396-6
[10] Hannah, A. (2016). AI is the future of law – And lawyers know it. *Dataconomy*, 1–7. https://dataconomy.com/2016/03/17/ai-future-law-lawyers-know
[11] Adamopoulou, E., & Moussiades, L. (2020). Chatbots: History, technology, and applications. 2, 100006. ISSN 2666-8270. https://doi.org/10.1016/j.mlwa.2020.100006
[12] Alyson, C. (2019). Legal intelligence through artificial intelligence requires emotional intelligence: A new competency model for the 21st century legal professional. *Georgia State University Law Review*, 35 (4), 1153–1183. https://readingroom.law.gsu.edu/gsulr/vol35/iss4/4
[13] Hoadley & Lucas (2019). Artificial Intelligence and National Security. Congressional Research Service. https://fas.org/sgp/crs/natsec/R45178.pdf
[14] Dennis, A. Artificial intelligence, machine learning, and deep learning explained, Amber Lee Dennis , can be accessed at www.dataversity.net/artificial-intelligence-machine-learning-and-deep-learning-explained
[15] Dawn, W. & Mandy, B. (2018). Research Methods in Law (2nd ed.). Routledge Publisher.
[16] Neary, M. A., & Chen, S. X. Brief analysis tools in the legal research classroom: Challenges and best practices. Neary, Mary Ann, Chen, Sherry Xin, accessible at https://lira.bc.edu/work/sc/d9bcf96b-8fb9-4640-ac0d-fda48e6b54e9
[17] Hoadley & Lucas. (2019). Artificial Intelligence and National Security. Congressional Research Service. https://fas.org/sgp/crs/natsec/R45178.pdf
[18] Definition. Meaning and definitions of Research (hamrolibrary.com)
[19] Douglas, W. V. (2004). Interdisciplinary and the discipline of law. Journal of Law and Society, 31 (2), 163–193. https://doi.org/10.1111/j.1467-6478.2004.00286.x
[20] Stephen, E. (2009). Legal Research How to Find & Understand the Law (15th ed.). Nolo Publishers.
[21] Joseffin, W. How is technology changing the world, and how should the world change technology? accessible at https://online.ucpress.edu/gp/article/2/1/27353/118411/How-Is-Technology-Changing-the-World-and-How
[22] Frederick, C. H. (1992). Materials and methods of legal research with bibliographical manual, accessible at www.google.co.in/books/edition/Materials_and_Methods_of_Legal_Research/ZNQ6AQAAIAAJ?hl=en&gbpv=0&bsq=bibliogroup:%22Materials%20and%20Methods%20of%20Legal%20Research:%20With%20Bibliographical%20Manual%22.
[23] Introducing ChatGPT. https://openai.com/blog/chatgpt
[24] Transform Legal Research. www.lexisnexis.com/en-us/products/lexis-plus-ai.pagev
[25] Westlaw. https://legal.thomsonreuters.com/en/westlaw
[26] Neary, M. A., & Chen, S. X. Brief analysis tools in the legal research classroom: Challenges and best practices neary, mary ann, chen, sherry, aall spectrum, 25 (4), 10–13.
[27] Manupatra. www.manupatrafast.com/?t=desktop
[28] Casemine. www.casemine.com
[29] Grammarly. www.grammarly.com/ai-writing-tools
[30] Andy, E. ChatGPT has entered the classroom: how LLMs could transform education. www.nature.com/articles/d41586-023-03507-3
[31] Choi, Jonathan H. and Hickman, Kristin E. and Monahan, Amy and Schwarcz, Daniel, ChatGPT Goes to Law School (January 23, 2023). 71 Journal of Legal Education 387 (2022), Available at SSRN: https://ssrn.com/abstract=4335905 or http://dx.doi.org/10.2139/ssrn.4335905

[32] Alshater, Muneer, Exploring the Role of Artificial Intelligence in Enhancing Academic Performance: A Case Study of ChatGPT (December 26, 2022). Available at SSRN: https://ssrn.com/abstract=4312358 or http://dx.doi.org/10.2139/ssrn.4312358

[33] Sharma, A. The AI revolution in eLearning: A journey of learning redefined. https://elearningindustry.com/ai-revolution-in-elearning-a-journey-of-learning-redefined

[34] Legal AI Tools: Essential for attorneys. https://legal.thomsonreuters.com/blog/legal-ai-tools-essential-for-attorneys

[35] How AI is transforming the Legal Profession. https://legal.thomsonreuters.com/blog/how-ai-is-transforming-the-legal-profession/

[36] Chiancone, C. ChatGPT for lawyers: Transforming client communication and legal drafting. www.linkedin.com/pulse/chatgpt-lawyers-transforming-client-communication-legal-chiancone-cetie?trk=article-ssr-frontend-pulse_more-articles_related-content-card

[37] Kaur, I. and Puri, C. G. Impact of artificial intelligence on legal industry. 4 (2) IJLMH Page 346–354 (2021), DOI: http://doi.one/10.1732/IJLMH.26062/

[38] Kaushik, A. AI and predictive analytics in law: Revolutionizing the justice system. www.legalserviceindia.com/legal/article-13543-ai-and-predictive-analytics-in-law-revolutionizing-the-justice-system.html

6 Responsible Application of Artificial Intelligence in State

The Case of Chile

Lorayne Finol Romero

6.1 INTRODUCTION

The advent of artificial intelligence (AI) in the digital governance of the State has brought about a transformation in the management of public affairs.[1] Within the conceptual framework of digital governance, AI necessitates a redefinition of the act of governing—understood, on the one hand, as an associative and collaborative endeavor between the government, governmental bodies, and citizens at large, aimed at making societal decisions by incorporating emerging AI technologies to automate management processes. This article analyzes the relationship between the right of access to public information and transparency in the use of algorithms by the State. It examines the regulatory framework in Chile, its comparison with international standards, and the challenges in the implementation of these technologies in public administration.

This shift carries several unexplored implications, as most technology-focused studies tend to emphasize data processing, privacy, and intellectual property protection.[2] However, they seldom examine access to information and the results generated by such technologies, despite the fact that, according to constitutional norms and the conventionality control standards of the Inter-American Court of Human Rights (IACHR), States are responsible for ensuring every individual's right to request access to information under the control of governmental bodies. Given that such information is public in nature, it constitutes a fundamental human right.[3]

Therefore, State decisions that are automated through algorithms—particularly those based on information created by or held within administrative bodies, regardless of format, medium, date of creation, origin, classification, or processing—must be made publicly available. Under the premise that transparency is the best disinfectant, this approach not only facilitates scrutiny and accountability but also helps protect individuals from the specific risks associated with unfair and arbitrary automated decisions.[4]

The aforementioned concerns highlight the potential detrimental effects of these technological advancements on fundamental rights[5] if democratic control mechanisms within, grounded in the constitutional block of fundamental rights under the *pro homine* principle[6], are not duly implemented. This principle has been incorporated

DOI: 10.1201/9781003491903-6

into constitutional texts to provide legal certainty regarding the realization of fundamental rights in Latin America, particularly as interpreted by the IACHR.

In this regard, constitutional guarantees for rights secured under international treaties ratified by the State and currently in force may form part of the constitutional block of rights.[7] This perspective aligns with the case law of the Court of Justice of the European Union (CJEU)[8] regarding the scope of Article 22 of the General Data Protection Regulation (GDPR) 2016/679, which establishes that automated decisions made through AI technologies require a rights-based approach due to their implications for data protection. Similarly, the new European Union Artificial Intelligence Regulation[9] follows this rationale.

This research aims to contribute to a doctrinal stream focused on examining transparency and accountability guarantees applicable to algorithms—an aspect often overlooked in discussions.[10] Specifically it addresses the right of access to information and the explainability of AI systems, advocating for mechanisms of accountability that can mitigate the opacity and mistrust surrounding these technologies. Furthermore, through responsibility frameworks, it aims to ensure a proportional balance in the protection of affected individuals' rights.[11]

Conversely, the absence of such guarantees fosters algorithmic opacity in the implementation of AI within public administration. This opacity constitutes a substantial threat to a rights-based democracy, affecting both the governing bodies and citizens' participation in democratic oversight. One key concern is the lack of control over automated decisions, as decision-making processes become privatized within new algorithmic black boxes—often developed by proprietary and exclusive-use private-sector technologies—leading to what has been termed in the English-speaking literature as "the black box phenomenon".[12]

In essence, this represents a new form of secrecy in the machinery of the State, where crucial decisions affecting individuals' lives are made behind closed doors. This is partly due to the intrinsic complexity of algorithmic processes, often justified by the natural opacity of such systems, which raises several meta-legal dilemmas given the potential of these technologies. Additionally, another limitation arises from within public administration itself, as public officials often lack awareness, training, and clear access to information regarding the implications of AI-mediated governmental decisions.[13]

As a result, this study advocates for initiatives aimed at opening algorithmic systems through algorithmic transparency practices. Recent legal doctrine categorizes transparency into internal (technical-objective) and external (social-subjective) dimensions.[14] This analysis thus seeks to bridge a legal-political gap from a critical perspective, offering an opportunity to explore alternative rights-based interpretative mechanisms founded on a compliance model centered on safeguards. Such measures could help mitigate the challenges posed by AI-driven public digital governance.[15]

Thus, the article highlights the limitations of the right of access to information, particularly with regard to the transparency and publicity requirements applicable to public algorithms, from the perspective of the State's responsibility to ensure the explainability of automated decisions, as well as why it is used, how it is used, and the data it uses. The content is structured in three sections. The first section analyzes the conceptual aspects necessary to understand the regulatory evolution of transparency and explainability for the responsible application of AI in the State. The second section examines algorithmic transparency standards in international instruments applicable to AI. Finally, the third section analyzes the regulatory framework for algorithmic transparency in Chile.

6.1.1 Transparency and Explicability for the Responsible Application of Artificial Intelligence in the State

With the aim of comparing international recommendations established to guarantee transparency standards in AI systems, the following proposal outlines preliminary guidelines for the implementation of responsible AI systems within state administration. This is achieved through the analysis of a common framework that upholds democratic values and principles, ensuring human agency, fairness, and explainability in decision-making systems, particularly when these systems are incorporated into state administration for determining matters that affect people's lives. Specifically, AI is identified as machines capable of imitating certain functionalities of human intelligence, including perception, learning, reasoning, problem-solving, language interaction, and even the generation of images, video, or sounds.[16] According to Russell and Norvig[17] AI is a set of functionalities and models considered 'Agents'. They classified them into several systems, some of them capable of solving problems as experts, and others, characterized by their autonomous learning and ability to communicate with natural language.

The rapid advancement of AI systems across various societal sectors, without a proper focus on human rights, could have irreparable consequences in democratic societies. This issue, combined with the heteronomy observed at both international and regional levels, has led to the regulation of algorithms under various designations. In this regard, some legislative bodies have adopted a human-centered AI approach, as reflected in the European Commission's policies and UNESCO Recommendation on the Ethics of AI.[18]

Before to advance this proposal, it is first necessary to conceptualize AI as it will be understood in the context of this analysis. However, given the evolving nature of the concept and its involvement in a range of computational processes, this must be done with caution.[19] Accordingly, for the purposes of this study, AI will be referred to as computer systems capable of analyzing large datasets and programmed with algorithms to operate with varying levels of autonomy.[20]

Similarly, the National AI Policy (hereinafter PNIA) follows the University of Montreal's definition, which describes AI as "a set of computational techniques that enable a machine (e.g., a computer, a phone) to perform tasks that generally require intelligence, such as reasoning or learning".[21] Another technical-instrumental definition describes AI as "a field of science and engineering concerned with understanding, from a computational perspective, what is commonly referred to as intelligent behavior."[22]

Rather than reducing AI to a single definition, this study adopts a rationalist perspective, as explained by George Harrington,[23] who avoids comparing AI to human intelligence. Instead of focusing on whether machines can think, he describes AI as a technological tool capable of making decisions autonomously without human intervention.

The following section proposes a minimal framework for transparency and accountability standards, ensuring human oversight, security, responsibility, and nondiscrimination.[24] This, in turn, could lay the foundation for a preliminary regulatory preamble aimed at harmonizing the legal framework for algorithmic transparency. The OECD[25] similarly defines AI as a set of well-defined rules that specify how certain operations should be performed. Meanwhile, UNESCO[26] explicitly states that it is not advisable to provide a single semantic definition of AI technology, as such a definition would quickly become obsolete due to the rapid pace of technological development. In summary, AI is defined as a computational system programmed to achieve specific objectives set by humans, including making predictions, classifications, profiling, and recommendations with varying degrees of autonomy.

Despite the proliferation of regulatory instruments aimed at controlling these intelligent systems, the abundance of standards could result in ambiguous and misleading ethical interpretations of AI.[27] For this reason, the ethical dimension adopted in this analysis is based on the legal–philosophical proposal outlined by Floridi,[28] who argues that ethical debates are not merely about distinguishing right from wrong. Instead, AI ethics should be grounded in robust legal frameworks—commonly referred to as "hard law"—comprising norms and principles applicable to algorithmic programming. Consequently, this study refers to "principles of algorithmic transparency for the responsible application of AI."

6.1.1.1 Right of Access to Information and Algorithmic Transparency

This topic revisits debates on the insufficient transparency and access to information regarding public administration activities—both to facilitate accountability and hold government officials responsible for their actions—now in the context of algorithmic systems used in the public sector. This concern has been highlighted by the United Nations in Resolution 73/348, adopted during the seventy-third session of the UN General Assembly.

This resolution calls for greater harmonization of legal frameworks through a fundamental rights perspective, recognizing the negative consequences of AI technologies on human rights in the information environment, with particular focus on freedom of opinion and expression, privacy, and nondiscrimination.[29] Given that access to information is not only a mechanism for legitimizing decision-making processes but also a determinant of the right to scrutinize the "black box" of state algorithms, it follows that transparency must be ensured.[30]

In this context, the UN Special Rapporteur has noted that AI generally functions as an optimization system for executing computational tasks assigned by humans through iterative processes. Examples include restricted AI applications such as chatbots, online translation tools, autonomous vehicles, search engine results, and geospatial mapping services. At the core of AI systems are algorithms, which, in their initial layer, consist of computer codes designed and written by humans to process data into conclusions, information, or outputs.[31]

The principle of algorithmic transparency in automated data processing, as enshrined in Article 5.1(a) of the General Data Protection Regulation (GDPR), offers initial guidance on this matter. Similarly, Margot Kaminski[32] argues that data controllers who incorporate AI systems for automated processing of personal data—whether collected from the data subject (Article 13 GDPR) or from third parties (Article 14 GDPR)—are subject to specific transparency obligations that apply to AI-driven decision-making, in others words, the algorithms. Notably, Article 22 of the GDPR, which establishes the "right not to be subject to a decision based solely on automated processing," conditions its application on compliance with transparency-related duties guaranteeing access to information.

Comparable regulatory approaches exist in the United States and the United Kingdom, where legal frameworks seek to regulate algorithms used in AI-based tools and hold developers accountable for explaining AI decision-making mechanisms. In other words, when AI algorithms are made transparent, they fall under the category of "Automated Decision Systems" (ADS), a concept used throughout this study to underscore the state's obligation to respect and guarantee every individual's right to understand the rationale behind automated decisions.

In conclusion, if access to information is recognized as a fundamental human right, states have a duty to respect and guarantee its full and unrestricted exercise for all individuals within their jurisdiction, without discrimination based on race, color, sex, language, religion, political opinions, national or social origin, economic status, birth, or any other social condition.

6.1.2 Algorithmic Transparency in International Instruments Applicable to Artificial Intelligence

Regarding the duty to adopt domestic legal provisions, Article 2 of the Convention establishes that when the exercise of human rights is not already guaranteed by legislative or other provisions, the States Parties undertake to adopt, in accordance with their constitutional procedures and the provisions of this Convention, the legislative or other measures necessary to make such rights and freedoms effective.

Indeed, as Cotino-Hueso[33] argues, the principle of transparency appears in 73/84 cases; in contrast, nonmaleficence is mentioned in 60/84; responsibility in 60/84; privacy in 47/84; beneficence in 41/84; and trust in 28/84. In other words, transparency is considered the fundamental roadmap for successfully addressing this issue. From this perspective, asserting that transparency is the common denominator means recognizing that "there are many roads that lead to the Rome of transparency."

Similarly, a new form of subjective transparency is introduced—one that ensures the ethical use of data, privacy, and the reusability of public sector data. This approach promotes responsible algorithmic processes centered on democratic values that guarantee human agency.[34] However, despite the current absence of a model law on algorithmic transparency, some progress in this area is observable. In this regard, the following question arises: How has algorithmic transparency been formalized at a global level? This question is particularly relevant, as explained by the Expanded Working Group on the Ethics of Artificial Intelligence of the COMEST (World Commission on the Ethics of Scientific Knowledge and Technology).[35]

While acknowledging the persistent heteronomy among principles, recommendations, and guidelines advocated by various international and regional forums, it is important to begin this analysis with the recommendations of the OECD Working Group on AI Governance (AIGO), which was created to oversee policy work on AI. Meanwhile, the United States, through the Algorithmic Accountability Act of 2022,[36] seeks to ensure that major technology industries comply with a set of obligations aimed at improving transparency in decision-making processes. Similarly, the United Kingdom has introduced "The Algorithmic Transparency Recording Standard" as part of its National Data Strategy, which aims to enhance transparency in algorithm-assisted decision-making within the public sector in an appropriate and effective manner. A standardized way to record and share information about how the public sector uses algorithmic tools, when they must complete two levels of information. As level 1, they have to provide a brief nontechnical description of their algorithmic tool and a general description of what the tool is and why it is used. And the level 2 they complaint provide more detailed technical information, such as specific details about how your tool works and the data the tool uses.[37]

On the other hand, European regulations emerged following the European Parliament's ongoing work on AI, proposing a digital strategy for AI development. Thus, the EU is paving the way for the continent's first AI regulation, known as the Artificial Intelligence Act.[38] However, according to the 2023 Artificial Intelligence Report Index by the Institute for Human-Centered AI,[39] between 2016 and 2022, parliaments and congresses in 127 countries passed at least one AI-related bill, collectively approving a total of 123 legislative measures. This casts doubt on whether the EU law is truly the first of its kind.

Meanwhile, the novelty of the European Commission's proposal lies perhaps in its extensive deliberative process, which began in 2018 with the establishment of the EU High-Level Expert Group (HLGE). This group produced the document COM (2019) 168, known as the Recommendations for Trustworthy Artificial Intelligence, which later led to the European Commission's White Paper on Artificial Intelligence. This White Paper, identified as COM (2020) 65 final, dated February 19, 2020, laid the foundational pillars applicable to AI technology developments with a European approach focused on excellence and trust.

Following this model, Latin American countries have also entered the race to regulate AI, aligning with the EU's approach, which emphasizes human rights and ethical principles across different societal sectors. This process is described by Bradford[40] as the "Brussels Effect," referring to the phenomenon wherein international organizations and states harmonize their laws with the EU model, inspired by the positive effects observed after the implementation of the 2016 GDPR.

In order to compare the nongovernmental initiatives that attempt to promote framework regulations of algorithmic systems. To achieve this, we rely on the methodological and analytical strategy proposed by García-Benítez and Ruvalcaba,[41] which consists of exposing and analyzing characteristics through the dimensions of ethics and human rights.

In this regard, it is crucial to examine other normative frameworks derived from the application of intelligent technology. The literature highlights the necessity of advancing the principle of transparency and explainability as the "missing piece of the puzzle," as Cotino-Hueso[42] called. This aligns with the four fundamental principles established by the Ethical Guidelines for Trustworthy AI, developed by the European Commission's Independent High-Level Expert Group on Artificial Intelligence.[43] These guidelines provide a set of basic principles that any attempt to regulate AI must incorporate. Thus, a comparison of algorithmic transparency standards reveals a degree of symmetry among the four main instruments, despite their association with different principles and objectives.

Indeed, the Organization for Economic Cooperation and Development (OECD), UNESCO, and the European Union (EU), as nongovernmental organizations initiating political debates and regulatory frameworks, propose five guiding principles to ensure that AI is applied transparently and responsibly. First, AI should benefit people and the planet by fostering inclusive growth, sustainable development, and well-being. Second, AI systems should be designed to uphold the rule of law, human rights, democratic values, and diversity. Third, transparency and disclosure of AI systems must ensure that individuals understand outcomes and can challenge them. Fourth, AI systems must function safely, with continuous assessment and management of potential risks. Fifth, organizations and individuals developing, implementing, and operating AI must be held accountable for its proper functioning.

The principles outlined in the analyzed instruments are considered essential for advancing AI regulation. However, this convergence also presents significant divergences regarding how these principles are interpreted, why they are deemed important, which domains or actors are obligated to comply with them, and how they should be implemented. A similar exercise, but with a broader sample of normative instruments, was conducted by Mantelero,[44] who concurs with Cotino-Hueso[45] that the principle of algorithmic transparency is present in 94% of reference documents on AI.

Thus, algorithmic transparency, as previously noted by Cotino-Hueso, constitutes the key piece in the regulatory puzzle of AI algorithms. He concludes that it could be the solution to one of the most serious legal threats: legal uncertainty, which—rather than providing security—exacerbates regulatory opacity and the inefficient piecemeal creation of rules. Despite the increasing integration of algorithmic processes and other AI systems, and their significant social and cultural implications, the prevailing approach favors the establishment of specific norms within regulatory frameworks based on principles and advances in public information transparency regulation.

For all these reasons, it can be argued that AI represents a new complex phenomenon whose dimensions are difficult to comprehend solely from a legal perspective. This calls for a fundamental rights-based approach, reinforcing the position that democratic principles such as publicity, access to information, and accountability should be applied as optimization mandates that states must uphold.[46]

6.1.3 The Regulatory Framework for Algorithmic Transparency in Chile

In Chile, the regulation of AI has been addressed through the National Artificial Intelligence Policy (PNIA) of 2021, as well as by the Council for Transparency (CPLT). Law 20.285 establishes that all information held by the State must be public, which implies that the algorithms used by the administration must also be transparent.

With a moderate approach, Chilean legislators have directed efforts toward regulating constraints applicable to AI applications, focusing on the protection of human rights. Thus, the required algorithmic transparency is that which guarantees the right of access to information. In this context, the 2021 National Artificial Intelligence Policy (PNIA), formulated by the Ministry of Science, Technology, Knowledge, and Innovation (CTCI) and published under Decree No. 20, marks a significant milestone in the comparative timeline of principles applicable to AI. This initiative positions Chile among the pioneering countries in AI regulation. The PNIA is designed as a ten-year instrument founded on four cross-cutting principles for AI development: (1) AI applications centered on human well-being, (2) Respect for human rights and security, (3) Sustainable and inclusive development, and (4) Global integration.

With this, the country ensures the incorporation of international principles for a reliable AI because they seek to open the black box of algorithms, through the requirement of the necessary safeguards so that their application is in accordance with the principles of "beneficence and non-maleficence". This, by means of guidelines for information governance of large datasets to enhance the great public value that these entail, centered on the human being to guarantee "human autonomy". And finally, ensuring equity through safety and security. In this regard, the work of the Chilean Transparency Council (hereinafter CPLT) in this area is particularly focused on the obligation to facilitate information disclosure for accountability regarding state agencies that implement Automated Decision Systems (ADS) in their processes. Additionally, it seeks to guarantee individuals' right of access to information. That is, protecting access to information through principles of transparency and explainability. As a result, Chile is considered the first country in the region to adopt algorithmic transparency practices as an indispensable legal principle.[47]

Furthermore, this approach is gaining traction particularly because the incorporation of algorithms in the state is advancing without adhering to formal requirements for establishing such obligations. That is, without an enabling law ensuring the application of this technology, despite Law 20.285, Article 5, stating that: "Pursuant to the principle of transparency in public administration, the acts and resolutions of state administration bodies, their rationale, supporting or supplementary documents, and the procedures used in their issuance shall be public."[48]

According to this provision, AI systems (ADS) constitute "information held by state administration bodies" and, therefore, the CPLT is obligated to guarantee the right of access to such public information, regardless of format, medium, date, origin, classification, or processing. Consequently, all information related to these systems must be published on the transparency portal, though there is still no certainty regarding how and where such information should be published.

Despite this, the enactment of the Algorithmic Transparency Resolution is considered the first source of law that enhance the obligations regarding algorithmic transparency.[49] Prior to this, the publication of information related to Algorithmic Transparency—concerning the type of information on Automated Decision Systems (ADS) that state administration bodies and obligated entities must disclose on their websites for responsible application—was voluntary.

In this initial phase at the national level, two types of information were required to be published on the transparency website. The first pertains to technical–instrumental aspects, while the second involves subjective information regarding the responsible public administration entities. Among the substantive information required is the identification of system names and the agencies responsible for their use. This also includes details about the services, programs, and benefits that utilize AI systems or the procedures influenced by them. If the ADS is owned by a third party, the system provider must be identified by name; otherwise, the entry should state "Not applicable." Additionally, a link to the provider's website may be included.

On the other hand, the technical–instrumental information covers aspects related to ADS operation. This includes specifying the system's internal identifier, distinguishing it from other ADS or IT systems used by the entity. If such an identifier does not exist, the entry should state "Not applicable," as should other required fields lacking relevant information. Furthermore, details about the ADS version, programming algorithm, and ownership rights over the ADS must be provided. If the state agency owns the rights, it should be stated as "Ownership of the entity"; otherwise, if a third-party provider holds the rights and the entity is merely a licensee, the entry should state "Licensed." The version release date of the ADS must also be included. Also, such as specific details on how the tool works and the data the tool uses, in in compliance of the new personal protection standard data that reformed.[50]

This marks progress in the first phase toward institutionalizing a legal framework that mandates active transparency obligations, allowing for the harmonization of AI technology use with the existing legal culture. That is, aligning with the norms, duties, and fundamental rights established under Law 20.285, which, beyond active transparency, facilitates oversight and evaluation of responsibilities arising from the application of this technology within state administration.[51] In other words, these obligations stem from the principle of publicity enshrined in Article 8 of the Constitution, as well as Articles 7 and 11 of Law 20.285.

This is particularly crucial in cases where AI-driven decisions have significant implications for individuals' lives, health, education, and freedom. The absence of algorithmic accountability can lead to various irregularities stemming from the rapid expansion of such systems. Therefore, it is justified that individuals should be able to access and understand the reasoning behind decisions made by AI systems.[52] Moreover, the imposition of specific technical–legal obligations is favorable for auditability, as it ensures the early and appropriate application of standards to address algorithmic opacity.[53]

This process aligns with international AI recommendations, such as the five OECD[54] recommendations discussed earlier, which have been adopted by pioneering national governments within their own legal frameworks. In this regard, the OECD's Observatory of Public Sector Innovation (OPSI)[55] cites Chile as the first country in Latin America to develop an open and participatory design for a "General Instruction on Algorithmic Transparency" through its Transparency Council.[56]

6.2 FINAL REFLECTIONS AND RECOMMENDATIONS

This article addresses some of the implications of the right of access to information, particularly with regard to the transparency requirements applicable to public algorithms, from the perspective of the State's obligation to ensure effective access to the explainability of automated decisions, as well as, justify what it is used for, how it is used and the data it uses. Specifically, it provides an overview of the state of the art in international law and a comparative analysis with Chile, emphasizing the need for greater transparency in AI in light of the risks and uncertainties it entails.

However, the most pressing issues revolve around accountability and ethical concerns, which remain unresolved in this analysis. This is because the article presents a synopsis of the process of approaching algorithmic transparency while also highlighting the persistent legal challenges arising from the integration of AI technology into public administration. Also presents a synopsis of the algorithmic transparency required in the context of the international principles of accountability, non-maleficence; beneficence and safety. In other words, transparency is seen as the fundamental roadmap for successfully addressing this issue.

Accordingly, it is argued that a comparative examination of international legal standards could serve as a description of advancing national regulation on algorithmic transparency and as a prelude to recognizing the right to explainability, which is necessary to ensure that this technology is both trustworthy and accountable. This issue reopens the longstanding debate on closed and opaque governments, underscoring the importance of making the decision-making processes of public-sector algorithms visible and subject to audit. This transparency is essential to ensure the explainability of the criteria associated with decision-making processes that impact the daily lives of individuals.

From a human rights perspective, access to information is a fundamental right that States are obliged to respect and guarantee, without discrimination and in full compliance with the principles of legality, transparency, and accountability. The United Nations has emphasized this in Resolution 73/348, which warns about the negative consequences of AI on rights such as freedom of opinion and expression, privacy and nondiscrimination. In this sense, access to information (technical, legal and substantive) not only legitimizes public decision-making processes, increasingly automated with algorithms but also serves as an enabling right to scrutinize the "black box" of AI systems used by the State.

Furthermore, due to the computational nature of AI and the ongoing debate about the displacement of human action by machines, there is an almost unanimous emphasis in various regulatory instruments on ensuring the responsibility of those developing algorithms, so that human intervention in administrative processes involving AI-based tools is safeguarded.

As a contribution, this article suggests that strengthening the right of access to information in the era of AI is an inescapable challenge for transparency and accountability in contemporary democracies. The regulation of algorithms used in public administration must advance through a human rights-based approach, ensuring that these technologies are not only efficient but also trustworthy, explainable, and subject to public scrutiny.

ACKNOWLEDGMENTS

This research is part of the project: "Algorithmic Transparency in the Public Sector," No. CIP2022015. I would like to express my gratitude to the Santander Foundation for the scholarship that supported my research stay at Florida International University (FIU) in the United States, as part of the College of Law Visiting Researchers Program.

NOTES

1 Meijer & Grimmelikjuisen (2022), p. 57.
2 Pentland Alex (2013), Contreras et al. (2022), and Azuaje-Pirela (2023).
3 Case of Claude Reyes and others vs. Chili. When "Article 13 of the Convention expressly stipulates the rights to "seek" and "receive" "information," this refers to the "dissemination of information held by the State [has] a very important role in a democratic society, as it enables civil society to control the actions of the government to which it has entrusted the protection of its interests." p. 58.
4 Simón Castellano (2023), p. 28.
5 Coddou & Smart (2021).
6 Aguilar Villanueva (2024), p. 4.
7 Nogueira Alcalá (2015), p. 325.
8 (§ 59) of the Judgment of the Court of Justice of the European Union (CJEU) of December 7, 2023. In: Cotino-Hueso, 2023. (21/01/2024). https://european-union.europa.eu/institutions-law-budget/institutions-and-bodies/search-all-eu-institutions-and-bodies/court-justice-european-union-cjeu_en
9 Artificial Intelligence Act. On March 13, 2024, the European Parliament finally approved Regulation (EU) 2024/1689, known as the Artificial Intelligence Regulation or Artificial Intelligence Act.
10 Diakopoulos (2020). "Accountability, transparency, and algorithms", pp. 20–22.
11 Diakopoulos (2020), Wieringa (2023), Llamas Covarrubias et al. (2023), and Miranzo-Díaz (2023).
12 Cotino-Hueso (2023) and Pasquale (2015).
13 Giest & Grimmellikhuijsen (2020).
14 Vestri Gabriell (2021), Ortiz De Zarate Lucía (2022), and Cotino-Hueso (2023b).
15 Burrel (2016), Pere Simon Castella (2023), Coglianese & Lehr (2019), and Castellanos-Ballesteros (2023).
16 Zlata Drnas (2022), p. 1.
17 Russell & Norvig (1994), p. 114.
18 Onu (2018), Resolución A/73/348.
19 Turner (2019), p. 7.
20 Recomendación OCDE de 2019 sobre inteligencia artificial.
21 Decreto Núm. 20. PNIA de 2021.
22 Kurzweil Ray (1992), p. 56.
23 Harrington (2017), p. 650.
24 Thus, in the United Nations Resolution 73/348, it has been stated that AI: "It is not a single thing, but rather a 'constellation' of processes and technologies that enable computers to complement or replace specific tasks that would otherwise be performed by humans, such as decision-making and problem-solving" (UN Resolution 73/348).
25 Recomendación OCDE de 2019 sobre inteligencia artificial.
26 UNESCO (2021). Recomendación sobre la ética de la inteligencia artificial, del 23 de noviembre de 2021.
27 García Benítez and Ruvalcaba-Gómez (2022), p. 7.
28 Floridi (2021), p. 619.
29 Baykurt (2022), p. 5.

30 Perel and Elkin-Koren (2017), p. 4.
31 Onu (2018), Resolución de la Asamblea General A/73/348.
32 Kaminski (2019), p. 192. "*The GDPR may prove to be an example, both good and bad, of a robust algorithmic accountability regime in practice*".
33 Cotino-Hueso (2023), p. 15.
34 Grant & Bruce (2021), OCDE (2019), and Cotino-Hueso (2023).
35 OCDE (2023). (Sitio web): https://oecd.ai/en/network-of-experts
36 US *Algorithmic Accountability Act de 2022.*
37 (Sitio Web) www.gov.uk/government/publications/algorithmic-transparency-template
38 Artificial Intelligence Act (EU), Regulation of the European Parliament and of the Council.
39 HAI Stanford University (2023), p. 5.
40 Bradford (2020), p. 68.
41 García Benítez and Ruvalcaba-Gómez (2021), p. 6.
42 Cotino-Hueso (2023), p. 20.
43 Libro Blanco de UE (2020).
44 Mantelero (2022), p. 390.
45 Cotino-Hueso (2023), p. 20.
46 Alexy (2002), pp. 86–87.
47 Mantelero (2022) and Jobin et al. (2019). A guarantor principle repeatedly invoked in 94% of the international instruments on AI regulation.
48 Law 20.285, Article 5.
49 CPLT Resolution No. 372 exempt from 2024.
50 Law No. 21.719 of 2024, published in official gazette No. 44.023.
51 Ortiz De Zárate (2023), p. 332.
52 OCDE (2023c).
53 CPLT (2021).
54 Recomendación OCDE de 2019 sobre inteligencia artificial.
55 OECD Observatory of Public Sector Innovation (OPSI) (OECD, 2023c), notes that "Governments should ensure that the underlying algorithms and data avoid bias and discrimination."
56 As of the date of this analysis, neither the special rules on transparency of algorithms nor the legal authorization for the incorporation of artificial intelligence in the Chilean State have been published, which is one of the limitations of this type of research in constant regulatory ferment.

REFERENCES

Aguilar Villanueva, Luis F. (2024). The New Public Governance: A Conceptual Overview. *Latin American Profiles* , *32* (63), 001. Epub July 29, 2024. https://doi.org/10.18504/pl3263-001-2024. Accessible at www.scielo.org.mx/scielo.php?script=sci_arttext&pid=S0188-76532024000100101

Intellectual property as a tool to promote transparency and prevent algorithmic discrimination. *Chilean Journal of Law and Technology* , *12* , pp. 1–34. https://doi.org/10.5354/0719-2584.2023.70131. Accessible at https://rchdt.uchile.cl/index.php/RCHDT/article/view/70131

Baykurt, Burcu (2022). Responsabilidad algorítmica en ciudades de EE. UU.: transparencia, impacto y economía política, *Big Data and Society,* 9 (2), 1–22.

Bradford, Anu (2020). *The Brussels Effect.* En: The Brussels Effect in Context', The Brussels Effect: How the European Union Rules the World (Oxford University Press).

Castellanos Ballesteros, Inmaculada (2023). Decisiones automatizadas y transparencia administrativa: nuevos retos para los derechos fundamentales. *Revista Española de La Transparencia*, 191–215. https://doi.org/10.51915/ret.250

Coddou Mc Manus, Alberto & Smart Larraín, Simon (2021). The Transparency and non-discrimination in the digital welfare State. *Revista Chilena De Derecho Y Tecnología*, *10*(2), 301–332. https://doi.org/10.5354/0719-2584.2021.61034

Coglianese, Cary & Lehr, David (2019). Transparency and algorithmic governance. *Administrative Law Review*, 71, 18–38. https://ssrn.com/abstract=3293008

Contreras, Pablo, Trigo, Pablo, & Ortiz, Luis (2022). Un sistema fragmentado: La protección sectorial de los datos personales en Chile. *Revista Derecho Administrativo Económico*, 35, 36–64. https://doi.org/10.7764/redae.35.2

Cotino-Hueso, Lorenzo (2023). Qué concreta transparencia e información de algoritmos e inteligencia artificial es la debida, *Revista española de la transparencia*, 16, 17–63.

Cotino-Hueso, Lorenzo (2023). Los usos de la inteligencia artificial en el sector público, su variable impacto y categorización jurídica, *Revista Canaria De Administración Pública*, 1, 211–242. https://doi.org/10.36151/RCAP.2023.7

Diakopoulos, N icholas. (2020). 'Transparency', in Markus D. Dubber, Frank Pasquale, and Sunit Das (eds), *The Oxford Handbook of Ethics of AI* . https://doi.org/10.1093/oxfordhb/9780190067397.013.11, accessed 13 Aug. 2025

García Benítez, Víctor Hugo, and Ruvalcaba-Gómez, Edgar A. (2021). "Análisis de las estrategias nacionales de inteligencia artificial en América Latina: Estudio de los enfoques de ética y de Derechos Humanos". *Revista de Gestión Pública*, 10 (1), 5–32.

Giest, Sarah and Grimmelikhuijsen, Stephan (2020). Algorithmic transparency in government: Towards a multi-level perspective. *Information Polity*, 25 (4), 409–417.

Harrington, Joseph (2017). "Developing competition law for collusion by autonomous artificial agents". *Journal of Competition Law and Economics,* 14 (4), 638–671.

Jobin, Anna, Ienca, Marcelo & Vayena, Effy (2019). The Global Landscape of AI Ethics Guidelines. Nature Machine Intelligence, 1, 389–399. https://doi.org/10.1038/s42256-019-0088-2

Kaminski, Margot E. (2019). *El derecho a la explicación, explicado*, 34, Berkeley *Tech.* LJ 189 *disponible en* https://scholar.law.colorado.edu/faculty-articles/1227. Fecha de consulta: 25.1.25.

Kurzweil, Ray (1992). The Age of Intelligent Machines. MIT Press.

Llamas Covarrubias, José, Mendoza, Enríquez, & Graff Guerrero, M. (2022). Enfoques regulatorios para la Inteligencia Artificial (IA). *Revista Chilena De Derecho*, 49 (3), 31–62.

Mantelero, Alessandro (2022). Beyond Data. Human rights, ethical and social impact assessment in AI. *Information Technology and Law Series, num*, vol. *36*. T.M.C. Asser Press, Springer.

Miranzo Díaz, Javier (2023). *Inteligencia Artificial Y Derecho Administrativo: Especial Referencia a Los Instrumentos de Colaboración Público-privada Y Contratación Pública.* (Editorial Tecno).

Nogueira Alcalá, Humberto (2015). "El bloque constitucional de derechos en Chile, el parámetro de control y consideraciones comparativas con Colombia y México: doctrina y jurisprudencia", *en Estudios Constitucionales*, 13 (2), 301–350.

Ortiz De Zárate Alcarazo, Lucía (2022). Explicabilidad (de la inteligencia artificial). *EUNOMÍA Revista En Cultura de La Legalidad*, 22, 328–344. https://doi.org/10.20318/eunomia.2022.6819

Pasquale, Frank (2015). The black box society: The secret algorithms that control money and information. *Business Ethics Quarterly: The Journal of the Society for Business Ethics*, *26*(4), 568–571. https://doi.org/10.1017/beq.2016.50

Perel, Maayan and Elkin-Koren, Niva (2017). Black Box Tinkering: Beyond Disclosure in Algorithmic Enforcement. *69 Fla. L. Rev.* Núm. 181, 2–42.

Turner, Jacob (2019). Robot Rules. Regulating Artificial Intelligence. Palgrave Macmillan.

Simón-Castellano, Pere (2023). Las evaluaciones de impacto algorítmico en los derechos fundamentales: hacia una efectiva minimización de riesgos. In C. H. Lorenzo y Claramaunt Castellanos Jorge (Ed.), Algoritmos abiertos y que no discriminen en el sector público (pp. 27–56). Tirant lo Blanch.

Vestri, Gagrielle (2021). La Inteligencia Artificial Ante El Desafío De La Transparencia Algorítmica. Una Aproximación Desde La Perspectiva Jurídico- Administrativa, Revista Aragonesa de Administración Pública, 56, 368–398

Wieringa, M. (2023). Hola SyRI, cuéntame sobre la responsabilidad algorítmica: lecciones de un caso histórico. *Data & Policy*, *5* (2), 1–24. https://doi.org/10.1017/dap.2022.39

Zlata Drnas de Clément (2022). Artificial intelligence in International Law, United Nations and European Union, *Revista de Estudios Jurídicos*, 22, 1–25.

Laws and Instruments Cited

CPLT. (2021). Transparencia algorítmica en el sector público. Disponible en: www.consejotransparencia.cl/wp-content/ Fecha consulta: 7/8/2021.

Decreto Núm. 20. PNIA de 2021. Política Nacional de Inteligencia Artificial, de 20 de septiembre de 2021.

OCDE. (2019). Recommendation of the Council on Artificial Intelligence. Disponible en: https://legalinstruments.oecd.org/en/instruments/OECD-LEGAL-0449

OCDE. (2023a). Informe OCDE destaca Instrucción sobre Transparencia Algorítmica del Consejo para la Transparencia. Disponible en: www.consejotransparencia.cl/informe-ocde-destaca-instruccion-sobre-transparencia-algoritmica-del-consejo/ Fecha de Consulta: 7/8/2023.

OCDE. (2023c). Observatory of Public Sector Innovation (OPSI) (OCDE, 2023c), Responsabilidad algorítmica. Nuevos aspectos de la transparencia. disponible en: https://oecd-opsi.org/publications/trends-2023/. Fecha de Consulta: 11/07/2023.

ONU. (2018). Promoción y protección de los derechos humanos: cuestiones de derechos humanos, incluidos otros medios de mejorar el goce efectivo de los derechos humanos y las libertades fundamentales, Resolución A/73/348 de 29 de agosto de 2018 Español.

UNESCO. (2021). Recomendación sobre la ética de la inteligencia artificial. Disponible en: https://bit.ly/3nTmLqN Fecha de Consulta: 11/07/2023.

7 Uncover the Potential of Artificial Intelligence in Legal System Flaking Crime Prevention

Breakthrough New Tools for Law Enforcement in the Digital Futuristic Arena

Bhupinder Singh and Christian Kaunert

7.1 INTRODUCTION

The artificial intelligence (AI)-powered risk assessment models evaluate various factors to predict individuals at a higher risk of criminal involvement (Singh, 2023). This allows for targeted preventive measures which offer an effective approach to crime prevention. It offers a cost-effective and flexible solution for monitoring large areas, acting as force multipliers for law enforcement (Singh & Kaunert, 2024). There are multifarious emerging trends such as biometric advancements, the potential impact of quantum computing, and the collaborative global law enforcement efforts that underscore the continuous evolution of AI in crime prevention (Singh, 2024). These futuristic tools hold the promise of further refining the effectiveness and scope of law enforcement practices (Cheng et al., 2021). AI in the legal system is redefining the landscape of crime prevention, and its breakthrough tools empower law enforcement with proactive capabilities, which offer a glimpse into a digital-futuristic arena (Muhlhoff, 2021). Although "intelligent machines" have long been a mainstay of science fiction, AI is now a reality that has a big influence on our daily lives (Saltz et al., 2019). AI is revolutionizing the way it interact with technology, impacting not only phones and automobiles but also banking and healthcare (Hoijtink & Planque-van Hardeveld, 2022). Applications for it may be found in many different fields, such as agriculture, industry, communications, finance, government, education, services, manufacturing, healthcare, and transportation (Dean, 2024). AI is also advancing criminal justice and public safety. For example, AI-driven traffic safety systems use traffic regulations to identify and punish transgressions, and predictive

DOI: 10.1201/9781003491903-7

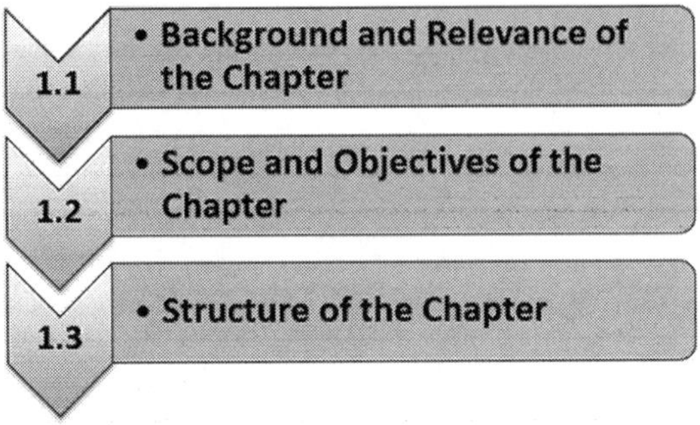

FIGURE 7.1 The dimensions of introduction split sections (source: original).

policing makes the best use of available resources (Utami et al., 2022). AI helps determine a person under criminal justice supervision's chance of committing another crime (Zhang et al., 2022).

7.1.1 Background and Relevance of the Chapter

There were numerous approaches being investigated to use AI as a resource for public safety. Facial recognition is a widely used application in both the public and private domains (Baker & Robinson, 2020). Face photos are a common tool used by intelligence analysts to identify and locate people (Aziz & Andriansyah, 2023). It takes a lot of work and is prone to human mistake due to exhaustion to properly and quickly analyze the enormous volume of potentially relevant photos and videos (Burrell et al., 2024). In contrast to humans, machines never weary (Attaran & Deb, 2018). Projects like the Janus computer vision project by the Intelligence Advanced Research Projects Activity entail trials where computers are trained to recognize faces and identify persons much like human analysts (Brotcke, 2022). AI is quickly becoming a key piece of equipment for fraud detection (Alnajim, et al., 2023). Large amounts of data are used by online retailers such as PayPal to regularly train their fraud detection algorithms to anticipate and spot unexpected trends as well as learn to recognize new ones (Abebe et al., 2020). The transportation department should be working to improve public safety through the study, creation, and testing of video-based automated traffic accident detection systems (Hagendorff, 2019). Under a variety of circumstances, such as shifting weather patterns, lighting conditions, and traffic patterns, this technology aids in maintaining safe and effective commuter traffic (Dash et al., 2022). In order to interpret radiological pictures, AI algorithms are also utilized in medicine (Britz, 2024). This might have a big influence on the criminal justice and medical examiner communities when it comes to identifying the cause and manner of death. Further research has been done on AI algorithms in forensic science fields including DNA analysis (Tyagi et al., 2020).

7.1.2 Scope and Objectives of the Chapter

AI is progressively becoming a useful instrument for prosecuting offenders and stopping illegal activity (Cao et al., 2021). The numerous law enforcement organizations throughout the world use cutting-edge methods to prevent crime; it is no longer just a theoretical idea (Williams & Burnap, 2023). "Facial recognition" is one such method that is frequently used in industries other than law enforcement to guarantee security (Yarkoni, 2024). AI in law enforcement refers to a framework that is assessed by computers and can help with ultimate decision-making. There is a lot of hope for the future of crime detection with this technology (Zhang et al., 2022). This chapter has the following objectives to:

- look into the existing integration of AI technology with law enforcement and crime prevention tactics. Investigating different AI techniques and how they may be used to anticipate, identify, and solve crimes is part of this (Lee & Shin, 2023).
- evaluate how well AI technologies work to lower crime rates and enhance public safety. This goal entails evaluating empirical data and case studies to ascertain how AI affects the outcomes of law enforcement (Li et al., 2020).
- determine the benefits and difficulties of integrating AI with the judicial system and crime prevention. Examining the operational, moral, and technological concerns raised by AI usage in law enforcement is part of this (Henke & Jacques Bughin, 2023).
- investigate the moral and legal ramifications of using AI to prevent crime. This goal is to make sure AI applications adhere to legal requirements, human rights, and privacy while also suggesting best practices for the ethical application of AI in law enforcement (Bao et al., 2022).
- make suggestions for the future use of AI in the judicial system and crime prevention. This entails making recommendations for best practices, legislative frameworks, and future study topics to maximize the application of AI in fostering safer societies and more effective legal systems (Odinet et al., 2024).

7.1.3 STRUCTURE OF THE CHAPTER

This chapter comprehensively explores the diverse arena for uncover the potential of artificial intelligence in legal system flaking crime prevention: breakthrough new

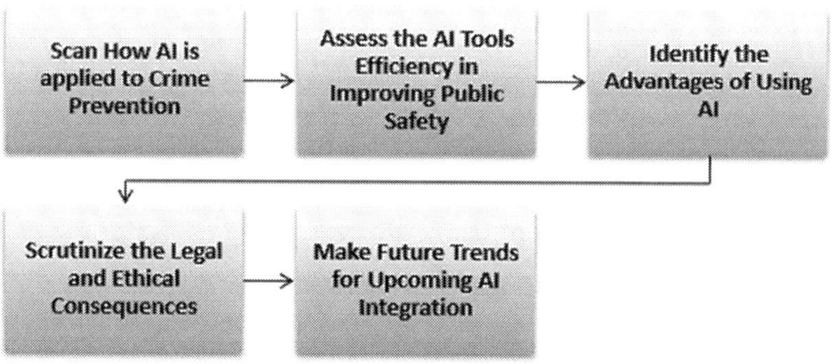

FIGURE 7.2 The objectives of the chapter (source: original).

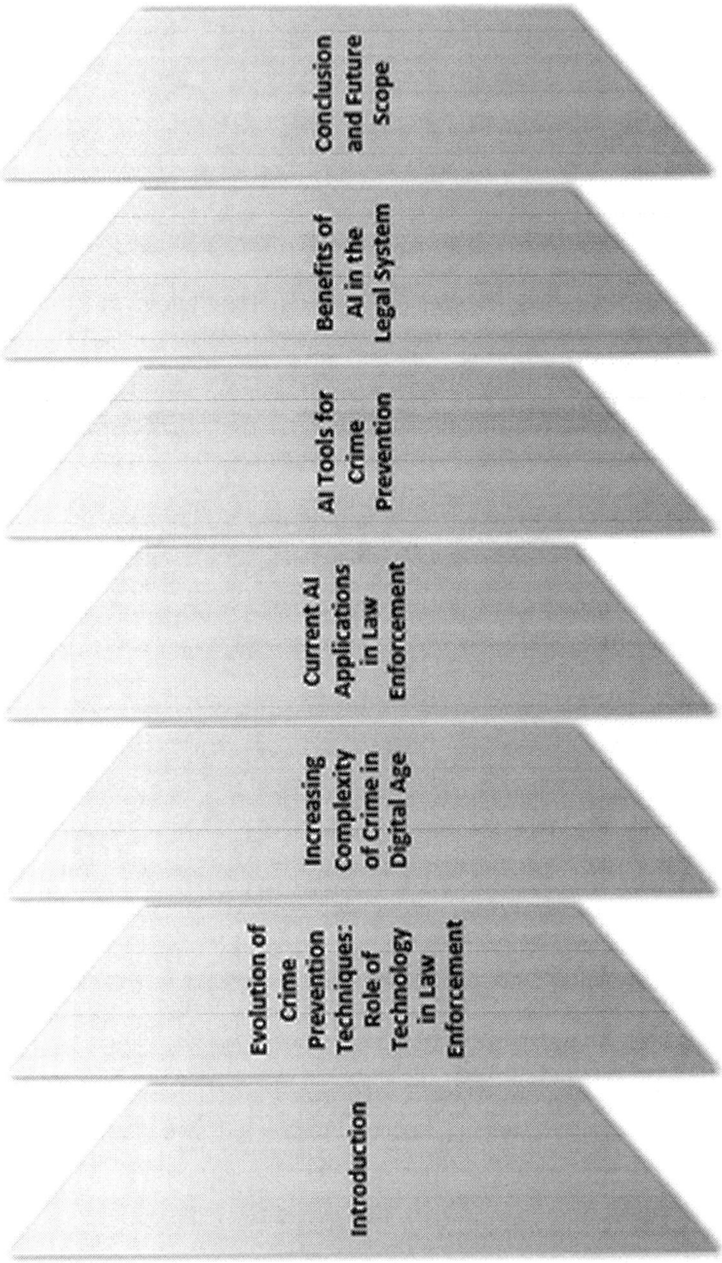

FIGURE 7.3 The flow of this chapter (source: original).

tools for law enforcement in the digital futuristic arena. Section 7.2 elaborates the evolution of crime prevention techniques: role of technology in law enforcement. Section 7.3 explores the increasing complexity of crime in digital age. Section 7.4 lays down the current AI applications in law enforcement. Section 7.5 specifies the AI tools for crime prevention. Section 7.6 highlights the benefits of AI in the legal system. Finally, Section 7.7 concludes the chapter with future scope.

7.2 EVOLUTION OF CRIME PREVENTION TECHNIQUES: ROLE OF TECHNOLOGY IN LAW ENFORCEMENT

The criminal justice and law enforcement sectors use video and image analysis to get data about individuals, items, and behaviors to aid in criminal investigations (McKendrick, 2019). However, this is a labor-intensive procedure that costs a lot of money to staff with specific knowledge (Varma et al., 2022). Also, human error might occur in video and image analysis due to the vast amount of data, the quick evolution of technology like smartphones and operating systems, and the scarcity of skilled experts (Gangadharan, 2021). These human mistakes may be avoided by AI technologies, which can operate as expert systems (Tippins et al., 2021). Conventional computer programs that aid people are restricted to preset characteristics, including eye color, shape, and distance between eyes for facial recognition or demographic data for pattern analysis. On the other hand, AI image and video algorithms are capable of learning intricate jobs and creating unique, autonomous facial recognition characteristics and parameters that surpass human-specified requirements (Ducas & Wilner, 2024). These algorithms are capable of facial recognition, item and weapon identification, and the detection of complicated events like crimes and accidents as both during and after the incident (Lui & Lamb, 2023). There is a need to improve contextual information and the speed, quality, and specificity of data collecting, imaging, and analysis in order to meet the demands of the criminal justice and law enforcement communities. Technology is evaluating human facial recognition and contrasting AI systems with skilled facial investigators (Schmitt, 2020).

AI-based facial recognition algorithms perform on par with human face examiners when recognition times are restricted to 30 seconds (Zhang et al., 2020). These results imply that AI algorithms can act as a "second pair of eyes" to improve the precision of knowledgeable human examiners and assist in data triage to maximize efficiency (Nassar & Kamal, 2021). AI algorithms are being developed to enhance identification, recognition, and detection, particularly for photographs in which a person's face is partially covered by masks, helmets, lamp posts, or lights, or shot at an angle that is not straightforward (Tene & Polonetsky, 2022). In order to improve face matching, these researchers are also working on improving low-quality facial photos, such as those with low ambient light levels and poor resolution (Grimm et al., 2021). These algorithms are presently being tested by the NIJ's test and evaluation department. Clear pictures of numerals and letters are gradually deteriorated in this method to simulate low-quality visuals (Dhoni & Kumar, 2023). After that, the deteriorated photos are represented mathematically and cataloged so that they may be identified by comparison with low-quality license plate photographs (Kordzadeh & Ghasemaghaei, 2022).

7.3 INCREASING COMPLEXITY OF CRIME IN DIGITAL AGE

The employment of current AI technologies is proven to be quite beneficial as crime rates rise (Sambasivan et al., 2021). The ability to forecast crimes and identify offenders is greatly aided by these algorithms (Singh, 2023). It is important to guarantee that their operating framework is both visible and logical (Singh, 2023). An international committee should be created, according to several scholars, to control the usage of AI. Every nation ought to make a contribution to the creation of this AI system (Passas et al., 2023). The protection of human rights also has to be taken into consideration. It's increasingly clear that law enforcement will require greater AI support. Even if this will become standard procedure, it is crucial to make sure that rules and laws do not violate people's rights (Zhang et al., 2023).

The criminal justice system has profited from two categories of technical advancements: hard technology and soft technology. Hard technology refers to improvements in the tools, supplies, and machinery that are used to either commit or prevent crimes (Katyal, 2019). Software, categorization schemes, methods for analyzing crime, and data sharing/system integration are all considered forms of soft technology (Irfan et al., 2023). Safety and crime detection have been transformed by incorporating technology into crime prevention measures, even if conventional law enforcement techniques and community watchfulness are still crucial (Selbst & Barocas, 2024). In an effort to maintain community safety, law enforcement organizations are progressively implementing technology strategies (Daugherty & Wilson, 2013). Facial recognition algorithms analyze digital images or videos to detect and identify individuals' faces, aiding in the identification of victims or suspects. This analysis may also involve comparing faces captured in surveillance footage or images from social media profiles with known databases to establish their identity (Swiakowska, 2020).

7.4 CURRENT AI APPLICATIONS IN LAW ENFORCEMENT

Technology plays a critical role in contemporary crime prevention tactics by offering creative responses to changing criminal activity (Berk et al., 2021). This study looks at the various ways that technology might be used to prevent crime (Asharf et al., 2023). It covers topics including community involvement, forensic science, surveillance, and predictive analytics (Vinayakumar et al., 2024). It emphasizes how technology helps law enforcement organizations, lawmakers, and communities inhibit criminal activity, improve public safety, and develop proactive crime prevention measures through a thorough analysis of scholarly research, empirical studies, and case examples (Khan et al., 2022). This article provides insights for policymakers, academics, and practitioners to fully harness the potential of technology in building safer societies by critically assessing the advantages, drawbacks, ethical issues, and future possibilities of technological interventions in crime prevention (Al-Garadi et al., 2020).

In the modern world, technology and crime prevention are becoming more and more intertwined, changing law enforcement tactics and community safety programs (Elhoseny et al., 2021). The use of technology is critical in improving the capacity of law enforcement agencies and communities to prevent and effectively respond to crimes (Kimbugwe et al., 2021). Examples of this include the use of surveillance technologies, the application of predictive analytics, and breakthroughs in forensic science (Saheed & Arowolo, 2021). An overview of technology's role in preventing crime is given in this introduction, along with a contextualization of its evolution, relevance, and implications for creating safer communities (Singh et al., 2021). AI is being used by law enforcement organizations more and more to increase the productivity of its agents. AI is helping a number of law enforcement activities and is quickly becoming an essential component (Waheed et al., 2020). It is employed for surveillance, monitoring anomalies in crowds, analyzing video to look for criminal activity, and successfully using facial recognition. It is projected that AI will significantly increase community trust and security in police. In addition to preventing crime, the police force's main objective is to solve it (Gao et al., 2023).

7.5 AI TOOLS FOR CRIME PREVENTION

AI has long since been incorporated into industries including energy, banking, healthcare, and transportation. In contrast to these industries, police forces are relatively new users of AI (Sarker, 2021). Numerous nations are aware of its benefits and potential in identifying crimes and apprehending offenders. While AI in law enforcement is still in its infancy, the outcomes are encouraging (Bout et al., 2021). AI is a

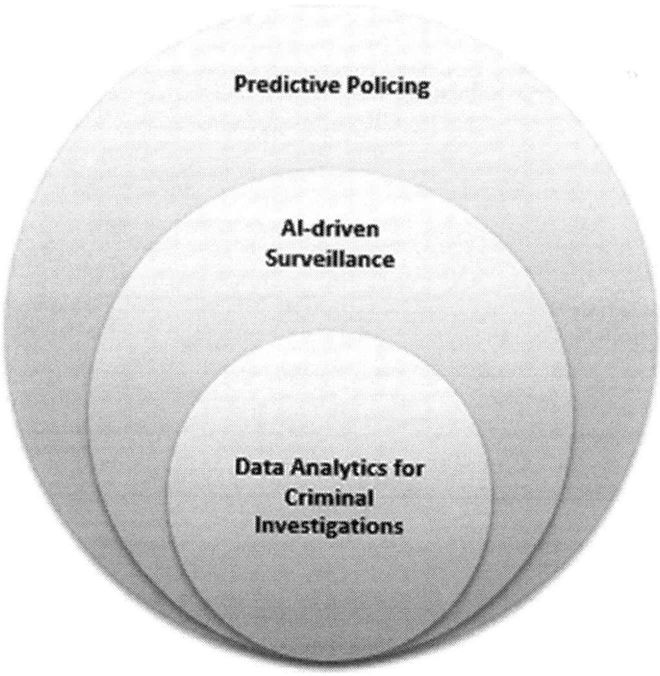

FIGURE 7.4 The major current AI applications in law enforcement (source: original).

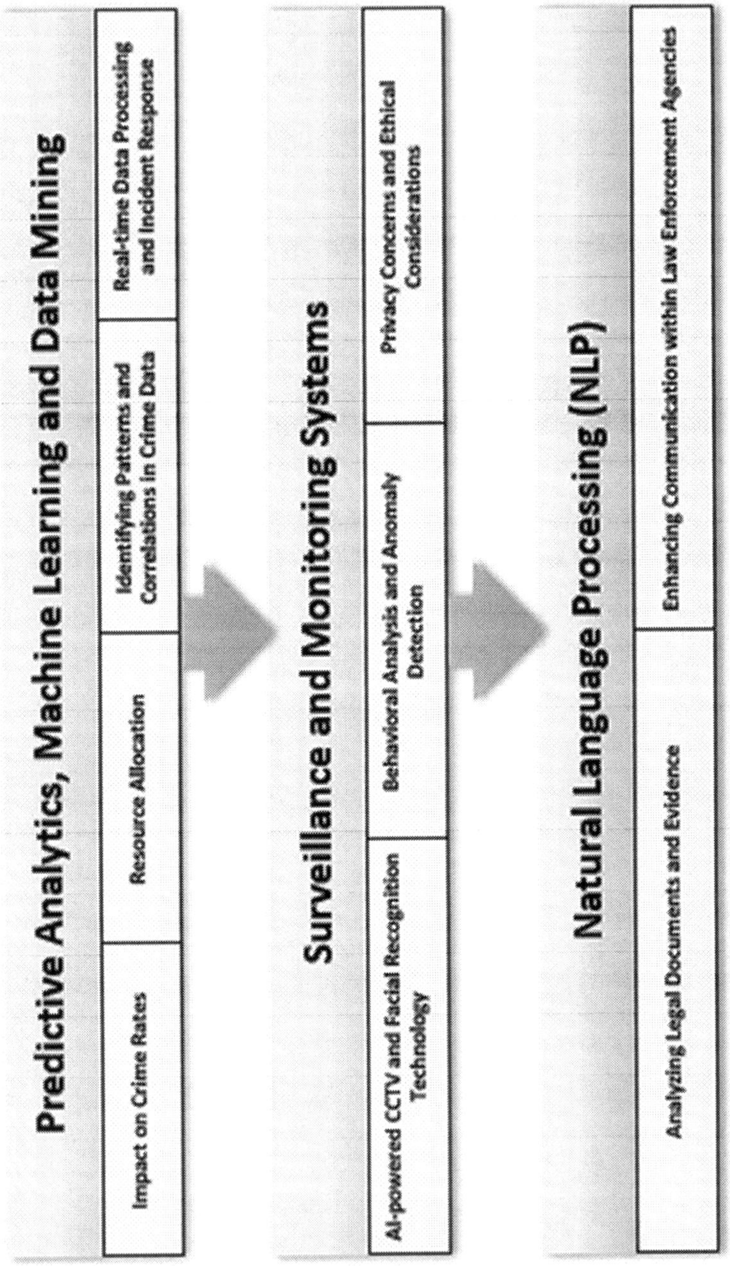

FIGURE 7.5 The AI tools for crime prevention (source: original).

potent tool since it can handle a variety of criminal activities. It enables law enforcement organizations to concentrate their efforts at certain times and in specified places. Understanding a site is essential before carrying out any operations there. Drones with sensors can be used to gather such important data (Aqeel et al., 2022).

Facial recognition software is one of the most widely used AI applications. A lot of work has gone into using this technology to assist in identifying criminals (Zhang et al., 2021). To detect and capture troublemakers, some nations have installed closed-circuit television systems using facial recognition technology in public spaces. It is also employed to keep an eye on the public and apprehend offenders in the act (Reddy et al., 2022). It is used in some cities for critical area surveillance, such train stations and airports. The application of AI in police has been gradually increasing as it improves law enforcement efficacy and yields beneficial outcomes (Oladipo et al., 2021).

AI cameras are used by police departments to help in crime scene surveying. Crime scenes can occasionally cover huge regions that are unapproachable on foot (Jagannath et al., 2022). AI in police can offer insightful information in these kinds of circumstances and assist in the search for leads following a crime (Singh et al., 2022). Law enforcement organizations use video technology in addition to cameras to keep an eye out for any threats at big events (Spaulding & Mohaisen, 2018). AI is frequently utilized to identify any unwanted activities at festivals and important sporting events. Facial recognition surveillance is another feature of video technology that makes it possible to detect faces in dense groups (Ahmad et al., 2021). In order to detect suspicious activities or threats, law enforcement relies on video equipment for extra monitoring, particularly during major events such as marathons and festivals. This technique has been implemented by several police agencies to help in facial recognition identification (Altaie et al., 2022).

7.6 BENEFITS OF AI IN THE LEGAL SYSTEM

AI improves surveillance in public areas like train stations and stadiums (Javeed et al., 2022). AI is essential in these situations since a small number of police personnel cannot scan a vast crowd efficiently and with the same impressive outcomes (Malik et al., 2022). The use of AI in robotics is another area of expertise and physical robots are currently used by many law enforcement organizations to carry out a variety of jobs, especially those deemed too risky for humans (Rudenko et al., 2022). Robots with AI capabilities may do difficult jobs like defusing bombs and entering dangerous environments to recognize and manage people or items (Tayfour et al., 2023). AI in police is a critical component of preserving human lives since robots with AI capabilities are better capable of handling illegal situations (Gokulakrishnan et al., 2023). Law enforcement organizations use a variety of AI techniques to help them spot suspicious trends that people might miss (Singh et al., 2024). With using "Artificial Neural Networks", AI is able to anticipate illegal activity. Security system regulators connect to millions of data points, such as social media postings, Wi-Fi networks, and internet IP addresses, in order to do these kinds of assessments. Currently, money laundering and other scams may be detected in law enforcement thanks to AI (Singh, 2024).

Big data sets are used in AI and machine learning to educate computers to carry out tasks that need human intelligence. Algorithms interpret patterns and trends in crime, giving law enforcement the ability to precisely predict and stop criminal activity (Arora et al., 2024). AI technology makes it possible for investigators to quickly and effectively go through enormous datasets and identify crucial evidence by quickly analyzing immense volumes of digital data, including files, emails, and communications (Bordeanu, 2024). Analytical methods are used in predictive policing to find possible victims and criminals. Law enforcement may identify people and places with a higher risk of crime by examining data (Inuwa & Das, 2024). The example is the sex offender management program, which enables parole and probation officials to keep an eye on an offender's mobile device and take prompt action if any illegal items are discovered, thereby averting further offenses (Singh et al., 2024).

Law enforcement may more efficiently deploy personnel and resources by using accurate and efficient crime analytics, which guarantee that these resources are always

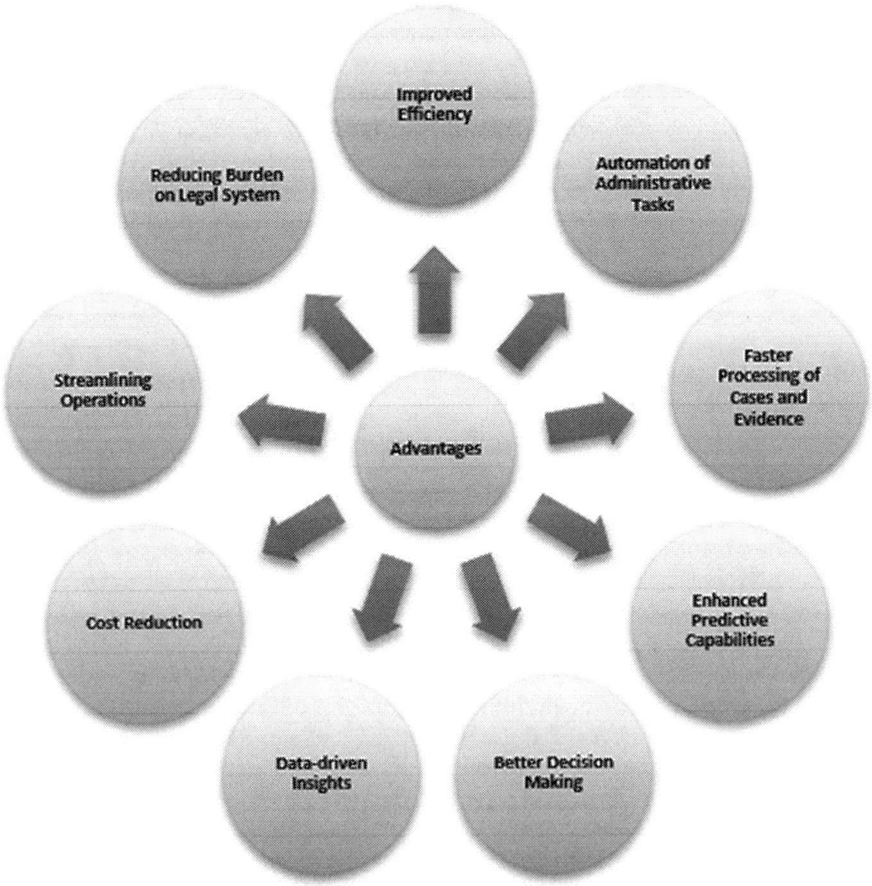

FIGURE 7.6 The benefits of AI in the legal system (source: original).

where they are most needed (Khansadurai et al., 2024). The geographical data required for this operation is provided by sophisticated mathematical models employing AI and heuristic approaches. Digital forensic software is capable of obtaining and keeping an eye on communications via mobile devices, web-based social media platforms, and the Internet (Xiao, 2024). This feature helps law enforcement look into financial crimes, drug crimes, sex crimes, and human trafficking over the internet. Cases frequently call for subscriber information and saved communications, including emails, instant messaging, browser histories, search records, and cloud data (Shang, 2024).

7.7 CONCLUSION AND FUTURE SCOPE

AI has the potential to become an integral part of our criminal justice system, offering investigative support and enabling criminal justice professionals to enhance public safety more effectively. The ability to learn from experience is one facet of human intelligence. An AI application called machine learning imitates this capacity, allowing computers and their software to gain knowledge from experience. This is especially important for the criminal justice system, as pattern detection is so important. Humans are excellent pattern recognizers and can identify things, people, complicated emotions, information, and circumstances on a regular basis via experience. AI uses computer hardware and software algorithms to try to mimic this skill. Self-learning algorithms, for example, use data sets to recognize individuals based on photos, carry out difficult computational and robotic operations, comprehend online purchase patterns and behaviors, diagnose medical disorders from complex radiological scans, and forecast trends in the stock market. AI should be used by other groups to aid in crime detection in addition to law enforcement. AI can detect products that are being transferred illegally, for instance. AI might be used by a delivery service to identify if a package includes any forbidden materials. If so, the service could notify law enforcement authorities so that the proper action can be taken. Retail establishments and pharmacies may identify suspicious consumers by utilizing a variety of AI technologies. Store owners should report large purchases of chemicals or other substances right away if they see them. With detecting containers used for unlawful human transit, shipping firms may utilize AI and their current data to combat human trafficking and perhaps save countless lives.

REFERENCES

Abebe, R., Barocas, S., Kleinberg, J., Levy, K., Raghavan, M., & Robinson, D. G. (2020). Roles for computing in social change. In *Proceedings of the 2020 conference on fairness, accountability, and transparency* (pp. 252–260).

Ahmad, W., Rasool, A., Javed, A. R., Baker, T., & Jalil, Z. (2021). Cyber security in IoT-based cloud computing: A comprehensive survey. *Electronics*, *11*(1), 16.

Al-Garadi, M. A., Mohamed, A., Al-Ali, A. K., Du, X., Ali, I., & Guizani, M. (2020). A survey of machine and deep learning methods for internet of things (IoT) security. *IEEE Communications Surveys & Tutorials*, *22*(3), 1646–1685.

Alnajim, A. M., Habib, S., Islam, M., Thwin, S. M., & Alotaibi, F. (2023). A Comprehensive survey of cybersecurity threats, attacks, and effective countermeasures in industrial internet of things. *Technologies*, *11*(6), 161.

Altaie, R. H., & Hoomod, H. K. (2022, December). Artificial intelligent management for internet of things: A review. In *2022 4th International Conference on Current Research in Engineering and Science Applications (ICCRESA)* (pp. 179–184). IEEE.

Aqeel, M., Ali, F., Iqbal, M. W., Rana, T. A., Arif, M., & Auwul, M. R. (2022). A review of security and privacy concerns in the internet of things (IoT). *Journal of Sensors, 2022.* Accessible at www.academia.edu/88304170/A_Review_of_Security_and_Privacy_Concerns_in_the_Internet_of_Things_IoT

Arora, S., Mittal, R., Shrivastava, A. K., & Bali, S. (2024). Blockchain-based deep learning in IoT, healthcare and cryptocurrency price prediction: A comprehensive review. *International Journal of Quality & Reliability Management, 41*(8), 2199–2225. https://doi.org/10.1108/IJQRM-12-2022-0373.

Asharf, J., Moustafa, N., Khurshid, H., Debie, E., Haider, W., & Wahab, A. (2023). A review of intrusion detection systems using machine and deep learning in internet of things: Challenges, solutions and future directions. *Electronics*, *9*(7), 1177.

Attaran, M., & Deb, P. (2018). Machine learning: The new 'big thing' for competitive advantage. *International Journal of Knowledge Engineering and Data Mining*, *5*(4), 277–305.

Aziz, L. A. R., & Andriansyah, Y. (2023). The role artificial intelligence in modern banking: An exploration of AI-driven approaches for enhanced fraud prevention, risk management, and regulatory compliance. *Reviews of Contemporary Business Analytics*, *6*(1), 110–132.

Baker, D. J., & Robinson, P. H. (Eds.). (2020). *Artificial Intelligence and the Law: Cybercrime and Criminal Liability*. Routledge.

Bao, Y., Hilary, G., & Ke, B. (2022). Artificial intelligence and fraud detection. In: Innovative Technology at the Interface of Finance and Operations, *Volume I*, pp. 223–247.

Berk, R., Heidari, H., Jabbari, S., Kearns, M., & Roth, A. (2021). Fairness in criminal justice risk assessments: The state of the art. *Sociological Methods & Research*, *50*(1), 3–44.

Bordeanu, O. C. (2024). *From Data to Insights: Unraveling Spatio-Temporal Patterns of Cybercrime using NLP and Deep Learning* (Doctoral dissertation, UCL (University College London)).

Bout, E., Loscri, V., & Gallais, A. (2021). How Machine Learning changes the nature of cyberattacks on IoT networks: A survey. *IEEE Communications Surveys & Tutorials*, *24*(1), 248–279.

Britz, M. (2024). *Computer forensics and cybercrime: An introduction, 2/e*. Pearson Education India.

Brotcke, L. (2022). Time to assess bias in machine learning models for credit decisions. *Journal of Risk and Financial Management*, *15*(4), 165.

Burrell, J. (2024). How the machine 'thinks': Understanding opacity in machine learning algorithms. *Big Data & Society*, *3*(1), 2053951715622512.

Cao, L., Yang, Q., & Yu, P. S. (2021). Data science and AI in FinTech: An overview. *International Journal of Data Science and Analytics*, *12*, 81–99.

Cheng, X., Liu, S., Sun, X., Wang, Z., Zhou, H., Shao, Y., & Shen, H. (2021). Combating emerging financial risks in the big data era: A perspective review. *Fundamental Research*, *1*(5), 595–606.

Dash, B., Sharma, P., & Ali, A. (2022). Federated learning for privacy-preserving: A review of PII data analysis in Fintech. *International Journal of Software Engineering & Applications (IJSEA)*, *13*(4).

Daugherty, P. R., & Wilson, H. J. (2023). *Human+ machine: Reimagining work in the age of AI*. Harvard Business Press.

Dean, J. (2024). *Big data, data mining, and machine learning: Value creation for business leaders and practitioners*. John Wiley & Sons.

Dhoni, P., & Kumar, R. (2023). Synergizing generative AI and cybersecurity: Roles of generative AI entities, companies, agencies, and government in enhancing cybersecurity. *Authorea Preprints*.

Ducas, E., & Wilner, A. (2024). The security and financial implications of blockchain technologies: Regulating emerging technologies in Canada. *International Journal*, *72*(4), 538–562.

Elhoseny, M., Selim, M. M., & Shankar, K. (2021). Optimal deep learning based convolution neural network for digital forensics face sketch synthesis in internet of things (IoT). *International Journal of Machine Learning and Cybernetics*, *12*, 3249–3260.

Gangadharan, S. P. (2021). Digital inclusion and data profiling. *First Monday*. *17*(5). https://doi.org/10.5210/fm.v17i5.3821. Accessible at https://firstmonday.org/ojs/index.php/fm/article/view/3821

Gao, M., Souri, A., Zaker, M., Zhai, W., Guo, X., & Li, Q. (2023). A comprehensive analysis for crowd counting methodologies and algorithms in Internet of Things. *Cluster Computing*, ***27***, 859–873 (2024). https://doi.org/10.1007/s10586-023-03987-y

Gokulakrishnan, S., Chakrabarti, P., Hung, B. T., & Shankar, S. S. (2023). An optimized facial recognition model for identifying criminal activities using deep learning strategy. *International Journal of Information Technology*, *15*(7), 3907–3921.

Grimm, P. W., Grossman, M. R., & Cormack, G. V. (2021). Artificial intelligence as evidence. *Northwestern Journal of Technology & Intellectual Property*, *19*, 9.

Hagendorff, T. (2019). From privacy to anti-discrimination in times of machine learning. *Ethics and Information Technology*, *21*(4), 331–343.

Henke, N., & Jacques Bughin, L. (2023). The age of analytics: Competing in a data-driven world. www.mckinsey.com/capabilities/quantumblack/our-insights/the-age-of-analytics-competing-in-a-data-driven-world

Hoijtink, M., & Planqué-van Hardeveld, A. (2022). Machine learning and the platformization of the military: A study of Google's machine learning platform tensor flow. *International Political Sociology*, *16*(2), olab036.

Inuwa, M. M., & Das, R. (2024). A comparative analysis of various machine learning methods for anomaly detection in cyberattacks on IoT networks. *Internet of Things*, *26*, Article 101162. https://doi.org/10.1016/j.iot.2024.101162.

Irfan, M., Elmogy, M., & El-Sappagh, S. (Eds.). (2023). *The impact of AI innovation on financial sectors in the era of industry 5.0*. IGI Global.

Jagannath, A., Jagannath, J., & Kumar, P. S. P. V. (2022). A comprehensive survey on radio frequency (rf) fingerprinting: Traditional approaches, deep learning, and open challenges. *Computer Networks*, *219*, 109455.

Javeed, D., Gao, T., Khan, M. T., & Shoukat, D. (2022). A hybrid intelligent framework to combat sophisticated threats in secure industries. *Sensors*, *22*(4), 1582.

Katyal, S. K. (2019). Private accountability in the age of artificial intelligence. *UCLA Law Review*, *66*, 54.

Khan, A. R., Kashif, M., Jhaveri, R. H., Raut, R., Saba, T., & Bahaj, S. A. (2022). Deep learning for intrusion detection and security of Internet of things (IoT): Current analysis, challenges, and possible solutions. *Security and Communication Networks, 2022*, Available at DOI:https://doi.org/10.1155/2022/40160.

Khansadurai, A. M., Veluchamy, A. D., Balasubramani, S., & Balasubramaniyan, K. (2024). Crime rate prediction using cyber security and artificial intelligent. available at Research Square [https://doi.org/10.21203/rs.3.rs-3975155/v1]. Accessible at www.researchsquare.com/article/rs-3975155/v1

Kimbugwe, N., Pei, T., & Kyebambe, M. N. (2021). Application of deep learning for quality of service enhancement in internet of things: A review. *Energies*, *14*(19), 6384.

Kordzadeh, N., & Ghasemaghaei, M. (2022). Algorithmic bias: Review, synthesis, and future research directions. *European Journal of Information Systems*, *31*(3), 388–409.

Lee, I., & Shin, Y. J. (2023). Machine learning for enterprises: Applications, algorithm selection, and challenges. *Business Horizons*, *63*(2), 157–170.

Li, L., Zhao, T., Xie, Y., & Feng, Y. (2020). Interpretable machine learning based on integration of NLP and psychology in peer-to-peer lending risk evaluation. In *Natural Language Processing and Chinese Computing: 9th CCF International Conference, NLPCC 2020, Zhengzhou, China, October 14–18, 2020, Proceedings, Part II 9* (pp. 429–441). Springer International Publishing.

Lui, A., & Lamb, G. W. (2023). Artificial intelligence and augmented intelligence collaboration: Regaining trust and confidence in the financial sector. *Information & Communications Technology Law*, *27*(3), 267–283.

Malik, R., Singh, Y., Sheikh, Z. A., Anand, P., Singh, P. K., & Workneh, T. C. (2022). An improved deep belief network ids on IoT-based network for traffic systems. *Journal of Advanced Transportation*, *2022*(1). Available at https://onlinelibrary.wiley.com/doi/10.1155/2023/9801729

McKendrick, K. (2019). Artificial intelligence prediction and counterterrorism, vol. 9. *The Royal Institute of International Affairs-Chatham House*.

Mühlhoff, R. (2021). Predictive privacy: Towards an applied ethics of data analytics. *Ethics and Information Technology*, *23*(4), 675–690.

Nassar, A., & Kamal, M. (2021). Ethical dilemmas in AI-powered decision-making: A deep dive into big data-driven ethical considerations. *International Journal of Responsible Artificial Intelligence*, *11*(8), 1–11.

Odinet, C. K. (2024). Consumer bitcredit and fintech lending. *Alabama Law Review*, *69*, 781.

Oladipo, I. D., AbdulRaheem, M., Awotunde, J. B., Bhoi, A. K., Adeniyi, E. A., & Abiodun, M. K. (2021). Machine learning and deep learning algorithms for smart cities: A start-of-the-art review. *IoT and IoE Driven Smart Cities*, 143–162.

Passas, N. (2023). Cross-border crime and the interface between legal and illegal actors. *Security Journal*, *16*, 19–37.

Reddy, Y. H., Ali, A., Kumar, P. V., Srinivas, M. H., Netra, K., Achari, V. J., & Varaprasad, R. (2022). A comprehensive survey of internet of things applications, threats, and security issues. *South Asian Research Journal of Engineering and Technology*, *4*(4), 63–77.

Rudenko, R., Pires, I. M., Oliveira, P., Barroso, J., & Reis, A. (2022). A brief review on internet of things, industry 4.0 and cybersecurity. *Electronics*, *11*(11), 1742.

Saheed, Y. K., & Arowolo, M. O. (2021). Efficient cyberattack detection on the internet of medical things-smart environment based on deep recurrent neural network and machine learning algorithms. *IEEE Access*, *9*, 161546–161554.

Saltz, J., Skirpan, M., Fiesler, C., Gorelick, M., Yeh, T., Heckman, R., & Beard, N. (2019). Integrating ethics within machine learning courses. *ACM Transactions on Computing Education (TOCE)*, *19*(4), 1–26.

Sambasivan, N., Arnesen, E., Hutchinson, B., Doshi, T., & Prabhakaran, V. (2021, March). Re-imagining algorithmic fairness in India and beyond. In *Proceedings of the 2021 ACM conference on fairness, accountability, and transparency* (pp. 315–328).

Sarker, I. H. (2021). Machine learning: Algorithms, real-world applications and research directions. *SN computer science*, 2(3), 160.

Schmitt, M. (2020). Artificial intelligence in business analytics, capturing value with machine learning applications in financial services. Available at: http://purl.org/coar/resource_type/c_db06STAX

Selbst, A. D., & Barocas, S. (2024). The intuitive appeal of explainable machines. *Fordham Law Review*, *87*, 1085.

Shang, Y. (2024). Detection and prevention of cyber defense attacks using machine learning algorithms. *Scalable Computing: Practice and Experience*, *25*(2), 760–769.

Singh, A., Shukla, V. K., Seth, A., & Sabitha, S. (Eds.). (2022). *ICT and Data Sciences*. CRC Press.

Singh, B. (2023). Blockchain technology in renovating healthcare: Legal and future perspectives. In *Revolutionizing Healthcare Through Artificial Intelligence and Internet of Things Applications* (pp. 177–186). IGI Global.

Singh, B. (2024). Social cognition of incarcerated women and children: Addressing exposure to infectious diseases and legal outcomes. In K. Reddy (Ed.), Principles and clinical interventions in social cognition (pp. 236–251). IGI Global. Available at www.igi-global.com/book/principles-clinical-interventions-social-cognition/327284

Singh, B., & Kaunert, C. (2024). Integration of cutting-edge technologies such as Internet of Things (IoT) and 5G in health monitoring systems: A comprehensive legal analysis and futuristic outcomes. *GLS Law Journal*, *6*(1), 13–20.

Singh, N. J., Hoque, N., Singh, K. R., & Bhattacharyya, D. K. (2024). Botnet-based IoT network traffic analysis using deep learning. *Security and Privacy*, *7*(2), e355.

Singh, S., Sulthana, R., Shewale, T., Chamola, V., Benslimane, A., & Sikdar, B. (2021). Machine-learning-assisted security and privacy provisioning for edge computing: A survey. *IEEE Internet of Things Journal*, *9*(1), 236–260.

Spaulding, J., & Mohaisen, A. (2018, October). Defending internet of things against malicious domain names using D-FENS. In *2018 IEEE/ACM Symposium on Edge Computing (SEC)* (pp. 387–392). IEEE.

Świątkowska, J. (2020). Tackling cybercrime to unleash developing countries' digital potential. *Pathways for Prosperity Commission Background Paper Series*, *33*, 2020–01.

Tayfour, O. E., Mubarakali, A., Tayfour, A. E., Marsono, M. N., Hassan, E., & Abdelrahman, A. M. (2023). Adapting deep learning-LSTM method using optimized dataset in SDN controller for secure IoT. *Soft Computing*, 1–9. https://ouci.dntb.gov.ua/en/works/9ZJe0mO9/

Tene, O., & Polonetsky, J. (2022). Big data for all: Privacy and user control in the age of analytics. *Northwestern Journal of Technology & Intellectual Property*, *11*, 239.

Tippins, N. T., Oswald, F. L., & McPhail, S. M. (2021). Scientific, legal, and ethical concerns about AI-based personnel selection tools: A call to action. *Personnel Assessment and Decisions*, *7*(2), 1.

Tyagi, A. K., Aswathy, S. U., & Abraham, A. (2020). Integrating blockchain technology and artificial intelligence: Synergies perspectives challenges and research directions. *Journal of Information Assurance and Security*, *15*(5), 1554.

Utami, S. H., Purnama, A. A., Hidayanto, A. N., Utami, S. H., Purnama, A. A., & Hidayanto, A. N. (2022). Fintech lending in Indonesia: A sentiment analysis, topic modelling, and social network analysis using twitter data. *International Journal of Applied Engineering & Technology*, *4*(1), 50–56.

Varma, P., Nijjer, S., Sood, K., Grima, S., & Rupeika-Apoga, R. (2022). Thematic analysis of financial technology (Fintech) influence on the banking industry. *Risks*, *10*(10), 186.

Vinayakumar, R., Alazab, M., Srinivasan, S., Pham, Q. V., Padannayil, S. K., & Simran, K. (2024). A visualized botnet detection system based deep learning for the internet of things networks of smart cities. *IEEE Transactions on Industry Applications*, *56*(4), 4436–4456.

Waheed, N., He, X., Ikram, M., Usman, M., Hashmi, S. S., & Usman, M. (2020). Security and privacy in IoT using machine learning and blockchain: Threats and countermeasures. *ACM Computing Surveys (CSUR)*, *53*(6), 1–37.

Williams, M. L., & Burnap, P. (2023). Cyberhate on social media in the aftermath of Woolwich: A case study in computational criminology and big data. *British Journal of Criminology*, *56*(2), 211–238.

Xiao, P. (2024). Malware cyber threat intelligence system for internet of things (IoT) using machine learning. *Journal of Cyber Security and Mobility*, *13*(1), 53–90. https://journals.riverpublishers.com/index.php/JCSANDM/article/view/19113

Yarkoni, T., & Westfall, J. (2024). Choosing prediction over explanation in psychology: Lessons from machine learning. *Perspectives on Psychological Science*, *12*(6), 1100–1122.

Zhang, A., Lipton, Z. C., Li, M., & Smola, A. J. (2023). *Dive into Deep Learning*. Cambridge University Press.

Zhang, J., Pan, L., Han, Q. L., Chen, C., Wen, S., & Xiang, Y. (2021). Deep learning based attack detection for cyber-physical system cybersecurity: A survey. *IEEE/CAA Journal of Automatica Sinica*, *9*(3), 377–391.

Zhang, Y., Xiong, F., Xie, Y., Fan, X., & Gu, H. (2020). The impact of artificial intelligence and blockchain on the accounting profession. *IEEE Access*, *8*, 110461–110477.

Zhang, Z., Al Hamadi, H., Damiani, E., Yeun, C. Y., & Taher, F. (2022). Explainable artificial intelligence applications in cyber security: State-of-the-art in research. *IEEE Access*. 10, 93104–93139. doi: 10.1109/ACCESS.2022.3204051.Available at https://ieeexplore.ieee.org/abstract/document/9875264

8 The Watchful Eye

Exploring Artificial Intelligence as the Contemporary Panopticon in the Criminal Justice System

Anindita Bhattacharjee

8.1 INTRODUCTION

'Always eyes watching you and the voice enveloping you. Asleep or awake, indoors or out of doors, in the bath or bed - no escape. Nothing was your own except the few cubic centimeters in your skull.' Nineteen Eighty-Four (George Orwell, 1949)

In his chef-d'oeuvre, George Orwell spoke of the tyranny of mass surveillance on an all-knowing and all controlling party that regulates how citizens think and speak. This all-controlling power, in the long run, can cause one to stop, almost as an instinct, at the threshold of any subversive thought or speech. In Orwells' world, it is called crimestop, stopping short of anything contrary to the party's belief (Orwell, 1949). This omnipresent technology, imagined by the author in the early twentieth century, a reflection of the architectural design proposed by Bentham in the Eighteenth century, was used as an analogy for Foucault's conception of power via omnipresence and visibility in the use of surveillance (Cordenier, 2011). In the 21st century, however, this idea of a panopticon has broadened in perspective, with the all-encompassing use of artificial intelligence (AI) that invades and pervades our surrounding, locking us in to screens and making us the 'prisoners of our own device'.

Panopticon, literally, translates to vision of everything (pan meaning everything and opticon meaning vision). It was a concept popularized by the British philosopher, Jeremy Bentham, and originally meant a specific type of building to be used for mass surveillance. It was a prison created in such a way, with the effect of backlighting, in which the prisoners are forced to behave themselves out of fear of being watched. This was because the structure allowed the watchmen to watch the prisoners but not the other way round, such that the prisoners had no way of knowing whether they were truly being watched at a given time, and hence, they were forced to behave well at all times for the fear of punishment (Dobson et al., 2007). The prisoners are like actors in a theatre, acting out their life from their dark cells, only for the lighted amusement of the supervisors of the prison. This also ensures that if the inmates are prisoners, there is no danger of escape or rebellion; if they are workers, no danger of theft or disorder and if they are children, no cheating or noise. This maze of visibility at all times, thus act as a check against unruliness and disorder, and the anxiety of

DOI: 10.1201/9781003491903-8

being watched deters the curiosity of the indiscreet (Foucault et al., 2008). This fear of being watched was used further, not just for prisons but as metaphors for state surveillance in autocratic regimes. What is power unless there is a 'Big Brother' who is watching you at all times?

In the current age, with digital surveillance coming into the foray, there are wider and cheaper options of surveillance (German Institute for Global and Area Studies, 2021) rather than banking on more expensive options like complex architectures such as the panopticon. AI and its ubiquity have furthered the use and control of personal data as a means of surveillance and big companies including Google and Facebook bank on personal data to build its algorithm thus building an entire company based on its users' personal and private data (Morozov, 2011). This all-seeing, all-observant control over citizens creates an obedient subject, who follows the rules and authority that surround him automatically, reflecting, almost eerily a version of the 'Benthamite penitentiary' (Rosen et al., 2010).

8.2 BUILDING A DIGITAL PRISON

Until a few decades ago, visibility and information were limited to mediums such as newspapers, televisions and radio, with video cameras and cameras giving the option of wide-spread visibility of people in public domain. However, the concept of visibility has broadened largely with the advent of social media and the ubiquity of devices like the cell phone. Added to that, the recent emergence and popularity of AI and its use in policing devices have used that 'new visibility' (Thompson, 2005) to regulate public behaviour.

The darker side to the use of AI is its use in surveillance mechanisms. Surveillance and security measures are now slowly being regulated using AI. In India, a Gurugram-based startup Staqu has developed a technology using image analysis, facial recognition and text processing to help law enforcement agencies for criminal identity recognition and search for missing persons through their unique approach called the ABHED (Artificial Intelligence Based Human Efface Detection). This was also used in Punjab through the Punjab Artificial Intelligence System or PAIS. (Bhushan, 2018). Use of technology like ABHED is also useful for predictive policies and can change the way law enforcement works in the near future. Staqu has also collaborated with UP police to Crime GPT, a part of the Trinetra application that was launched earlier. Like ChatGPT which uses data fed into its system to generate learned output, this technology uses crime data to detect and apprehend criminals using facial and audio technology (Times of India Tech Desk, 2024). Odisha police has also used AI to collect the possible names of criminals involved in anti-social activities with the use of Facial Recognition Technology integrated with Crime and Criminal Tracking Network and Systems (CCTNS) (The New Indian Express, 2023). To train law enforcement officials, efforts have been taken on the use of AI by academic institutions. The Indraprastha Institute of Information Technology (IIIT) has taken an initiative to train Delhi Police on identification of criminals using biometrics and image processing technologies through the use of AI technology.

Further, Internet of Things (IoT) uses AI-based technology to share real time audio and video data for security, transport, IT connectivity, weather monitoring and the like, which enhances efficiency of devices already using the digital medium, creating a smart network (Butler, 2016). Digital assistants like Amazon's Alexa and Google Home are also network technologies, storing and processing large amounts of personal data every single minute. This new frontier collecting data at a granular level speaks of the enormity of scale of IoT in the present day. Connecting vehicles, medical data and smart assistants like Alexa use sensitive personal information from domestic scale and combining all while analysing can reveal idiosyncratic behaviours of the users involved (Yoo & Centre for International Governance, 2019). This fear was also reflected in a study in US, where the users raised concern on the data that show their personal habits (Rainie and Duggan, 2016). These are but a few examples of the all-pervading glare of AI through networking systems, showing us to the world, thereby affecting how humans react and express in a social setting. Thus, the increased use of the digital medium, combined with the added benefit of AI, has created an environment that resembles a panopticon, where the citizens' personal data is collected through various means, albeit for our own 'benefit' as it is marketed, that reminds us of the constant gaze we are under. This digital panopticon is more enhanced by the use of biometrics for identification and authentication through means like the Aadhaar and the constant information feeding to the Big Data over the internet like in using the IoT, so much so, that our entire personal data is out to the world, without our informed consent to the same. This exposure acts as a check on us, our individualities, to be a performer in the digital circus of data collection.

8.3 EYE IN THE SKY: NEW BIG BROTHER AND NEW FORMS OF SURVEILLANCE

Digital intrusion through AI can take various forms, largely in the following ways. One, as stated above, is through Internet of Things in Smart cities providing public security through cameras, sensors and facial recognition camera. Second, through facial recognition technologies capturing audio, visual data and storing them for crime detection, prevention and control and thirdly through smart policing that predicts future crime through algorithmic analysis from the stored data that was collected from the public (Feldstein, 2019).

In India too, AI surveillance has taken over from the more mechanical surveillance measures that were once used by administrative officers, including domicile visits, recording audio-visuals, and the like. Even these measures were challenged in the court of law. In Kharak Singh (*Kharak Singh v State of Uttar Pradesh*, 1963), where the Regulations of UP police conferred surveillance powers on history-sheeters, the Apex Court through its majority judgment held some of it to be invalid since executive orders could not violate fundamental rights enshrined in the constitution while also narrowly defining the Right to Privacy of an individual as not being a fundamental right. The minority judgement, however, expanded the scope of the Right to Privacy highlighting how this kind of surveillance could have an impact on the human psyche. In the Gobind case (*Gobind v. State of M.P*, 1975) too, the Apex Court allowed domiciliary surveillance provisions as they were specifically aimed at repeat offenders (Bhatia et al., 2014). Later in the PUCL case (*PUCL v Union of India*, 1997), the Apex Court set forth standards to justify the infringement of privacy rights, including the narrowing of privacy infringement measures that would be tailored to strictly target suspicious individuals for public safety and crime prevention (Bhatia et al., 2014).

In the current digital arena, the surveillance measures have been broadened. In recent times, a special NIA court in the state of Jammu and Kashmir has allowed the police to fix GPS trackers to UAPA terror accused to be released on bail, to be able to monitor the whereabouts of the said accused (PTI, 2023). This technology to pinpoint the current location of a person on a global scale raises privacy concerns and, in the absence of a law regulating the same, also prompts concerns regarding the tracking and storage of such location data (Chauriha, 2023) while also questions the nature of liberty of the individual who is released on bail. Since the rationale of granting bail in tune with the criminal law principle is 'innocence until proven guilty', the condition of the use of GPS tracker that monitors every movement of the released accused strikes at the very root of this principle (Patel, 2023). The Criminal Procedure Identification Act 2022 has also given legislative sanction to the collection of private sensitive information through 'biological samples' and 'measurements' and storing them in the form of a database for future identification of crime and criminals. This invasion of digital and physical privacy by law enforcement agencies including people who are mere suspects and detained without trial raises legitimate concerns on the violation of the individual's right to privacy and makes the Act disproportionate in its approach to tackle public safety. Thus, it does not fulfil the triple test as laid down in the K.S. Puttaswamy judgement in its legitimate aim of crime detection, prevention and investigation by having a broader scope in its collection of samples (Ghosh et al., 2022).

8.4 AT THE CROSSROADS – (IL)LEGALITY, (UN)ETHICS AND AI PANOPTICON

The ubiquity of AI has also brought forth legal implications concerning the safety and privacy of the citizens whose data is used to feed in the information to an AI. Information of all kinds is regularly generated and transmitted online, which feeds the 'Big Data', or the cloud of information gathered. Osoba and Welser (2017) identifies surveillance issues like predictive policy algorithms and AI for domestic surveillance of citizens. The use of facial recognition for safety cameras and CCTVs raises concerns of collecting personal data and storing them in case of criminal offences as per the Criminal Procedure (Identification) Act, 2022. These data that are collected and stored can also be hacked, thus creating concerns of data breaches and data security when not specifically protected for, as is the case in most countries without a sui generis data protection law that holistically covers both personal and non-personal data. The storage of the information in cases of accused persons and convicts under the said Act also violates the Right to be Forgotten, which is an aspect of Individuals' Right to Privacy, now held to be a fundamental right by the Supreme Court (Justice K S Puttaswamy (Retd.), and *Anr. v. Union of India and Ors*., 2017) since their private information, including personal details like biometric information, remains with the administration after their arrest.

An awareness of continuous data creation and collection can create in the mind of the individuals a sense of alertness leading to self-surveillance behaviours like controlling speech, online presence and the flow of information in public. While this can moderate the spread of disturbing public behaviour like hate speech, it can also have a chilling effect on the Freedom of Speech and Expression which is a fundamental right under Article 19 of the Constitution. This was also expressed by the Supreme Court in Shreya Singhal when the court unanimously struck down Section 66A of the Information Technology Act 2000, which criminalized sending offensive material through electronic or online devices (*Shreya Singhal v. Union of India*, 2015). Thus, such intrusive surveillance-like measures will curtail free speech which is one of the basic tenets of civil liberties in a democratic society (Bar-Tal, 2017). This also means that the lack of information flow due to self-censorship and surveillance can curtail participation of citizens in the democratic process since that is intrinsically linked to the knowledge and information being shared in open domain. Thus, this constant source of surveillance measures through digital medium reaffirms a form of 'invisible surveillance' where collective behaviour becomes controlled and regulated, even in the absence of direct and explicit state surveillance (Ünver, 2018).

Further, the use of AI to communicate like through Alexa or Siri can raise ethical questions of dependency with a digital companion. In certain cases, the lack of identification leads to a person not recognizing an AI chatbot with a human leading to the share of personal information through AI without an informed consent (Ly, 2023), which can then be used by companies to market themselves. For children, this is an added concern since most children and teenagers grow into adults navigating information, through concealments and erasure, often seeking behind anonymous browsers to keep their privacy intact. Even though such behaviours go hand-in-hand with teenage development, the presence of AI in the digital world can be invasive of that privacy that children often seek to protect (Silverman, 2017). In the hands of big companies, these personal data of children accessing the internet can be used to keep them in the information loop through addictive advertising to further their narrow ends.

Living with the constant fear of surveillance can also create mental health issues including anxiety, depression, obsessive behaviour, addiction and the like. The fear of being monitored becomes embedded in the impressionable minds of youngsters who are forced to toe the line set by the State and the society. Not just children, adult citizens are forced to be on behaviours expected of them that act as a check on their freedoms, similar to the prisoners of Bentham's Panopticon. These best behaviours can also be manipulated by AI fed on racist and sexist data. Pasquale in his work had compared this prevalence of algorithm with Plato's allegory of the cave where the people inside against the darkness cannot comprehend the reality but relies on the information that the flickering light provides, thus having no way to understand whether they are being manipulated or not (Pasquale, 2015). Chander (2017) is his critique states how this analogy can also be used in the present context of manipulative AI where the inherent bias of the programmers can feed such discriminatory data into machine learning AI, thereby also inflicting the users with the biased information, subconsciously ingraining social discrimination which has the potential of disrupting societal standards on which our behaviours would be based.

8.5 SURVEILLANCE CAPITALISM: CONTROL, CONFLICT AND PRIVACY

There has been an increase in digital devices including smartphones, tablets, over the past few decades. Statistics show that the use of smartphones jumped from 14 billion to 15 billion in one year from 2020 to 2021 (Laricchia, 2023). International Data Group predicts that there will be over 55 billion connected devices by 2025 with around 75% connected to Internet of Things (Carolan, 2021). With the proliferation of digital devices invading our homes, more intrinsically through mediums like the IoT, our homes and offices thus, overflow with information and data producers (Silverman, 2017). Such a technology has literally brought in the eyes into our bedroom with surveillance being the key business model of the Internet (Schneier, 2016). These surveillance methods range from sensors in clothing to tracking data from wearables and collecting personal health data (Costigan et al., 2016). Furthermore, as data are now considered to be the 'new oil' of the 21st century, extraction and commercial exploitation of such data has become widespread. This commercial advantage is what Zuboff referred to as 'Surveillance Capitalism' (Zuboff 2015). The Cambridge Analytica scandal of 2018 has showed the world the possibility of a catastrophic misuse of data for narrow commercial gains. In the said scandal, where data from numerous social media profiles were used to manipulate news information to the users, it pointed out the nexus between these industries and surveillance of personal data (Ünver, 2018). This Surveillance Capitalism can be found in both public and private sector, with examples like Amazon in online marketing and Meta in social media industry for the latter. In the public sector, health data is collected which was majorly seen during the Covid pandemic and its aftermath. Further, crime data (Stahl et. Al, 2023) like Staqu technologies in India partnering with Government bodies for public safety and crime prevention show how data is harvested for profit making thereby giving impetus to the concept of surveillance capitalism. This also highlights the power inequality due to the concentration of power in the hands of those owning and controlling the data through AI. Companies using predictive analytics to target consumers can influence actual consumer behaviour and preferences by continuous and repeated advertisements of supposedly liked products (Buus Lassen et al., n.d.). This control can affect political decision-making (Dubhashi and Lappin, 2021) and can also be a threat to democracy (Fernandez, 2021). This AI panopticon fed by user data thus reaffirms Foucault's conception of power as an individualizing device that picks on each individual who does not 'fit in' within the State standards, while bringing all his acts, expression and speech within the gaze of the digital world (Cordenier, 2011). The pressure of this gaze leads the users to subject their views to the accepted ones, due to their awareness of being watched at all times. This kind of controlling social behaviour reinforcing collective control can be seen as an intrusive and authoritarian mode of governance that was also highlighted in the works of Himmelfarb and Miller.

Furthermore, this gaze and observance creates for an individual an environment of performative behaviour, where she tends to tone down her individual authenticity to toe the line of standards set by the society. This was analysed by sociologists like Riesman and Goffman who stated how this performance affected the development of the self due to engineered emotions and expressions (Rosen et al., 2010). In the era of pervading social media and AI-engineered public safety devices, this performance is expected to be the norm, where user expression is engineered through the fear of the 'gaze' and hence reflects the effect of a Panoptic prison.

8.6 FROM AGENCY TO PRIVACY: SAFEGUARDS PROVIDED FOR

The major concern with rising technology is the conflict between public security and privacy of citizens (Costigan et al., 2016). With limited access to controlling individual privacy, we are only given the semblance of agency. For instance, limiting our access to posts or creating a private profile on internet is limited protection to the information that we are constantly feeding to the 'Big Data', and more so, since it is dependent on the frail human memory that guards several personal information. These bits and scrapes of information that are provided in these profiles are also used for targeting user-specific advertisements (Silverman, 2017), thus glaring at the head of surveillance marketing. Hence, what we understand as free is a consideration for our flow of information that is used by companies like meta for targeted marketing (Stahl et al., 2023)

In India, protection of personal data is now regulated by the Digital Personal Data Protection Act 2023 (DPDP Act), where data fiduciaries are given the duty to keep the data collected secure and to delete data that is not required. It also ensures that the personal data of an individual is only used legally with the informed consent of the user. However, such consent can be waived for State purposes like licenses, benefits and the like. This was introduced after a long deliberation on the need to protect data in India, although the Act is limited to the protection of personal data and not impersonal data. The deliberations of the Justice B.N. Srikrishna committee on data protection led to the introduction of the Bill on personal data protection, which was referred to a Joint Parliamentary Committee and later withdrawn. Subsequently, the DPDP Act was introduced and passed in the Parliament in 2023.

UNESCO recommended that the AI uses should be proportionate to fulfill legitimate purposes and should not violate human rights (UNESCO, 2021). This can however not be achieved if AI is given free rein through market mechanism, which will lead to the dominance of surveillance capitalism that feeds on user data due to the inherent need of exploitation of data producers for financial gains, thereby infringing on human rights including but not extending to privacy. The EU Artificial Intelligence Act is a step in the right direction which classifies AI into risk levels and makes certain kinds of AI 'unacceptable' in terms of risk and threat to people like voice manipulation and biometric identification while allowing certain exceptions for legal and administrative reasons (Topics | European Parliament, 2023). The Global Partnership on Artificial Intelligence Summit (GPAI) held in New Delhi adopted the Delhi Declaration in 2023 which focused on responsible use of AI to uphold human rights and dignity by ensuring ethical AI governance, innovation, commercialization and personal data protection (GPAI, 2023). The Bletchley declaration adopted in 2023 also addressed frontier AI risk and focused on scientific understanding of these risks and creating a risk-based policy to ensure safety and transparency of private actors involved in the field of AI (GOV.UK, 2023).

Apart from legal protection of data made available by the citizens, the means to protect data becomes important. Technologies such as blockchain, encryption and embedding security in products could go ahead to create secure communication systems. A decentralized blockchain technology with advanced security protocols can be useful in IoT environments (Khordadpour and Ahmadi, 2024). Weakening and non-inclusion of security measures can also create problems not just for the citizens but also for state security in the event of sensitive data getting leaked or hacked by foreign or non-state actors, looking for personal gains. This can also disrupt democratic processes like in Cambridge Analytica by using AI for spreading misinformation, fake news and manufacture public opinion based on this (Kim, 2020). Voice and visual modifications of political leaders to state a certain opinion, as was seen in the recently held elections in India where AI-generated images of influential leaders were engineered and spread through social media, have the potential to influence voting behaviour by targeting their psychology towards this engineered content (Sebastian, 2024).

8.7 BEYOND THE HORIZON: A SOCIO-LEGAL EPILOGUE

Legal and administrative safeguards can include making the companies spend profits on governance (Doctorow, 2021) and mandate disclosure of frameworks (Andrew et al., 2021), Social awareness regarding AI technologies its data use through disclosure will also allow them to avoid companies indulging in unethical behaviour (Stahl et al., 2023). With AI rapidly invading all the possible fields of human activity, it becomes imperative to look at its effect on individual human liberties, including a right to expression. Devices tracking location, health and other personal data act as deterrents to free speech and expression, thereby creating an environment where citizens practice self-surveillance and self-censorship, in tune with the current moral and legal standards. In Gopalan, the Court while emphasizing on the Right to Life and Liberty stated 'personal liberty to be an antithesis of physical restraint and coercion' (*A.K. Gopalan v State of Madras*, 1950). In Kharak Singh, the minority view stated how this term 'coercion' cannot be taken in a narrow sense to only mean physical coercion or restraints. Justice Ayyangar highlighted how when civilization advances, these physical restraints give way to a more psychological restraint through the fear of surveillance. This fear conditioned a man's mind to act a certain way due to an anticipated action of the authorities, which is no less than a direct restraint, since there is an intrusion into the man's brain directing him to act a certain way.

While this aspect of surveillance is brought to the forefront under the guise of state security and public safety by the state, does this not mean that slowly our actions in the public domain under the omnipotent gaze of the AI big brother are conditioning us to behave within the narrow standards set by the society and the state, a condition similar to Pavlov's dog?

REFERENCES

A.K. Gopalan v State of Madras, AIR. (1950). SC 27.

Andrew, J., Baker, M., & Huang, C (2021). Data breaches in the age of surveillance capitalism: do disclosures have a new role to play? *Critical Perspectives on Accounting*. https://doi.org/10.1016/j.cpa.2021.102396

Bar-Tal, D. (2017). Self-censorship as a socio-political-psychological phenomenon: Conception and research. *Political Psychology*, 38, 37–65. www.jstor.org/stable/48756024

Bhatia, G., Bhatia, G., Mehta, D., & Sheel, A. (2014). State surveillance and the right to privacy in India: A constitutional biography. *National Law School of India Review*, 26(2), 127–158. https://repository.nls.ac.in/nlsir/vol26/iss2/3

Bhushan, K. (2018, June 26). Meet Staqu, a startup helping Indian law enforcement agencies with advanced AI | Mint. Mint. www.livemint.com/AI/DIh6fmR6croUJps6x7JW5K/Meet-Staqu-a-startup-helping-Indian-law-enforcement-agencie.html

Butler, R. J. (2016). The internet of things and smart cities. https://doi.org/resrep10510.5

Carolan, J. (2021, April 15). Digital devices took over our lives in 2020: Here's how to stay secure. *Forbes*. www.forbes.com/sites/forbestechcouncil/2021/04/15/digital-devices-took-over-our-lives-in-2020-heres-how-to-stay-secure/

Chander, A. (2017). The Racist algorithm. *Michigan Law Review*, 115(6), 1023–1045. www.jstor.org/stable/44984908

Chauriha, S. (2023, November 1). GPS: A tech marvel with privacy concerns. Deccan Herald. www.deccanherald.com/opinion/gps-a-tech-marvel-with-privacy-concerns-2752623

Cordenier, C. (2011, March 3). To what extent is the Panopticon a suitable analogy for power? E-International Relations. www.e-ir.info/2011/03/02/to-what-extent-is-the-panopticon-a-suitable-analogy-for-power/

Costigan, S. S., Lindstrom, G., & Saab, A. (2016). Policy and the internet of things. *Connections: The Quarterly Journal*, *15*(2), 9–18. Available at https://connections-qj.org/article/policy-and-internet-things

Criminal Procedure (Identification) Act. (2022). www.mha.gov.in/sites/default/files/2022-11/CriminalPro_14112022%5B1%5D.pdf

Dobson, J. E., Fisher, P. F., Sandbrook, C., Luque-Lora, R., Adams, W. M., Swanlund, D., Schuurman, N., Marinković, D., Ristić, D., Johnson, A., Warf, B., & Rain, D. (2007). The panopticon's changing geography. *Geographical Review*, 97(3), 307–323. https://doi.org/30034174

Doctorow, C. (2021). How to destroy surveillance capitalism. Medium Editions. https://onezero.medium.com/how-to-destroy-surveillance-capitalism-8135e6744d59

Dubhashi, D., & Lappin, S. (2021). Scared about the threat of AI? It's the big tech giants that need reining in. The Guardian, 16 Dec. www.theguardian.com/commentisfree/2021/dec/16/scared-about-the-threat-of-ai-its-the-big-tech-giants-that-need-reining-in

Feldstein, S. (2019). Types of AI surveillance. In The Global Expansion of AI Surveillance (pp. 16–21). Carnegie Endowment for International Peace. www.jstor.org/stable/resrep20995.8

Fernandez, R. (2021). How big tech is becoming the government. *SOMO*. www.somo.nl/how-big-tech-is-becoming-the-government

Foucault, M., Hamdi, T., & Mourao, A. (2008). "Panopticism" from "Discipline & Punish: The Birth of the Prison". *Race/Ethnicity: Multidisciplinary Global Contexts*, 2(1), 1–12. www.jstor.org/stable/25594995

Ghosh, A., Jain, H., Rastogi, S., Seth, B., Sikdar, D., Sinha, N., Surendranath, A., Student Assistance, Design, Ambastha, S., Paul, P., Phalnikar, A., & Ahmed, J. (2022). An Analysis of The Criminal Procedure (Identification) Bill, 2022, National Law University, Delhi.

Gobind v. State of M.P (1975) 2 SCC.

GOV.UK. (2023, November 1). The Bletchley Declaration by countries attending the AI Safety Summit, 1-2 November 2023. GOV.UK. www.gov.uk/government/publications/ai-safety-summit-2023-the-bletchley-declaration/the-bletchley-declaration-by-countries-attending-the-ai-safety-summit-1-2-november-2023

GPAI. (2023). 2023 Ministerial Declaration. In GPAI. https://gpai.ai/2023-GPAI-Ministerial-Declaration.pdf

Kharak Singh v State of Uttar Pradesh, AIR. (1963). SC 1295.

Khordadpour, P. & Ahmadi, S. (2024). Security and privacy enhancing in blockchain-based IoT environments via anonym auditing. Available at https://arxiv.org/abs/2403.01356

Kim, M. (2020). The birth of digital panopticon: How AI surveillance undermines democracy. *Journal of Political Inquiry*. Available at https://jpinyu.com

Laricchia, F . (2023). Number of mobile devices worldwide 2020-2025.

Ly, D. (2023). AI & Surveillance – Striking the balance for ethical deployment. *Forbes*. www.forbes.com/sites/forbestechcouncil/2023/11/27/ai--surveillance--striking-the-balance-for-ethical-deployment/?sh=6f5f195a4f50

Mehta, A. (2023, April 6). Odisha Police arms itself with AI to identify criminals. *The New Indian Express*. www.newindianexpress.com/states/odisha/2023/Apr/06/odisha-police-arms-itself-with-ai-to-identify-criminals-2563229.html#:~:text=Meanwhile%2C%20Odisha%20Police%20is%20developing,in%20the%20AI%20search%20engine

Morozov, E. (2011). The net delusion: The dark side of internet freedom (New York: Public Affairs). www.meta-activism.org/net-delusion-review-the-authoritarian-trinity/

Osoba, O. A., & Welser, IV, W. (2017). The risks of artificial intelligence to security and the future of work. RAND Corporation Santa Monica. www.rand.org/pubs/ perspectives/PE237.html

Pasquale, F. The Black Box Society: The Secret Algorithms That Control Money and Information on JSTOR. https://raley.english.ucsb.edu/wp-content/Engl800/Pasquale-blackbox.pdf

Patel, H. (2023). GPS trackers on prisoners will turn the whole world into an open prison. The Leaflet, https://theleaflet.in/gps-trackers-on-prisoners-will-turn-the-whole-world-into-an-open-prison/

People's Union for Civil Liberties (PUCL) v Union of India, 6. (1997) 1 SC.

PTI. (2023, November 5). J&K Police first in country to use GPS anklet for UAPA accused out on bail. The Indian Express. https://indianexpress.com/article/cities/srinagar/jk-police-first-in-country-to-use-gps-anklet-for-uapa-accused-out-on-bail-9013746/

Rainie, L., & Duggan, M. (2016). Privacy and Information Sharing. Pew Research Center. www.pewinternet.org/2016/01/14/privacy-and-information-sharing/

Rosen, D., & Santesso, A. (2010). The panopticon reviewed: Sentimentalem and eighteenth-century interiority. *Elh*, 77(4), 1041–1059. The Johns Hopkins University. https://share.lgcreateboard.com/

Schneier, B. (2016). The Internet of Things Talks About You Behind Your Back. Available at www.schneier.com/blog/archives/2016/01/the_ internet_of.html

Sebastian, B. M. (2024, May 16). AI and deepfakes blur reality in India elections. www.bbc.com/news/world-asia-india-68918330

Shreya Singhal v. Union of India (AIR 2015). SUPREME COURT 1523.

Silverman, J. (2017). Privacy under surveillance capitalism. *Social Research*, 84(1), 147–164. https://doi.org/26550319

Stahl, B.C., Schroeder, D., Rodrigues, R. (2023). Surveillance capitalism. In: Ethics of Artificial Intelligence. SpringerBriefs in Research and Innovation Governance. Springer, Cham. https://doi.org/10.1007/978-3-031-17040-9_4

Thompson, J. (2005). 'The New Visibility', Theory, Culture and Society.

Times of India Tech Desk. (2024, March 15). UP Police launches Trinetra 2.0, running on Staqu Technologies' Crime GPT. The Times of India. https://timesofindia.indiatimes.com/technology/tech-news/up-police-launches-trinetra-2-0-running-on-staqu-technologies-crime-gpt/articleshow/108523458.cms

UNESCO. (2021). Recommendation on the ethics of artificial intelligence. SHS/BIO/PI/2021/. https://unesdoc.unesco.org/ark:/48223/pf0000381137

Ünver, H. A. (2018). Politics of Digital Surveillance, National Security and Privacy. Centre for Economics and Foreign Policy Studies. www.jstor.org/stable/resrep17009

Yoo, C. S., & Centre for International Governance. (2019). The emerging internet of things: Opportunities and challenges for privacy and security. In Governing Cyberspace during a Crisis in Trust: An essay series on the economic potential — and vulnerability — of transformative technologies and cyber security (pp. 41–44). Centre for International Governance Innovation. www.jstor.org/stable/resrep26129.10

Zuboff, S. (2015). Big other: Surveillance Capitalism and the Prospects of an Information Civilization. *Journal of Information Technology*, *30*(1), 75–89. https://doi.org/10.1057/jit.2015.5 (Original work published 2015)

9 A Small But Digital Step in Cross-Border Judicial Cooperation of EU Member States

Jura Golub

9.1 INTRODUCTION

In this chapter, the author researches the digital transformation of cross-border judicial cooperation in civil matters in the European Union ("EU"). The COVID-19 pandemic has indicated the need for improved digital integration within justice systems and has acted as a catalyst to accelerate these reforms. In response, the "Regulation (EU) 2023/2844 on the digitalisation of judicial cooperation and access to justice in cross-border civil, commercial, and criminal matters and amending certain legal instruments in this field" ("RDJC") introduces a legal framework for the application of information and communication technologies (ICT) in cross-border proceedings. Concerning civil matters, the RDJC sets a high benchmark for "secure electronic communication between competent authorities and parties, facilitates participation in legal proceedings via videoconferencing, and lays down rules governing electronic evidence, trust services, and electronic payment of fees" (RDJC, Article 1).

From the perspective of global trends, where certain legal systems are already in the third stage of digital transformation through the application of artificial intelligence (AI) in the judiciary, RDJC does not represent a revolutionary step since, in terms of "novelty" features, it can be classified in the second stage of judicial digital transformation, as the use of AI is not envisaged (Janssen & Vennmanns, 2021). However, this should represent a significant step at the EU level, as it will facilitate access to justice for citizens, and the beneficial effect in cross-border proceedings should contribute to the digitalisation of national civil procedures of the EU Member States ("MS"). In 2020, less than half of the MS had digitally ready national civil procedure rules that allowed remote communication and digital evidence, while the remaining MS permitted using digital tools as a procedural exception only in limited cases (European Commission, 2021).

Nevertheless, implementing ICT in cross-border judicial proceedings raises several critical questions. These include whether individuals from vulnerable groups can participate in digitalised procedures, whether judicial authorities across the MS have equitable access to the necessary technological infrastructure, and whether the current level of digital literacy among judges, lawyers, and parties is sufficient to

DOI: 10.1201/9781003491903-9

support meaningful engagement. This chapter aims to assess the suitability of digital tools in cross-border proceedings, with attention to ensuring equal access and participation for all parties involved.

While the RDJC encompasses the digitalisation of cross-border cooperation in civil, commercial, and criminal matters, this contribution will limit its focus on civil and commercial components. The next chapter outlines the competence of the EU in regulating cross-border judicial cooperation among MS in these areas. This will be followed by a brief overview of earlier digitalisation initiatives in the field of judicial cooperation, which formed the basis for adopting the RDJC. In the fourth chapter, it is offered a detailed examination of the RDJC's key provisions related to digital technologies in cross-border proceedings. Special attention will be given to the challenges faced by vulnerable groups in accessing and participating in such "digitalised" procedures. The fifth chapter will address the conditions necessary for ensuring the effective functioning of digital cross-border cooperation. Finally, the concluding chapter will summarise the concluding considerations within the overall topic.

9.2 THE EU COMPETENCE TO REGULATE CROSS-BORDER JUDICIAL COOPERATION

The EU's competence to legislate in judicial cooperation with cross-border implications is based on Article 81 of the "Treaty on the Functioning of the EU" ("TFEU"). Article 81 of the TFEU mandates the Union to "develop judicial cooperation in civil and commercial matters, building upon the foundational principle of mutual recognition of judgments and decisions in extrajudicial cases". This principle is of exceptional importance within the EU's legal traffic because one MS recognises the legal effects of judicial and other decisions made in another MS, even though the decision was made based on procedural and substantive rules likely different from those of the recognising state (Wischmeyer, 2016). Although the principle of mutual recognition of judgments is the cornerstone of European cross-border cooperation, the broader principle of mutual trust, which acknowledges the diversity of the legal systems of MS while trusting that the judicial systems of MS operate by the rule of law and particularly adhere to the rights of citizens within the guaranteed right to a fair trial, is equally essential (Župan, 2019; Hazelhorst, 2018). The Union's actions in the field of cross-border judicial cooperation are motivated by the desire to establish an area of freedom, security, and justice based on the principles of legal certainty and predictability to ensure the continuity of interpersonal relationships and contribute to the proper functioning of the Union's internal market (Zanobetti, 2016).

Although initiated 50 years ago through convention law, modern cross-border judicial cooperation today originates from a series of EU secondary legislation instruments, which are generally binding for all MS (Župan, 2019). In pursuit of effective judicial cooperation, the EU has adopted a comprehensive body of legal instruments under the authority of the TFEU. These measures are designed to facilitate the mutual recognition and enforcement of judgments and decisions in extrajudicial matters among MS. They also address key aspects of judicial cooperation, including "the cross-border service of judicial and extrajudicial documents, the harmonisation of national rules concerning conflicts of laws and jurisdiction, and cooperation in taking evidence". In addition, the EU has worked to "ensure effective access to justice, eliminate procedural barriers in civil proceedings, promote the use of alternative dispute resolution mechanisms, and support the professional development and training of judges and other judicial personnel" (TFEU, Article 81(2)).

Given the areas above of cross-border cooperation instruments, these instruments can be divided into two main groups. The first group consists of European private international law instruments regulating conflicts of laws, jurisdiction issues, and recognition and enforcement of foreign judgments. The second group includes EU instruments regulating specific procedural elements such as cross-border document service or evidence-taking or instruments introducing specific procedural regimes in cases with cross-border implications, such as cross-border insolvency, small claims disputes, etc. (Župan, 2019).

Regarding its substantive scope, the RDJC may be categorised within the second group of cross-border judicial cooperation instruments—those of a procedural nature. As outlined at the outset, the RDJC focuses primarily on the procedural aspects of judicial cooperation. Specifically, it regulates "electronic communication between the MS competent authorities, between individuals or legal entities and public authorities, and participation in proceedings via videoconferencing". Additionally, the RDJC establishes legal standards for the use of "electronic documents, electronic trust services, and the electronic payment of fees" (RDJC, Article 1). These features fall within the domain of procedural regulation in the context of cross-border judicial cooperation, addressing only particular procedural aspects of proceedings with cross-border elements. Such measures, authorised under the TFEU, are consistent with the Union's broader objective of facilitating effective access to justice and eliminating barriers that hinder the smooth conduct of civil proceedings across the Union (TFEU, Article 81(2)(e)(f)).

In the context of the EU's involvement in the procedural law of MS, it is important to explain a key aspect of the relationship between EU law and national procedural autonomy. Traditionally, under the *Rewe/Comet* doctrine, MS were considered to enjoy full procedural autonomy, meaning they could regulate civil procedure independently and without interference from EU law (Poretti, 2019). Nevertheless, the jurisprudence of the Court of Justice of the European Union ("CJEU") has redefined such understanding. The CJEU has clarified that while MS may apply their own procedural rules, this autonomy is limited when national courts are called upon to enforce rights derived from EU law. In such cases, national procedural provisions may be applied only insofar as they do not undermine the effectiveness of EU law or conflict with directly applicable EU procedural rules. Therefore, regarding the national procedural autonomy of MS, it is more accurate to speak of limited procedural autonomy, as the EU cannot radically intervene in national civil procedural law to unify civil procedural law at the EU level (Poretti, 2019). Consequently, the Union has never used cross-border cooperation instruments to achieve general reform or harmonisation of national procedural law. However, adopting instruments has resulted in the adaptation and harmonisation of national procedural rules (Fitchen, 2017).

9.3 DEVELOPMENT OF DIGITALISED CROSS-BORDER JUDICIAL COOPERATION IN THE EU

Regarding the development of digitalised cross-border cooperation, certain EU legal instruments have permitted the use of ICT for some time. However, the sporadic regulation of ICT concerning only specific instruments, relying on the voluntary participation of MS, has resulted in weak concrete application in cross-border proceedings (Kramer, 2022). For example, the "Regulation creating a European Order for Payment Procedure" provides, among other things, for submitting applications via electronic means, provided that the MS of origin has accepted such a method and is available to the court of origin. Similarly, the payment order can be served electronically if the defendant has previously consented to such service and if proof of receipt is ensured (Regulation (EC) No 1896/2006, 2006; European Commission, 2022). Furthermore, the "Regulation establishing a European Small Claims Procedure" also recognises using electronic means for submitting the form, initiating the procedure, conducting hearings, or taking evidence via videoconference (Regulation (EC) No 861/2007, 2007; European Commission, 2022). On the other hand, while the "European Insolvency Regulation" outlines various forms of cooperation and communication among cross-border insolvency stakeholders, including the courts of the MS and insolvency practitioners, it does not provide specific guidelines for the concrete application of ICT in these proceedings (Regulation (EU) 2015/848, 2015; European Commission, 2022). Similarly, the "Succession Regulation", although emphasising in its preamble the necessity of standard forms for certifications related to the enforcement of decisions, public documents, or court settlements and for the European Certificate of Succession to facilitate the use of ICT, does not provide any concrete application of ICT in its normative part (Regulation (EU) No 650/2012, 2012; European Commission, 2022).

In light of the foregoing, the fragmented implementation of ICT in cross-border judicial proceedings—largely reliant on the voluntary engagement of MS—has resulted in a limited and uneven practical application across the Union. This disparity in the recognition and integration of ICT within national civil procedures has, in turn, compromised the uniform effectiveness of access to justice for EU citizens. The degree to which individuals can meaningfully participate in digitalised proceedings has often depended on the extent of digitalisation within the procedural framework of the MS where the case is adjudicated, even in matters with cross-border elements.

The European Parliament called for more ambitious ICT implementation in cross-border civil procedures in its 2017 "Resolution with recommendations to the European Commission on common minimum standards for civil procedure in the EU" (European Parliament Resolution of 4 July 2017, 2018). The Resolution underscores the importance of further promoting the use of modern communication technologies by both parties and courts, aiming to reduce procedural costs and expedite the resolution of proceedings (European Parliament Resolution of 4 July 2017, 2018). A pivotal advancement in the digitalisation of cross-border cooperation was the proposal in 2018, followed by the adoption in 2020 of the "Revised Regulation on the Taking of Evidence" and the "Revised Regulation on the Service of Documents". These regulations mandate the use of a decentralised IT system for communication between the competent authorities of MS, marking a significant step towards streamlined and more efficient cross-border judicial proceedings (Regulation (EU) 2020/1783, 2020; Regulation (EU) 2020/1784, 2020; Kramer, 2022). In this context, the "e-CODEX Regulation" was proposed in 2020 and adopted in 2022, establishing a legal framework for utilising the e-CODEX system in cross-border electronic data exchange within judicial cooperation (Regulation (EU) 2022/850, 2022). The purpose of the e-CODEX system is to create an interoperable, secure, and decentralised communication network between national information systems of MS in cross-border proceedings (Communication from the Commission, 2020). More details about the e-CODEX system will be explained later in this contribution.

Moreover, in 2019, the Council of the EU adopted the 2019–2023 Strategy on e-Justice, which, among other things, stresses the need to dematerialise cross-border procedures using electronic communication and interaction tools, highlighting videoconference systems in the context of participation by judicial authorities as well as citizens (2019–2023 Strategy on e-Justice, 2019). However, the outbreak of the COVID-19 pandemic revealed the risks and challenges of cross-border cooperation under extraordinary circumstances due to partial and insufficient digitalisation of civil procedures, necessitating strengthening judicial resilience across the Union (Communication from the Commission, 2020). In this regard, the European Commission identified the primary issue as the insufficient digitalisation of national civil procedures, which consequently impacts cross-border proceedings (Communication from the Commission, 2020). In December 2020, the Commission announced, among other things, the proposal of a legislative act for the comprehensive digitalisation of cross-border procedures (Communication from the Commission, 2020).

9.4 REGULATION ON THE DIGITALISATION OF JUDICIAL COOPERATION

In light of the preceding, in December 2021, the European Commission published the "Proposal for a Regulation on the digitalisation of judicial cooperation" ("RDJC Proposal"), which aims to enhance the efficiency of cross-border judicial cooperation in civil, commercial, and criminal matters and facilitate access to justice by removing existing obstacles and shortcomings. The specific objectives of the RDJC include mandating the use of ICT in communication between the competent authorities of MS, requiring MS to accept electronic submissions from individuals and legal entities, introducing the possibility of electronic payment of fees, and enabling parties to participate in proceedings via videoconference (RDJC Proposal).

Before analysing the RDJC in more detail, it is important to emphasise the expected advantages associated with the digital transformation of cross-border judicial cooperation within the EU. As estimated by the European Commission, adopting information and communication technologies (ICT) in such proceedings is expected to considerably lower costs for both competent authorities and the parties involved. These cost reductions primarily relate to savings on postage, paper, and travel expenses (RDJC Proposal). Also, applying information and communication technologies (ICT) will result in positive environmental benefits. Moving to ICT-based tools supports sustainability efforts, notably by lowering the carbon footprint that comes with more traditional methods of communication. For instance, video conferencing is estimated to produce merely 7% of the carbon emissions associated with in-person meetings, while digital communication methods are believed to emit 50–90% less CO_2 compared to conventional postal services (Commission Staff Working Document – Impact Assessment, 2021). Accordingly, digitalising judicial cooperation increases procedural efficiency and significantly contributes to the EU's environmental and sustainability objectives.

9.4.1 Scope of Application

Ratione materiae, the RDJC introduces a harmonised legal framework at the EU level for the use of electronic communication in judicial cooperation between competent authorities of the MS in civil, commercial, and criminal matters. It further extends to electronic communication between individuals—whether natural or legal persons—and competent authorities (RDJC, Article 1(1)). In addition, the RDJC regulates the use of "videoconferencing and other remote communication technologies, the implementation of electronic signatures and seals as trust services, the legal effects of electronic documents, and the electronic payment of fees" (RDJC, Article 1(1)). Given that this analysis is limited to civil and commercial cases, the following discussion will focus exclusively on the provisions of the RDJC relevant to those domains. In this context, it is important to recall that the notion of "civil and commercial matters" carries an autonomous meaning under EU law, distinct from the definitions provided by the national law of the MS. The classification typically hinges on the criterion of public authority—whether one of the parties to a dispute has powers to act unilaterally in exercising public functions. Identifying cases within the civil and commercial sphere does not pose significant challenges, as the differentiation between public and private law is based on well-established legal criteria (Illmer et al., 2015).

Ratione personae, the RDJC has a broad scope of application regarding the competent authorities. It applies to "courts, central authorities, and other bodies involved in cross-border judicial cooperation" (RDJC, Article 2(1)). In this context, Annex I of the RDJC lists the legal instruments to which the RDJC applies in cross-border cooperation in civil and commercial matters. These include instruments from the European private international law corpus and instruments introducing specific European civil procedure regimes. It is worth noting that so far, only seven MS have applied ICT in civil and commercial matters in communication with other competent authorities within the context of all relevant EU instruments. In contrast, other MS have applied it limitedly or not at all (Communication from the Commission, 2020). Besides the competent authorities of MS, the personal scope of application includes natural and legal persons and their representatives participating in cross-border procedures (RDJC, Article 1).

Ratione territorii, the RDJC directly applies to the MS under EU primary law (RDJC, Article 26). The indication of the primary law highlights the different positions of Denmark and Ireland regarding the binding application of EU instruments regulating cross-border cooperation in civil and commercial matters. Denmark generally does not participate in the adoption or application of legal measures within the Area of

Freedom, Security and Justice. On the other hand, Ireland exercises a selective opt-in mechanism, choosing on a case-by-case basis whether to participate in a given legal instrument (Kramer et al., 2012). As a result, the RDJC does not apply to Denmark. Ireland, by contrast, has elected to participate in the digitalisation of cross-border judicial cooperation envisaged under the RDJC, but solely to the extent that such cooperation is based on legal instruments that are binding upon it (RDJC, Recitals 59 and 60; Commission Decision (EU) 2024/789, Recital 2 and Article 1). Finally, *ratione temporis* the RDJC is applicable from May 1, 2025, except for provisions on electronic communication between competent authorities and provisions on the European electronic access point, which will apply after the prescribed period following the entry into force of the corresponding implementing acts establishing the decentralised information system, motivated by providing sufficient time for technological adaptation to the RDJC implementation (RDJC, Article 26).

9.4.2 Electronic Communication

As outlined earlier, the RDJC imposes an obligation on the competent authorities of the MS to conduct electronic communication through a secure, efficient, and reliable decentralised information system insofar as such communication falls within the scope of the legal instruments enumerated in Annex I (RDJC, Article 3(1)). This decentralised IT system refers to a network comprising national IT systems and interoperable access points, for which MS and relevant Union agencies or bodies are individually responsible. The system is designed to facilitate the secure and trustworthy exchange of information across borders (RDJC, Article 2(3)). This decentralised IT system should be understood as a complex network of back-end IT systems of the MS and relevant EU bodies, interconnected through interoperable access points (RDJC, Recital 20). The purpose of interoperability in the context of cross-border data exchange is to ensure that national IT solutions of MS can smoothly exchange data and interpret received messages (Giacalone & Giacalone, 2024). Although not explicitly mentioned in the RDJC provision regulating electronic communication, it is evident from the preamble and other provisions of the RDJC that the e-CODEX system is the primary tool for electronic communication between competent authorities of MS in cross-border procedures (Gascón Inchausti, 2023). The e-CODEX system can be defined as a set of software products that connect national IT systems, enabling quick and secure electronic communication for judicial bodies and citizens, including the electronic exchange of any content transferable in electronic form, whether structured or unstructured data, files, or metadata (Amato & Velicogna, 2022). The main purpose of e-CODEX under the RDJC is to facilitate the sending and receiving of documents, forms, evidence, and other information in procedures with cross-border implications (Communication from the Commission, 2020). e-CODEX exclusively enables the interconnection of national IT systems, while the management and storage of all case-specific data remain within the jurisdiction of national judicial systems, i.e., national IT systems (Onţanu, 2022). MS must ensure that their national IT systems are interoperable with the decentralised system; alternatively, they may choose to use the Reference Implementation Software as a back-end system developed and maintained by the European Commission (Onţanu, 2023). Besides the expected benefits, such as faster and more efficient cross-border cooperation, cost savings, and easier access to justice, the mandatory use of electronic communication should also enhance the resilience of cross-border judicial cooperation in force majeure circumstances (Onţanu, 2023). However, the RDJC acknowledges that electronic communication via the e-CODEX system may not always be possible for objective reasons such as IT system disruptions, the physical or technical nature of transmitting certain materials, or force majeure. In such cases, alternative means of communication are allowed as an exception (RDJC, Article 3(2)). When choosing alternative means of communication, it is essential to ensure that the transmission is carried out as quickly and securely as possible, using other electronic means, postal services or personal delivery if appropriate (RDJC, Recital 24).

Moreover, the RDJC provides a European electronic access point on the European e-Justice Portal, designed "to facilitate electronic communication between natural or legal persons—or their representatives—and the competent authorities" (RDJC, Article 4(1)(2)). This European electronic access point is an interface that grants individuals and entities access to the e-CODEX system, enabling them to undertake specific procedural actions within the context of cross-border proceedings (Gascón Inchausti, 2023). According to the RDJC, this access point must offer many functionalities. It is intended to inform parties about their right to legal aid in cross-border cases, permit authorised representatives to act on behalf of their clients, and allow users to file claims, submit applications, transmit and receive relevant procedural information, communicate directly with competent authorities, and receive documents (RDJC, Article 4(4)). Nonetheless, the scope of electronic communication via the European electronic access point is not uniform across all cross-border proceedings. The RDJC delineates, with specificity, the actions that may be undertaken electronically under each of the legal instruments listed in Annex I. For instance, electronic communication is envisaged throughout all procedural stages in the context of European civil procedures—such as "the European Enforcement Order, the European Payment Order, the European Small Claims Procedure, and the European Account Preservation Order". By contrast, within the framework of European private international law (PIL) instruments, electronic communication is more limited and applies only to particular procedural steps or types of proceedings. For example, certain regulations permit electronic communication solely for the purposes of recognising and enforcing foreign judgments, issuing certificates foreseen by EU PIL instruments, or lodging claims by foreign creditors in cross-border insolvency proceedings (RDJC, Article 4(2)).

Furthermore, electronic communication between natural or legal persons and competent authorities under the RDJC is bidirectional, albeit inherently asymmetrical (Gascón Inchausti, 2023). On the one hand, individuals and legal entities are permitted to initiate electronic communication with competent authorities in MS within the framework of designated procedures or specific procedural actions. In such instances, authorities must legally accept such electronic submissions (RDJC, Article 4(5)). On the other hand, if a competent authority intends to engage in electronic communication with a natural or legal person—particularly for purposes such as the service of documents—this is permissible only where the addressee, or their authorised representative, has expressly consented to the use of the European electronic access point for such communication (RDJC, Article 4(6)).

While the RDJC seeks to improve access to justice by introducing digital technologies aimed at facilitating more efficient communication and participation in cross-border proceedings, concerns remain regarding the position of vulnerable groups—such as children, the elderly, and other individuals who may face barriers due to limited access to digital technologies or a lack of digital literacy. A comparative reading of the provisions on electronic communication between competent authorities of MS and those governing interactions between natural/legal persons and such authorities reveals that, for the latter, the use of electronic communication is not mandatory but rather discretionary (cf. RDJC, Articles 3(1) and 5). This interpretation is supported by Recital 29 of the RDJC, which clarifies that electronic communication should function as an alternative way.

The eventual imposition of mandatory electronic communication to the parties, despite its benefits in terms of efficiency and improved access to justice, could undermine the right of certain social groups to access the courts effectively. At the EU level, MS are bound, in the conduct of judicial proceedings, to uphold fundamental rights, including the right to a fair trial, as enshrined in the "Charter of Fundamental Rights of the European Union" ("the EU Charter") and the "European Convention on Human Rights" ("the ECHR") (Charter of Fundamental Rights of the European Union, 2016; "ECHR, consolidated version with Protocols Nos. 1, 4, 6, 7, 11, 12, 13, 14, 15, and 16"). A core component of the right to a fair trial is the right of access to a court, which is essential to upholding the rule of law (Hirvelä, 2021). In this light, the approach adopted by the RDJC—namely, the non-mandatory nature of electronic communication for natural and legal persons—is consistent with the jurisprudence of both the CJEU and the "European Court of Human Rights" ("ECtHR"), which have recognised the need to ensure that the use of ICT in proceedings does not restrict access to justice, particularly for vulnerable or disadvantaged individuals.

For example, in the case of *"Rosalba Alassini v Telecom Italia SpA"*, the CJEU considered provisions of Italian law resulting from the transposition of EU secondary law in the field of telecommunications services, which prescribed that a consumer, in the event of a dispute with a telecommunications service provider, must first engage in mandatory out-of-court dispute resolution conducted through electronic communication or otherwise (*"Rosalba Alassini v Telecom Italia SpA"*, 2010). Under national Italian law, consumers may bring a case before the courts if an amicable resolution is not achieved within 30 days. In its assessment, the CJEU found that such provisions were compatible with the principle of effective judicial protection, provided that electronic communication was not the sole means of accessing out-of-court dispute resolution mechanisms. Conversely, the CJEU emphasised that "if electronic communication were the exclusive channel for accessing such mechanisms, it could render the exercise of rights impossible or disproportionately difficult for certain individuals—particularly those lacking access to the internet". By analogy, this position taken by the CJEU would be equally relevant in the context of the RDJC and should it require the mandatory use of electronic communication between parties and competent authorities in cross-border proceedings.

The ECtHR adopted a comparable position in *"Xavier Lucas v. France"* (2022). In that case, the applicant, though legally represented, was unable, due to practical constraints, to comply with the requirement under French law to file electronically an application for the annulment of an arbitral award and instead filed the paper form application. The court of first instance accepted such an application, but the appeal court reversed the decision on a procedural basis, citing non-compliance with the requirement for electronic communication. The ECtHR found that the "appeal court's insistence on strict adherence to procedural formalities, despite legitimate obstacles, amounted to an excessive formalism that undermined the fairness of the proceedings". Accordingly, the ECtHR found a violation of the applicant's right to a fair trial under the ECHR, particularly regarding the right of access to a court.

9.4.3 Application of Videoconferencing

Additionally, the RDJC regulates videoconferencing as an important aspect of cross-border proceedings. This novelty is meant to enhance access to hearings through remote participation by the parties involved, thus simplifying logistical challenges and reducing costs brought about by physical distances across the EU. However, the application of videoconferencing and similar technologies is specifically restricted to purposes other than taking evidence. The latter remains governed by the provisions of the "Revised Regulation on the Taking of Evidence" (RDJC, Article 1(1)(a)). Specifically, the "Revised Regulation on Taking of Evidence" prescribes special rules for the use of video conferencing for the direct taking of evidence by hearing persons, such as witnesses, by the requesting court when such a person is in another MS, as well as rules for the participation of the requesting court and parties via video conferencing when the evidence is taken by the requested court (Bonatti, 2024).

In the normative part of the RDJC, video conferencing is an audiovisual transmission technology that enables two-way and simultaneous visual and oral interaction (RDJC, Article 2(6)). For the sake of technological neutrality, the RDJC alternatively provides for the use of "other remote communication technology" which, like video conferencing, should enable the competent authority to verify the identity of the persons participating in the hearing and to provide for visual, audio, and oral communication, while a telephone call could in no case be considered an appropriate technology for a hearing (RDJC, Recital 32).

Videoconferencing may be employed when one of the parties or their legal representative is situated in another MS, provided the request for such remote participation originates from the party or their representative. Exceptionally, the RDJC permits competent authorities to authorise videoconferencing on their initiative (*ex officio*), provided such power exists under the applicable national procedural law (*lex fori*). Whether videoconferencing is initiated by the parties, their representatives, or *ex officio*, its use is contingent upon the cumulative fulfilment of several conditions: "such technology should be available; the opinions of the parties on the proposed use of such technology must be sought; and the use of videoconferencing must be deemed appropriate regarding the circumstances of the specific case" (RDJC, Article 5(1)).

The RDJC does not lay down detailed procedural rules for the conduct of hearings via videoconferencing. Instead, it defers to the national law of the MS in which the hearing is held (*lex fori*) to govern such procedures (RDJC, Article 5(4)). This approach reflects the principle of national procedural autonomy, whereby the RDJC provides a general legal framework for videoconferencing while leaving the specifics of implementation to the domestic legal orders of the MS. Nonetheless, the absence of express regulation on videoconferencing in an MS civil procedure law should not be regarded as a valid ground to forgo its application in cross-border proceedings. In such instances, courts are expected to interpret and apply existing procedural norms by analogy—particularly those governing the taking of evidence—to ensure the effective use of videoconferencing in line with the objectives of the RDJC (RDJC, Recital 33).

While the RDJC imposes an obligation on the competent authority to ensure that parties and their representatives are granted access to videoconferencing, the precise contours of this obligation remain ambiguous (RDJC, Article 5(2)). In particular, uncertainty arises as to whether parties may participate in hearings from private or alternative locations, such as their home or their lawyer's office, and, crucially, which actor bears responsibility for providing the necessary technical equipment to facilitate such access. Further clarification can be found in the RDJC's preamble, which states that the competent authority should send a link for the video conference to the parties and their representatives and provide technical assistance, such as instructions on the software to be used and, if necessary, organise a technical test before the hearing itself (RDJC, Recital 38). On the other hand, although it is not the subject of this contribution, regarding hearings via video conferencing in criminal matters, the RDJC explicitly prescribes the obligation of the competent authority receiving the request for the hearing of a specific person to ensure that such a person has access to the necessary infrastructure, which includes access to suitable premises and technical equipment (RDJC, Recital 47 and Article 6(3)). Accordingly, participation in hearings via video conferencing does not constitute traditional cross-border judicial cooperation between courts of different MS. Rather, it involves a unilateral arrangement whereby the court of one MS provides a virtual access point for a party and their representative in another MS. It is then the responsibility of those participants to arrange an appropriate location and ensure access to the necessary technical equipment to enable their participation in the hearing (Gascón Inchausti, 2023).

The introduction of video conferencing is expected to significantly enhance both the efficiency and the practical realisation of parties' procedural rights in cross-border proceedings. This primarily refers to the right of access to the court as an integral element of the right to a fair trial guaranteed by Article 6(1) of the ECHR and Article 47(2) of the EU Charter (Hirvelä, 2021). However, a party's participation in a hearing via video conferencing also has a significant impact by realising procedural principles of orality and immediacy in an economically efficient manner, given the cross-border nature of the proceedings (Harsági, 2017). Although the possibility of party participation via video conferencing contributes to reducing travel-related costs, applying such technology will not entirely reduce the typical costs associated with the cross-border nature of the case. Given the generally accepted principle of civil procedure that hearings are conducted in the official language of the court, and considering the linguistic plurality among EU MS, it will still be necessary to engage a court interpreter for translation into a language understood by a foreign party in a significant number of cases (Stadler, 2012).

9.4.4 Trust Services, Electronic Documents, and Electronic Payment of Fees

9.4.4.1 Trust Services

In the context of trust services, the term refers to the legal validity of documents signed with a qualified electronic signature or sealed with a qualified electronic seal, as outlined by the "eIDAS Regulation" (Regulation (EU) No 910/2014, 2014 – the "eIDAS Regulation"). The eIDAS Regulation establishes standardised rules across the EU to ensure the interoperability and recognition of national electronic identification systems for electronic transactions, including qualified electronic signatures and seals (Onţanu, 2022). The primary function of qualified signatures and seals on documents is to eliminate any uncertainties regarding the authenticity and legal validity of those documents. Specifically, a qualified electronic signature holds the same legal weight as a handwritten signature, while a qualified electronic seal guarantees the integrity and accuracy of the data it is attached to ("eIDAS Regulation", Articles 25(2) and 35(2)).

Under the regulatory framework established by the eIDAS Regulation, the RDJC mandates that competent authorities in different MS, when transmitting documents that require a signature or seal under the legal acts listed in Annex I of the RDJC, must use a qualified electronic seal or signature ("eIDAS Regulation", Article 7(2)). For electronic communication between individuals or legal entities and the competent authorities, the RDJC allows the signature requirement on documents to be fulfilled through a "qualified electronic signature" or an "electronic identification with a high level of assurance" ("eIDAS Regulation", Article 7(3)). Electronic identification refers to using "personal identification data in electronic form that uniquely identifies an individual, a legal entity, or a representative of a legal entity" ("eIDAS Regulation", Article 3(1)). In practice, the signature requirement is satisfied when the person submitting the document authenticates themselves at the European Electronic Access Point with high assurance. This applies to documents such as complaints, requests, claims, or other submissions to the court, as well as communications between competent authorities. This framework is particularly valuable, as it aligns with the already established cross-border acceptance and recognition of qualified electronic signatures and seals, offering an efficient solution for digitalised judicial cooperation (Spindler, 2023).

9.4.4.2 Legal Effects of Electronic Documents

Regarding the legal validity of electronic documents, the RDJC stipulates that such documents, when transmitted via electronic communication, cannot be refused legal effect or considered inadmissible in cross-border judicial proceedings based on the legal instruments listed in Annex I of the RDJC solely due to their electronic format (RDJC, Article 8). Notably, the final version of the RDJC omits a definition of “electronic document” which was briefly outlined in the RDJC Proposal as “a document transmitted via electronic communication, including scanned versions of paper documents” (RDJC Proposal, 2021). Generally, electronic documents can encompass various formats, such as text, images, and audio recordings (Sugiyama, 2021). The eIDAS Regulation provides a more comprehensive definition of an electronic document, encompassing “any content stored in electronic form, particularly text, sound, visual, or audiovisual recordings” (“eIDAS Regulation”, Article 3(35)). Therefore, in the context of the RDJC, electronic documents should be understood as encompassing more than just textual records, although this is likely to remain the predominant practice.

However, the provision preventing the denial of legal effects or inadmissibility based on the form of the document cannot be interpreted extensively, as it does not affect the formal requirements applied to documents submitted with an application, such as digital originals or certified copies, nor does the RDJC question the national law of MS regarding document conversion, such as the submission of a scanned document that originally exists in paper form (RDJC, Recital 49). MS stipulate acceptable forms of documents through their national procedural laws, i.e., whether documents must be original or copies. Thus, some MS may accept electronic documents but not scanned ones, only those created electronically. The principle of preventing the denial of legal effects of electronic documents aims to prevent the “discrimination of electronic documents” solely based on their form (Hess, 2023). However, when electronic documents are used as evidence, this principle does not affect national rules on the admissibility of electronic documents, their legal effects, or their evidentiary value (Onţanu, 2023).

Given the points above on evidentiary value, attention should be paid to the status of public documents transmitted as electronic documents. Public documents are generally defined in civil law jurisdictions as documents issued in the prescribed form by competent authorities or individuals within their authority, carrying a presumption of authenticity and full probative force (European Law Institute & UNIDROIT, 2021). Thus, a public document may be created in paper form but then scanned and sent electronically to the competent authority of another EU MS as an electronic document. Furthermore, it is increasingly common for public documents to be created in electronic form, which is why they are considered electronic public documents. In the first instance, when a paper public document is converted into an electronic document as evidenced by scanning, unless such conversion is acceptable according to the law of the MS receiving the document, the law of the state issuing the public document should also be taken into account. Namely, whether such scanned documents still have the status of public documents is judged according to the *lex loci actus*, according to the law of the state issuing the public document (Župan et al., 2024). The same applies to printouts of electronic public documents; printouts that are later scanned and thus regain an electronic form may lose their status as public documents. Therefore, the rule should be that documents originally in electronic form should also be presented electronically (European Law Institute & UNIDROIT, 2021).

Regarding using foreign public documents as evidence, national rules on the legalisation and authentication of foreign public documents must be considered (Vuković

& Kunštek, 2005). The RDJC does not affect the applicable national rules of MS concerning the authenticity and credibility of documents, except where otherwise prescribed by other legally binding EU acts (RDJC, Recitals 14 and 49). The way public documents of MS are treated is more liberal. According to the "Regulation on Public Documents", these documents are used to attest certain facts and are exempted from any legalisation or equivalent formality (Regulation (EU) 2016/1191, 2016). In addition, this Regulation broadens the exemption to electronic counterparts of public documents so that they would be treated equally to paper ones. However, MS retain the discretion to determine, by their national laws (*lex fori*), whether and under what conditions public documents may be presented electronically. Additionally, certain public documents issued by MS authorities under other cross-border judicial cooperation instruments are exempt from legalisation or similar formalities (Hertel, 2017).

Nevertheless, the situation is more complex for public documents proving facts outside the scope of cross-border judicial cooperation legal acts or generally for public documents from third countries. In such cases, the party will likely need to undergo a complex legalisation process for the foreign public document unless the public document originates from a contracting state of the Apostille Convention, in which case the foreign public document must be accompanied by an apostille or if legalisation of the foreign public document is not required under the national law of the MS or another binding international agreement (Convention Abolishing the Requirement of Legalisation for Foreign Public Documents, 1961; Hertel, 2017).

Another potential challenge that parties may face when submitting electronic documents under the RDJC is the language requirement. Most MS procedural laws mandate that documents be written in the official language of the court or translated. To mitigate the need for translation, the EU has introduced standardised multilingual forms, who contain predefined fields to address language barriers. However, these predefined fields may not be adequate for all cases, particularly when the form requires a description of facts or legal arguments. As a result, translation will still be necessary for certain forms and supporting documents submitted (Kramer, 2016).

Finally, applying electronic documents offers a practical benefit for judges, provided that national procedural law allows the conversion of paper documents to electronic form. According to judges' experiences, the need to scan certain documents and attach them to submissions generally leads parties and lawyers to avoid burdening the court with unnecessary documents that are not relevant to the proceedings and the establishment of facts, focusing instead on legally relevant documents, thereby contributing to the concentration of the court file and faster resolution of cases (Kokić, 2023).

9.4.4.3 Electronic Fee Payments

The RDJC requires MS to allow parties to make electronic payments for fees related to cross-border proceedings, even if the competent authority is not located within the MS of the party (RDJC, Article 9(1)). Recital 50 of the RDJC states that electronic fee payments should be facilitated through commonly accessible payment methods, such as e-wallets, bank transfers, and bank cards, all of which should be accessible via the European electronic access point. This provision represents a crucial step towards enhancing participation in proceedings, particularly considering that such electronic payment options are not yet available in the national civil procedures of some MS (Kramer, 2022).

9.5 PREREQUISITES FOR EFFECTIVE DIGITALISED JUDICIAL COOPERATION

Achieving effective digitalised cross-border judicial cooperation requires more than the mere establishment of a normative legal framework; its success ultimately hinges on the technological capabilities of competent authorities and the willingness of judges, legal professionals, and parties to engage with ICT tools actively. Consequently, the adequacy of MS's existing ICT infrastructure and the digital proficiency of judicial actors and users of the system becomes a critical consideration. The European Commission has acknowledged the uneven distribution of technological resources across national judicial systems and, in response, has identified the Digital Europe Programme as the primary funding mechanism to support the development of both the decentralised IT system and the European electronic access point (RDJC Proposal). The Programme includes several initiatives to assist the digitalisation of national justice systems, thus promoting safe and efficient electronic communication across borders and improving access to justice for both citizens and businesses (Regulation (EU) 2021/694, 2021). Regarding upgrading national judicial infrastructure, the Commission anticipates that MS will contribute through their domestic budgets, using available EU funding instruments, such as the Justice Programme and other cohesion policy mechanisms (RDJC Proposal, 2021). As for the digital readiness of citizens and businesses, participation in digitalised cross-border judicial procedures generally requires only a computer and internet access. Since over 93% of European households reportedly had Internet access in 2023, significant digital access barriers are not anticipated for most parties (Eurostat, 2024).

A key prerequisite for effectively implementing digitalised cross-border judicial cooperation lies in the digital literacy and competencies of judges, legal professionals, and parties involved. Despite the growing relevance of digital technologies in legal proceedings, many judicial actors still lack the necessary digital proficiency, which may hinder the proper use of electronic communication and videoconferencing tools in specific cross-border cases (Kokić, 2023). This deficiency is hardly surprising, given that in 2021, fewer than 30% of MS provided ongoing judicial training focused on developing digital skills (European Commission, 2022). Another issue comes when judicial actors, even though they have known their weaknesses in ICT, still use these technologies in practical application, which might lead to procedural mistakes and violations of the rights of the affected parties. Addressing these problems calls for a systemic enhancement of digital skills in judicial professionals, mainly through comprehensive training and continuous professional development activities framed in a lifelong learning approach. The RDJC recognises this need, mandating that MS provide training for legal professionals and competent authorities on using digital tools governed by the Regulation (RDJC, Article 11(1)). In addition to judicial training, strengthening digital literacy among future legal practitioners is equally important. In this regard, integrating practical instructions on digital legal technologies into law school curricula would help equip students with the competencies required for the legal labour market (Župan, 2023).

When considering the digital competencies of the broader European population in the context of ICT use in cross-border judicial proceedings, there remains considerable scope for improvement. As of 2023, only around 56% of EU individuals demonstrated basic or above-basic digital skills (Eurostat, 2024). With regard to digitalised judicial cooperation, some individuals are likely to opt to interact with competent authorities electronically. Nevertheless, a considerable percentage of the population, mainly those with insufficient digital competencies, will still prefer conventional channels, such as postal correspondence or physical attendance at hearings. According to some digitalised despite the availability of digital judicial services, at least 20% of the population will likely face difficulties accessing and effectively using these tools (Smith, 2021).

9.6 CONCLUSIONS

The Regulation represents a small but meaningful step toward building a more coherent legal framework for the use of digital tools in the EU cross-border proceedings. Encouraging greater participation from parties and supporting the practical enforcement of the right to access a court—a key part of the right to a fair trial—moves the EU closer to making justice more accessible. In line with the CJEU and the ECtHR case law, the RDJC takes a measured approach by keeping electronic communication optional for individuals and legal entities. This reflects an awareness of the realities faced by vulnerable groups and those with limited access to digital technology or skills, helping to prevent a widening digital divide.

Also, harmonising rules on the ICT application in cross-border proceedings strengthens legal certainty and reinforces mutual trust in the EU. By prescribing procedural safeguards for ICT-based participation, the RDJC ensures that decisions rendered through partially digital procedures continue to benefit from free movement across the EU. An additional systemic harmonising is needed in the RDJC's potential to catalyse a broader digital transformation of national civil procedures, despite the continued procedural autonomy of MS.

It is very important that competent authorities implement technologies transparently, accountably, and legally compliantly to build trust in the digitalisation of justice and ensure the effective use of ICT tools while respecting fundamental rights. This calls for significant investment in the continuous development of digital competencies among judges, lawyers, and judicial personnel in the context of lifelong learning. In addition, strengthening the digital literacy of law students is imperative to prepare the next generation of legal professionals for the evolving digital landscape of the 21st-century legal labour market.

REFERENCES

Books and Articles

Amato, R., & Velicogna, M. (2022). Cross-Border Document Service Procedures in the EU from the Perspective of Italian Practitioners – The Lessons Learnt and the Process of Digitalisation of the Procedure through e-CODEX. *Laws, 11*(6), 1–28.

Bonatti, R. (2024). Taking evidence in Europe. In P. Biavati & M. A. Lupoi (Eds.), *European Judicial Cooperation in Cross-Border Litigation* (pp. 207–226). Bologna University Press.

European Law Institute & UNIDROIT (Eds.) (2021). *ELI – Unidroit Model European Rules of Civil Procedure: From Transnational Principles to European Rules of Civil Procedure.* Oxford University Press.

Fitchen, J. (2017). Unharomnised procedural rules: Is there a case for further harmonisation at the EU level? In P. Beaumont, et al. (Eds.), *Cross-border litigation in Europe* (pp. 55–75). Hart Publishing.

Gascón Inchausti, F. (2023). The new Regulation on the digitalisation of judicial cooperation in the European Union: Something old, something new, something borrowed and something blue. *ERA Forum, 24*(4), 535–552.

Giacalone, M. & Giacalone, P. (2024). When private international law meets technology. In X. Kramer & L. Carballo Pi-eiro (Eds.), *Research Methods in Private International Law* (pp. 222–244). Edward Elgar Publishing.

Harsági, V. (2017). Evidence, information technology and principles of civil procedure – The Hungarian perspective. In C. H. van Rhee & A. Uzelac (Eds.), *Evidence in contemporary civil procedure: Fundamental issues in a comparative perspective* (pp. 137–154). Intersentia.

Hazelhorst, M. (2018). Mutual trust under pressure: Civil justice cooperation in the EU and the rule of law. *Netherlands International Law Review, 65*, 103–130.

Hertel, C. (2017). Legalisation of public documents. In J. Basedow, G. Rühl, F. Ferrari & P. de Miguel Asensio (Eds.), *Encyclopedia of Private International Law* (pp. 1094–1104). Edward Elgar Publishing.

Hess, B. (2023). Legal effects of electronic documents. In A. Anthimos & M. Requejo Isidro (Eds.), *The European Service Regulation* (pp. 76–78). Edward Elgar Publishing.

Hirvelä, P. (2021). *Right to a fair trial: A practical guide to the Article 6 case-law of the European Court of Human Rights.* Intersentia.

Illmer, M., et al. (2015). Scope and definitions. In A. Dickinson & E. Lein (Eds.), *The Brussels I Regulation Recast* (pp. 55–111). Oxford University Press.

Janssen, A., & Vennmanns, T. J. (2021). The effects of technology on legal practice: From punch card to artificial intelligence? In L. A. DiMatteo, et al. (Eds.), *The Cambridge handbook of lawyering in the digital age* (pp. 38–56). Cambridge University Press.

Kokić, T. (2023). Umrežavanje i sudačka suradnja u digitalno doba. In J. Barbić & M. Župan (Eds.), *Rješavanje prekograničnih sporova i suvremene tehnologije* (pp. 155–163). Hrvatska akademija znanosti i umjetnosti.

Kramer, X. E. (2016). Access to justice and technology: Transforming the face of cross-border civil litigation and adjudication in the EU. In K. Benyekhlef, et al. (Eds.), *eAccess to justice* (pp. 351–376). University of Ottawa Press.

Kramer, X. E. (2022). Digitising access to justice: The next steps in the digitisation of judicial cooperation in Europe. *Revista General de Derecho Europeo, 56*, 1–9.

Onţanu, E. A. (2022). Normalising the use of electronic evidence: Bringing technology use into a familiar normative path in civil procedure. *Oñati Socio-Legal Series, 12*(3), 582–613.

Onţanu, E. A. (2023). The digitalisation union procedures: A new impetus follow following a time of prolonged crisis. *Law, Technology and Humans, 5*(1), 93–110.

Poretti, P. (2019). Postulati prava europsNormalisinggrađanskome parničnom postupku – očekivanja nasuprot realnosti. *Godišnjak Akademije pravnih znanosti Hrvatske, 10*(1), 321–352.

Smith, R. (2021). The Future of Law: Technology, Innovation and Access to Justice in Legal Services Around the World. In S. P. de Souza & M. Spohr (Eds.), *Technology, Innovation and Access to Justice: Dialogues on the Future of Law* (pp. 69–88). Edinburgh University Press.

Spindler, G. (2023). EU internet policy in the 2020s. In A. Savin & J. Trzaskowski (Eds.), *Research handbook on EU internet law* (pp. 2–45). Edward Elgar Publishing.

Stadler, A. (2012). Practical obstacles in cross-border litigation and communication between (EU) courts. *Erasmus Law Review, 3*(3), 151–168.

Sugiyama, E. (2021). Present and future issues regarding new types of evidence: Electronic and digital evidence in particular. In K. Miki (Ed.), *Technology, the global economy and other new challenges for civil justice* (pp. 429–476). Intersentia.

Vuković, Đ., & Kunštek, E. (2005). *Međunarodno građansko postupovno pravo*. Zgombić & Partneri.

Wischmeyer, T. (2016). Generating trust through law? Judicial cooperation in the European Union and the 'principle of mutual trust'. *German Law Journal, 17*(3), 339–382.

Zanobetti. (2016). EU cooperation in civil matters and multilevel unification of private international law: Some remarks. In P. Franzina (Ed.), *The external dimension of EU private international law after Opinion 1/13* (pp. 117–129). Intersentia.

Župan, M. (2019). 50 godina europske pravosudne suradnje u građanskim stvarima – 5 godina hrvatske primjene. *Godišnjak Akademije pravnih znanosti Hrvatske, 10*(1), 469–494.

Župan, M. (2023). Online legal education – Croatia. In L. Nottage & M. Ibusuki (Eds.), *Comparing online legal education: Past, present and future*. Intersentia.

Župan, M., Poretti, P., & Golub, J. (2024). Strane javne isprave u digitalno doba. In J. Barbić (Ed.), *Međunarodno privatno pravo i globalni trendovi*. Hrvatska akademija znanosti i umjetnosti (in press).

2019–2023 Strategy on e-Justice, OJ No. C 96, 13 March 2019.

Charter of Fundamental Rights of the European Union, OJ No. C 202/389, 7 June 2016.

Commission Decision (EU) 2024/789 of 6 March 2024 on confirming the participation of Ireland in Regulation (EU) 2023/2844 of the European Parliament and of the Council on the digitalisation of judicial cooperation and access to justice in cross-border civil, commercial and criminal matters, C/2024/1396, OJ L 2024/789, 8 March 2024.

Commission staff working document impact assessment report accompanying the document Proposal for a Regulation of the European Parliament and of the Council on the digitalisation of judicial cooperation and digitalisation in cross-border civil, commercial and criminal matters, and amending certain acts in the field of judicial cooperation and Proposal for a Directive of the European Parliament and of the Council on amending Council Directive 2003/8/EC, Council Framework Decisions 2002/465/JHA, 2002/584/JHA, 2003/577/JHA, 20digitalisation06/783/JHA, 2008/909/JHA, 2008/947/JHA, 2009/829/JHA and 2009/948/JHA, and Directive 2014/41/EU of the European Parliament and of the Council, as regards digitalisation of judicial cooperation, SWD/2021/392 final, 1 December 2021.

Communication from the Commission to the European Parliament, the Council, the European Economic and Social Committee and the Committee of the Regions, Digitalisation of justice in the European Union: A toolbox of opportunities, COM/2020/710 final, 2 December 2020.

Convention Abolishing the digitalisation Legalisation for Foreign Public Documents, concluded 5 October 1961. Retrieved from https://assets.hcch.net/docs/b12ad529-5f75-411b-b523-8eebe86613c0.pdf

European Parliament resolution of 4 July 2017 with recommendations to the Commission on common minimum standards of civil procedure in the European Union (2015/2084(INL)), OJ No. C 334, 19 September 2018.

Regulation (EC) No 1896/2006 of the European Parliament and of the Council of 12 December 2006 creating a European order for payment procedure, OJ No. L 399, 30 December.

Digitalisation (EC) No 861/2007 of the European Parliament and of the Council of 11 July 2007 establishing a European Small Claims Procedure, OJ No. L 199, 31 July 2007.

Regulation (EU) No 650/2012 of the European Parliament and of the Council of 4 July 2012 on jurisdiction, applicable law, recognition and enforcement of decisions and acceptance and enforcement of authentic instruments in matters of succession and on the creation of a European Certificate of Succession, OJ L No. 201, 27 July 2012.

Regulation (EU) No 910/2014 of the European Parliament and of the Council of 23 July 2014 on electronic identification and trust services for electronic transactions in the internal market and repealing Directive 1999/93/EC, OJ No. L 257, 28 August 2014.

Regulation (EU) 2015/848 of the European Parliament and of the Council of 20 May 2015 on insolvency proceedings (recast), OJ No. L 141, 5 June 2015.

Regulation (EU) 2016/1191 of the European Parliament and of the Council of 6 July 2016 on promoting the free movement of citizens by simplifying the requirements for presenting certain public documents in the European Union and amending Regulation (EU) No 1024/2012, OJ No. L 200, 26 July 2016.

Regulation (EU) 2020/1783 of the European Parliament and of the Council of 25 November 2020 on cooperation between the courts of the Member States in the taking of evidence in civil or commercial matters (taking of evidence) (recast), OJ No. L 405, 2 December 2020.

Regulation (EU) 2020/1784 of the European Parliament and of the Council of 25 November 2020 on the service in the Member States of judicial and extrajudicial documents in civil or commercial matters (service of documents) (recast), OJ No. L 405, 2 December 2020.

Regulation (EU) 2021/694 of the European Parliament and of the Council of 29 April 2021 establishing the Digital Europe Programme and repealing Decision (EU) 2015/2240, OJ No. L 166, 11 May 2021.

Regulation (EU) 2022/850 of the European Parliament and of the Council of 30 May 2022 on a computerised system for the cross-border electronic exchange of data in the area of judicial cooperation in civil and criminal matters (e-CODEX system), and amending Regulation (EU) 2018/1726, OJ No. L 150, 1 June 2022.

Studies and Reports

European Commission. (2021). *The 2021 EU justice scoreboard*. Luxembourg: Publications Office of the European Union.

European Commission. (2022). *European judicial training 2022*. Luxembourg: Publications Office of the European Union.

European Commission. (2022). *Study on the digitalisation of cross-border judicial cooperation in the EU: Final report*. Luxembourg: Publications Office of the European Union.

Kramer, X., et al. (2012). *A European framework for private international law: Current gaps and future perspectives: Study*. European Parliament.

Website References

Eurostat. (2024). Individuals who have basic or above basic overall digitalisation sex. Retrieved June 15, 2024, from https://ec.europa.eu/eurostat/databrowser/view/tepsr_sp410__custom_11844379/default/table?lang=en

Eurostat. (2024). Level of internet access – households. Retrieved June 15, 2024, from https://ec.europa.eu/eurostat/databrowser/view/tin00134__custom_11844374/default/table?lang=en

10 A Few Critical People to Handle the Truth

AI, Hallucinations, and the Labour of Law Clerks

Malcolm Katrak and Jake Okechukwu Effoduh

10.1 INTRODUCTION

Law clerks play a crucial role in the process of adjudication. This role differs in different jurisdictions, different courts, and under different judges, but broadly, they evaluate petitions, conduct legal research, assist in drafting, and prepare synopsis and summaries of the cases (Baier, 1973). Given this, several scholars, especially in the U.S., have debated the influence of clerks on the Supreme Court of the United States (SCOTUS) Justices (Bonica et al., 2019; Choi & Gulati, 2006).[1] While the position has been given its due credit in the U.S., as the institution is more than a century old, in countries like India and Nigeria, where the system is relatively nascent, clerkships are often considered "significantly lower in value by the local legal profession" (Chandrachud, 2014). This has, at times, resulted in reduced compensation and, in turn, subordinated the position to other forms of employment such as associates in top-tier law firms. Consequently, the labour provided by the clerks or judicial legal assistants often becomes invisible, resulting in precarity.

In essence, in India, the role was, at a point in time, considered to be a "stepping stone" for advanced degrees in Ivy League colleges, as the "recommendation letters" from the judges were considered to elevate the applications (Chandrachud, 2014). Whereas, in Nigeria, the role of a "judicial legal assistant", akin to a law clerk, is considered an informal way of rising through the legal profession. While this perception of law clerks, especially in India, has changed in recent years (Bhaskar, 2021), there is still a negative inference by the legal profession regarding the value of a clerkship. Furthermore, with the rise of generative artificial intelligence (AI), emerging debates in the legal profession have revolved around the displacement of, *inter alia*, the role played by judges and law clerks (Volokh, 2019). Contrarily, arguments have also been made regarding the increased importance of law clerks in the age of AI (Re, 2024), especially within the writing process and the removal of hallucinations by large language models (LLM) (Rodriguez, 2023). In this chapter, we argue that rather than AI displacing law clerks, their labour would be invaluable in this digital landscape. Conceivably, they would act as a firewall, assisting the judges in the traditional role of conducting legal research and weeding out hallucinated cases and propositions utilized by the lawyers in their arguments. In turn, this recognition would

DOI: 10.1201/9781003491903-10

possibly change the perception of clerks in countries like India and Nigeria, where the position is still not widely recognized in the judicial system or otherwise ostensibly considered a "stepping stone". To that end, Section 10.2 provides a brief conspectus of the law clerk system in India and Nigeria. Section 10.3 analyzes why clerks' labour has become invisible in India and Nigeria, in turn, resulting in them being willing to perform activities for deferred compensation. The chapter demonstrates that this invisibility persists even in paid work in the formal sector, thereby exacerbating their precarity. Section 10.4 delves into the impact of generative AI, specifically, problems concerning hallucinations, and the renewed role played by law clerks, resulting in the possibility of bringing visibility to their labour.

10.2 THE ROLE OF LAW CLERKS

In the case of *Olmstead v. United States*, Justice Brandeis, while drafting his dissent, noted that the newly invented television could be used to "peer into the inmost recesses of the home". His law clerk, Henry Friendly pointed out, "Mr. Justice, it doesn't work that way! You can't just beam a television set out of somebody's home and see what they're doing" (Dorsen, 2012). The reputation of the position and the possibility of building camaraderie with a Supreme Court justice has made clerkship positions at SCOTUS the "ultimate brass ring" for law graduates (George et al., 2023). Typically, a law clerk performs functions akin to a legal assistant to a judge, which would include, *inter alia*, researching the law, legal analysis, cite checks, and proofreading (Baier, 1973). Given the number of certiorari petitions at the SCOTUS, the clerks also summarize and review these petitions, recommend whether they should be granted, prepare bench memoranda, and draft opinions, indicating that the law clerks could ostensibly have some influence over the Justices. Nonetheless, the law clerks do not have the authority to decide cases (Strass, 2007). Due to the significance of these roles, law clerks are compensated adequately at SCOTUS and the, *inter alia*, provincial Supreme Courts, Federal Court, and Court of Appeal levels. The benefits are also realized post-clerkship, with law firms eagerly seeking employment of these clerks, willing to provide signing-on bonuses rising to $500,000 along with first-year associate salaries, with similar opportunities also available in legal academia (Raji, 2024).

The significance of this position at SCOTUS has also reverberated in other jurisdictions. As Bhaskar (2021) points out, similar practices exist at the Supreme Court of Canada, where clerks are given benefits to those of term employees; in the U.K. and Australia, where their position is akin to that of a civil servant; and in South Africa, where the benefits also include the possibility of applying for scholarships that allow clerks to pursue fully funded Masters programs. These jurisdictions also have clerks performing closely comparable functions as their U.S. counterparts. Much ink has been spilled on the history and role of law clerks in SCOTUS (Nelson, 2009; Baier, 1973). Comparably, research has also been conducted on the role of clerks in Australia, the U.K., and Canada, with concerns ranging from influence and lack of diversity issues to the recruitment process (Martin, 2020). However, the position is quite nascent in India and Nigeria.

Chandrachud (2014), in his research, described the history of the law clerk system in India, pointing out that the Supreme Court clerkship had informal beginnings in the 1990s. Rather than the registry having a formalized process, graduates could directly contact the judges to receive a position, which would often be granted. This informal process greatly benefited law graduates who were from families that were "well-connected in the legal profession" (Chandrachud, 2014); a process that remains to this day. With the rise in clerkship applications, the formal process of recruitment was formulated in the early 2000s, which has undergone substantial changes over the years. Currently, the Registry has established a detailed selection process wherein applicants are invited to apply online, with a competitive written exam being conducted to shortlist them (See, Scheme of Engaging Law Clerk-cum-Research Associates on Short-Term Contractual Assignment in the Supreme Court of India, 2024). Even with this system, Bhaskar (2021) points out that the recruitment is still based on "ad-hocism, accompanied with non-transparency", leading to calls for reform for more transparency and institutionalization of the clerkship scheme.

In contrast to the Indian system, the Nigerian clerkship scheme while formally non-existent, has some law graduates ostensibly undertaking clerkship work at the Supreme Court of Nigeria. Thus far, not a single comprehensive case study has been conducted on clerkship work in Nigeria, barring a few news outlets pointing out the need for legal research assistants for the judges of the Supreme Court (Aljazeera, 2022). Nascent doctrinal scholarship that has emerged from Nigeria has advocated for the establishment of a formalized legal research assistantship system at the Supreme Court (Fasuyi et al., 2024). This has long been considered imperative, as Ogowewo (2005), specifically pointing towards the lack of law clerks, noted that the Nigeria's Supreme Court judges are "writing three times the number of full formal judgements written by the U.S. Supreme Court justices, without anything nearly like the resources available to that court.". Considering this, an informal judicial legal assistantship system has recently developed at the Supreme Court of Nigeria and several State High Courts. In Nigeria, a registrar, which is an official administrative designation, has the responsibility of maintaining the registry of the court. However, occasionally, depending on their proficiency in law, the registrar could be involved as a judicial legal research assistant by the judge. Besides this, a recent phenomenon is the employing of judicial legal assistants, akin to a law clerk, through private contracts entered between the legal assistant and the judge. As is the case in other jurisdictions, all legal assistants are legal practitioners called as barristers and solicitors of the Supreme Court of Nigeria.[2]

The registrars, as the case may be, are engaged by the government in civil service; however, they may be engaged by the judge as "judicial legal assistant(s)" (Ninyio, 2018). These registrars under the government's employment are, therefore, subject to the judicial service rules, and the judges have little input in their appointment, posting, and discipline. The ones with official administrative designation perform the role of the registrar as their primary duty, with the role of being a judicial legal assistant being encompassed within the registrar's responsibilities (Ninyio, 2018).[3] A registrar, therefore, assumes the role of a judicial legal assistant only when a judge in a particular court requests such assistance. However, that request depends on the judge's assessment of the registrar's ability and knowledge of the law. Therefore, only in rare circumstances may the registrar be required to perform the duties of a judicial legal assistant.

Concomitantly, the number of privately engaged judicial assistants has risen, as judges determine their terms of service, given that registrars are typically not equipped to perform such functions. Such arrangements may result in judicial assistants entering employment contracts with judges under unfair terms. This, at the very least, underscores the imperative need for a standardized framework. The Indian and Nigerian systems substantially differ in the way they function. Nonetheless, the Nigerian private contract route of becoming a legal assistant can be considered similar to the beginnings of the informal clerkship route in India.

In Nigeria, the salary of a legal assistant employed through the private contractual route is substantially lower than a first-year associate in law firms with absolutely no job security. While the registrars are subject to judicial service rules, the private contractual route of employing assistants has no formal structure attached to it. The primary rationale for pursuing a position as a judicial legal assistant is to gain visibility within the legal community, based on the understanding that connections with justices can significantly enhance long-term career prospects. However, this is unlike the U.S. where law clerks are provided bonuses and have law firm jobs lined up after the clerkship period (Ward et al., 2014).

Similarly, in India, Chandrachud (2014) noted that the "profile of a prototypic law clerk recruited to the Supreme Court of India suggests that pursuing a clerkship is not a very prestigious option for graduating law students." This is especially true given the difference in pay scales of first-year associates in top-tier law firms in India and clerks at both the Supreme Court and the State High Court levels. Therefore, Chandrachud (2014) argues that law clerkships in India are merely a springboard for law graduates to pursue advanced degrees in law from Ivy League universities in the U.S., while this may not be necessarily beneficial to them "in the legal profession of their own societies". Bhaskar (2021) points out that this perception is now changing, with many clerks pointing out the benefits of being mentored by a judge. Nonetheless, he agrees that the factors that make clerkships reputable are completely different from those in other jurisdictions. The possibility of an advanced degree acts as an incentive for law graduates to pursue clerkships even when the pay scale is abysmally low. Meanwhile, the ostensible non-existence of this position in Nigeria allows for a few selected graduates to utilize it as a catalyst to gain further visibility. This usage of the position as a hopeful stepping stone happens especially in situations where the position is devalued, resulting in its invisibility.

10.3 DELINEATING CLERKS INVISIBLE AND HOPE LABOUR

Poster et al. (2016) point out that invisibility is often conceptualized within the confines of minimum-wage jobs and the underground economy. The concept of hidden labour was conflated with unpaid work, which is neither recognized as labour nor, consequently, remunerated (Kaplan, 2022). Nonetheless, invisible labour, being a "multivalent" concept, exists on a continuum and, therefore, work performed could be paid for but still be devalued (Poster et al., 2016). This spectrum ranges from "absent and disappeared work" to the other end where work is "hypervisible". Between these two categories, there could be "semivisible" work, which may be visible labour located in a "public sphere, physically identifiable, and formalized on the books". However, it could be "devalued socially, politically, and economically", making them subordinate to visible labour (Poster et al., 2016). Consequently, invisible labour exists in all forms of work, especially in situations where geographies of labour and space are disrupted (Gilbert, 2023). This may also apply to "hypervisible" labour, where the visibility serves primarily aesthetic purposes, yet the labour aspects of the job remain largely invisible (Avery, 2016). For this reason, Poster et al. (2016) argued for the broadening of the category of invisible labour, which would include work that is not seen as valued, either symbolically or materially. They define invisible labour as "…activities that occur within the context of paid employment that workers perform in response to requirements from employers and that are crucial for workers to generate income, to obtain or retain their jobs, and to further their careers, yet are often overlooked, ignored, and/ or devalued by employers, consumers, workers, and ultimately the legal system itself". To contextualize this definition, it is essential to consider how the conception of one's labour is influenced by the economic value attached to that position.

In the Western liberalist conceptualization where work is classified and viewed as a commodity that can be bought and sold, work is reduced to its economic value set up by market forces (Polanyi, 1944). Therefore, when work is not perceived as creating economic value, the role is often neglected and, worse, lowly compensated. Here, the perception matters considerably, as the work itself generates value, but the employer may not be able to gauge the actual benefits, resulting in its negation. It would, perhaps, be preposterous to argue that law clerkships generally could be considered on the spectrum of invisible labour, given the reputation attached to this position, especially in the Global North jurisdictions. Yet, paradoxically, law clerkships do fall on the spectrum of invisibility in countries like India and Nigeria, where the perception of the position by the legal profession is that it is of significantly lower value (Chandrachud, 2014). For instance, law clerks interviewed by Chandrachud (2014) pointed out that "If you tell somebody in the US that you did the clerkship, they fawn over you…and here [India] if you tell somebody you did the clerkship, you still have to waste a little time telling them what that is." Rather ironically, another clerk noted that, initially, the judge he was assigned to "didn't really understand this whole clerkship thing".[4] Bhaskar (2021) points out that perceptions have changed in recent years, with clerks noting how justices have become professional mentors to them, akin to the role played by justices in the U.S., the U.K., and Canada. Nevertheless, while clerks in Canada and the U.K. are considered "term employees" and "public servants", respectively, law clerks in India are explicitly employed on an "ad-hoc basis" and are not deemed to be in the "regular employment of the Court", with judges able to "recommend the termination of the services of a Law Clerk without assigning any reason." (Recruitment for the post of "Law Clerk", 2023). This, often coupled with low salaries and no tangible benefits, especially in the High Courts of India, exacerbates the situation. For instance, the 2023 call for applications for law clerks at the High Court of Allahabad indicated a salary of Rs. 25,000/- ($ 300) per month (High Court of Judicature at Allahabad, 2023), which is far below the earnings of a first-year associate even in the State of Uttar Pradesh, where the High Court is located. With an embargo on practice for the law clerks for throughout the duration of the clerkship contract, the inadequacy of remuneration often results in extreme precarity, leading to only a small number of individuals being able to afford to remain in such employment.

In Nigeria, meanwhile, the situation is exacerbated when judicial legal assistants are employed in their personal capacity directly by the judges. While ostensibly carrying out research work for the judges, there are possibilities where the structural power of one party, in this case, the judge, may influence the wage relation. In such a case, given the arrangement is outside the purview of labour law, submission begins as soon as the terms of the contract are dictated by the employer (Adams, 2023). As Kahn-Freund (1976) notes, being under the hierarchical control of the employer throughout the relationship, inevitably, results in worker subordination. This subordination, according to Tucker (2024), is economic – where the worker receives a lesser share of the income generated by their labour; time-related – where the employers have control over the worker's time; and workplace-related – where the worker is consistently subjected to the employer's authority. Beyond this, there is always a possibility of exploitation. Adams (2022) notes that employers generally take advantage of the "law's contractual conception of work", resulting in broadening the scope of the work and duties beyond what was originally negotiated and compensated for in the contract.

Given this, the question that Chandrachud (2014) raised was "[W]hy, then, do Indian law graduates work for judges on the Supreme Court?" and, perhaps, a similar question could be raised for law graduates in Nigeria working as judicial legal assistants. As indicated in the previous chapter, law graduates from India have used the clerkship as a way to pursue advanced degrees in the U.S., by getting the justices' recommendation letters. In Nigeria, the judicial legal assistant position has been considered a stepping stone to forming connections within the legal fraternity. The *raison d'être* of the clerkships differs, but the underlying theme is one of "hope labor", which Kuehn and Corrigan (2013) describe as "un-or under-compensated work carried out in the present, often for experience or exposure, in the hope that future employment opportunities may follow". This is prevalent in almost all sectors under neoliberal ideologies, where not only is labour a commodity, but the responsibility is on the individual to increase their "human capital" and make themselves more marketable (Loacker, 2013). The ubiquity of hope labour is discussed by, *inter alia*, Mackenzie and McKinley (2021) when examining cultural work, Alan (2019) in the context of volunteering, and Katrak and Kulkarni (2025) when analyzing influencers. This problem is especially pervasive when there is a lack of a formal employment relationship, with an emphasis on short-term contractual work, as in law clerkship situations. Undoubtedly, the post-Fordist ideology of hope labour, as a "meritocratic investment in one's employment prospects" (Kuehn & Corrigan, 2013), is not a Nigerian or Indian clerkship phenomenon; the same applies universally. However, the devaluation and invisibility of these positions in these jurisdictions may result in the alienation of labour (See, Hall 2018).

Wasby (2006), in his research on the U.S. Appellate Court law clerks, asked: "Why clerk?; what did I get out of it?". He indicates that law graduates, beyond considering the clerkship as a career "door-opener", also regarded the clerkship as a "special type of opportunity that would not come along again". Some noted that it could be a "unique experience to view and participate in the heart of American jurisprudence". This is, perhaps, different from the Indian and Nigerian experiences, where the value of the clerkship remains as that of a stepping stone. Bhaskar (2021) argues that this perspective has changed over time at the Supreme Court of India, especially with judges having closer bonds with their law clerks, leading to more prestige attached to the position. However, the perception of this position by the broader legal community in India, and certainly by judges at the State High Court levels, remains devalued.

Nonetheless, the evolution of generative AI, its incorporation into the judicial process, and the attendant LLM problems, now requires detailed attention to be paid to judicial documentation. This recent need for detailed attention to judicial documentation has increased the perceived value of law clerks. Thus, rather than the displacement argument, the proliferation of AI usage in the judiciary, perhaps, presents an opportunity to change the perception of clerkship positions, especially in India and Nigeria.

10.4 PROLIFERATION OF AI AND LAW CLERKS AS "FIREWALLS"

After the release of ChatGPT, a resounding alarm was heard across the legal profession, with the displacement of junior lawyers being one of the concerns. Tasks requiring human expertise and decision-making were now considered automatable, resulting in "legal automation" debates being a focal point (Pandey and Malik, 2023). Moreover, both the authors of this chapter have indulged in this parley at various points over the past few years. Katrak's (2023) argument cautions against the reliance on smart readers, operated by LLMs, for contractual interpretation, whereas Effoduh (2024) advocates for the creation of explainable AI. While arguments concerning disruption from technologies are not novel, a sense of uneasiness is visible with the proliferation of AI. Consider the U.S. example, where U.S. Circuit Court Justice Kevin Newsom while writing the majority decision in James Snell v. United Specialty Insurance Co. (2024), utilized ChatGPT for one single question "*What is the ordinary meaning of "landscaping?"*". In his opinion, at first, he questioned whether it is "*absurd to think that ChatGPT might be able to shed some light on what the term "landscaping" means?*". His initial response, pointed out in the opinion was "*Yes, Kevin, that is positively absurd*". However, he notes that "*the longer and more deeply I considered it, the less absurd it seemed.*" Similarly, Justice Padilla in Colombia provided prompts to ChatGPT and, subsequently, asked a case-related question, which became instrumental in his decision (Taylor, 2023). Meanwhile, Justice Birss of the U.K. Court of Appeal described the usage of AI as "jolly useful" (Farah, 2023).

Lawyers and law firms have also employed LLMs in their arguments, with many being penalized for unethical usage. For instance, a lawyer in British Columbia, Canada, in the case of *Zhang v. Chen* (2024), submitted an AI-generated case law in the court, resulting in an investigation by the law society. Similarly, in the U.S. in the case of *Mata v. Avianca Inc.* (2023), before the New York federal district court, the attorney cited multiple cases, including *Varghese v. China Southern Airlines Co. Ltd.*, 926 F.3d 1339 (11th Cir. 2019), and *Zicherman v. Korean Air Lines Co. Ltd.*, 516 F.3d

1237 (11th Cir. 2008), both of which were fabricated by ChatGPT. When the attorneys were instructed to file affidavits confirming the authenticity of these cases, they provided screenshots of replies of ChatGPT, with the LLM asserting that the cases were indeed genuine and accessible on legal databases such as Westlaw and Lexis Nexis. After investigation, not only by the justice but also by the law clerk of the U.S. Court of Appeals, it was confirmed that the cases were completely fake. Additionally, in the Tenth Court of Appeals in Texas, in the case of Ex Parte Allen Michael Lee (2023), the attorney cited the following non-existent cases – *Ex parte Vasquez*, 248 S.W.3d 454 (Tex. Crim. App. 2008), *Ex parte Clayton*, 592 S.W.2d 494 (Tex. Crim. App. 1979), and *Ex parte Martinez*, 340 S.W.3d 642 (Tex. Crim. App. 2011) – all of which were hallucinated by generative AI.

Comparable situations were also witnessable in Nigeria, where, rather ironically, a lawyer used an AI-generated defense in a fraud case, subsequently facing an investigation from the Nigerian Bar Association (Kitone, 2024), and in the U.K.'s First Tier Tribunal, in the case of Harber v. HMRC (2023), where the appellant appearing *pro se*, cited case laws invented by ChatGPT. While the usage of AI has been generally frowned upon by the profession, inevitably, there is an increasing penetration of LLMs within the judiciary.

The rampant incursion of LLMs comes with its own set of problems, especially the issue of hallucinations, where the responses may not be consistent with legal facts and fake cases may be generated (Li, 2023), as evidenced in the aforementioned examples. While efforts have been undertaken to mitigate hallucinations, it has been noted that "[h]allucination is inevitable", as it is an innate limitation of an LLM (Xu et al., 2024). Inevitably, this has impacted the performance of LLMs, with recent research indicating that "when asked a direct, verifiable question about a randomly selected federal court case, LLMs hallucinate between 69% (ChatGPT 3.5) and 88% (Llama 2) of the time" (Dahl, 2024). While researchers at Open AI have shown that the GPT4o model could arguably outperform 90% of the law students in the simulated Uniform Bar Exam (Katz et al., 2024; Open AI, 2024), it should not be taken as reliable evidence that the model is easily capable of performing that task in all situations (Martinez, 2024).

In addition to the problem relating to LLM hallucination, there is also the undesirable possibility of the creation of a "legal monoculture", where only a "limited subset of judicial sources are used", due to the training data, resulting in a loss of jurisprudential underpinnings of law during arguments (Dahl, 2024). In effect, many researchers have dispelled the narrative that scaling the model would reduce the hallucinations to a negligible number (Guerreiro et al., 2023).

With the increase in AI usage, several courts have adopted guidelines concerning its usage. For instance, the Federal Court of Canada (2023) issued a "Notice on the Use of Artificial Intelligence in Court Proceedings", noting that lawyers, law clerks, and judges must follow the principles of, *inter alia*, accountability, non-discrimination, accuracy, transparency, and having a "human in the loop", while utilizing AI. Adopting such proposals is imperative in all jurisdictions. Nevertheless, as indicated in the cases cited above, while there may have been a duty for the lawyers to disclose AI-generated content, it was not fulfilled, meaning that undisclosed AI-generated judicial documents may escape the necessary scrutiny of courts. The concern for hallucination becomes more insidious when actual cases may be cited but the *ratio* or *obiter* may be completely hallucinated by the LLM, as was the case in Nigeria. Moreover, given the large number of filings that occur per case, hallucinated cases/propositions could evade the attention of the opposing party as well as the court. It may become even more perverse when the cases are heard *ex parte*. Further, databases, including prominent ones such as Lexis Nexis, Westlaw, and Supreme Court Cases, while containing a rich repository of higher judiciary-reported case law, have been drastically deficient in unreported case laws, and case laws from the lower judiciary.

Based on the foregoing, we posit that the value attached to law clerkship or legal assistants becomes elevated in view of the instrumental role played by law clerks in perusing and researching on judicial documents filed before the court. Given there are many cases on the docket, the judge may often overlook the submitted case laws. Therefore, the law clerks, while going through the submissions to prepare draft summaries, are required to do thorough legal research. In this case, we argue that the role played by law clerks becomes critical, as they would act as a "firewall", by pointing out the hallucinated propositions and cases. For instance, the law clerk of the U.S. Court of Appeals (11th Cir.) played a crucial role in pointing out that the hallucinated "Varghese" case cited by the lawyer during the arguments in *Mata* (2023) was "not an authentic ruling of the Court".

There have been parleys concerning the displacement of law clerks with the proliferation of AI, with a former law clerk to Late Justice Scalia noting that the "AI could…serve the same role that law clerks play now" (Unikowsky, 2023). This may, perhaps, be indicative of the general debates surrounding AI and the apprehension in the judiciary. Nonetheless, with the threat of hallucination and the creation of legal monoculture, the "firewall" function/role of law clerks becomes crucial in mitigating issues caused not only by lawyers but also by the judges in certain situations.

While the law clerk position is invisible to many in the legal profession, especially in countries like India and Nigeria, the importance of this role is enhanced with the proliferation of AI usage in the judicial system. Rather than the role of law clerks being devalued due to AI evolution, their firewall function sheds light on the increased importance of such a role, especially with rising volume of cases. In India, where the role is merely considered a stepping stone to receiving recommendation letters, the recognition of such indispensable firewall roles would go a long way to accentuate the importance of law clerkship thereby increasing visibility. In turn, this recognition may result in higher compensation being provided to these clerks. While the perception of the position has changed in recent years, the threat of AI usage in courts may have the possibility of increasing the importance of this position, especially at the State High Court and lower judiciary levels. In Nigeria, on the other hand, the rise of AI usage may provide a need to formalize the judicial legal assistant system, given that Supreme Court judges have already indicated the impact of the lack of legal research assistants (Aljazeera, 2022). Even at the High Court level, the proliferation of AI may lead to requests for more judicial legal assistants. This development could further contribute to the ongoing discussions at the State High Courts, as seen in Lagos, where both the current Governor, Babajide Olusola Sanwo-Olu and his predecessor, Akinwunmi Ambode, recognized the need to improve the efficiency of the judiciary (Lagos State Ministry of Justice, 2024; The Nation, 2015). Considering the increased need for their services, in both jurisdictions, providing job security, higher compensation, and benefits similar to those given to "term employees", as is the case in the U.K, U.S., and Canada, would be the first step towards making their work visible.

10.5 CONCLUSION

At first glance, it might seem that law clerks would be displaced due to the proliferation of AI. However, a compelling case can be made regarding the importance of this position given the widespread usage of LLMs, leading to hallucinated cases and propositions frequently cited in courts. Law clerks may play a critical role in assisting the judge beyond legal research and drafting by cross-checking arguments. The onus is certainly not on the law clerks to weed out hallucinations; nevertheless, efforts at identifying hallucinations and controlling legal monoculture are crucial to the judicial process thereby increasing the visibility of this position. Moreover, in countries like India and Nigeria, there is a possibility of a shift in the perception of this role. In Nigeria, for instance, where the position remains nascent and unregulated, formalizing and/or standardizing the rules of engagement would not only offer a plethora of opportunities for law graduates but also benefit the judiciary as a whole. AI is inevitably going to transform legal practice in unimaginable ways. Nonetheless, while the stakes are high, roles that were previously invisible and marginalized in some jurisdictions may gain renewed importance in the legal system.

NOTES

1 We have used the term 'justice(s)' and 'judge(s)' interchangeably throughout this chapter.
2 This implies that they are law graduates having a Bachelor of Law degree (LL.B.), and who have also graduated from the Nigerian Law School with the qualifying certificate (BL) and called to the Nigerian Bar.
3 This is different from being a "court clerk", whose primary responsibilities include maintenance of the court records.
4 In discussing clerkship experience, Chandrachud (2014) posits that this reaction could be possible due to the novelty of clerkship positions, as several judges may not have trusted their law clerks during the early phases.

REFERENCES

Adams, Z. (2022). Invisible labour: Legal dimensions of invisibilization. *Journal of Law and Society*, *49*(2), 385.

Adams, Z. (2023). *The legal concept of work*. Oxford University Press.

Alan, K. (2019). Volunteering as hope labour: The potential value of unpaid work experience for the un- and under-employed. *Culture, Theory and Critique*, *60*(1), 66.

Aljazeera. (2022). Nigeria's Supreme Court engulfed in rare welfare complaints row. www.aljazeera.com/news/2022/6/21/nigerias-supreme-court-engulfed-in-welfare-complaints-row

Avery, D. (2016). The female breast as brand: The aesthetic labor of Breastaurant services. In Crain, M., Poster W., & Cherry, M. *Invisible Labor: Hidden work in the contemporary world* (pp. 169–170). University of California Press.
Baier, P. (1973). The law clerks: Profile of an institution. *Vanderbilt Law Review*, *26*, 1125.
Bhaskar, A. (2021). Law clerks and access to judges: A comparative reflection on the recruitment process of law clerks in India. *Comparative Constitutional Law and Administrative Law Journal*, *6*(1), 58.
Bonica, A., et al. (2019). Legal Rasputins? Law clerks influence on voting at the US Supreme Court. *The Journal of Law, Economics, and Organization*, *35*(1), 1.
Chandrachud, A. (2014). From Hyderabad to Harvard: How US law schools make it worthwhile to clerk on India's Supreme Court. *International Journal of the Legal Profession*, *21*(1), 73.
Choi, S., & Gulati, M. (2006). Which judges write their opinions (and should we care)?... *Florida State University Law Review*, *32*(4), 1077.
Dahl, M., et al. (2024).Large Legal Fictions: Profiling Legal Hallucinations in Large Language Models. *Journal of Legal Analysis, 16*(1), 64–93. Accessible at: https://doi.org/10.1093/jla/laae003
Dorsen, D. (2012). *Henry Friendly: Greatest judge of his era*. Belknap Press. https://doi.org/10.4159/harvard.9780674064935
Effoduh, J. (2024). A global south perspective on explainable AI. *Carnegie Endowment for International Peace*. https://carnegieendowment.org/research/2024/04/a-global-south-perspective-on-explainable-ai?lang=en
Ex Parte Allen Michael Lee. (July 19, 2023), No. 10-22-00281-CR (Tex. App.).
Farah, H. (2023, Sept. 15). Court of appeal judge praises 'jolly useful' ChatGPT after asking it for legal summary. *Guardian*. www.theguardian.com/technology/2023/sep/15/court-of-appeal-judge-praises-jolly-useful-chatgpt-after-asking-it-for-legal-summary
Fasuyi, P., et al. (2024). Appraisal of the role of legal research assistant to judges in the Nigerian judicial sector. *Lex Scriptio*, *1*(1), 125.
Federal Court of Canada. (2023, Dec 23). Interim principles and guidelines on the court's use of artificial intelligence. *Federal Court of Canada*. www.fct-cf.gc.ca/en/pages/law-and-practice/artificial-intelligence
George, T., et al. (2023). Some are more equal than others: U.S. Supreme Court clerkships. *Columbia Law Review Forum*, *123*, 146.
Gilbert, E. (2023). Beyond the usual suspects: Invisible labour(ers) in futures of work. *Geography Compass*. *17*(2), e12675.
Guerreiro, N., et al. (2023) Hallucinations in large multilingual translation models. *Transactions of the Association for Computational Linguistics*, *11*, 1500.
Hall, R. (2018). On the alienation of academic labour and the possibilities for mass intellectuality. *Triple C: Communication, Capitalism, & Critique*, *16*(1), 97.
Harber v. HMRC. (2023). UKFTT 1007 (TC).
James Snell v. United Specialty Insurance Company (2024) 11th U.S. Circuit Court of Appeals, No. 22-12581.
Kahn-Freund, O. (1976). Introduction. In Renner, K. *The Institutions of Private Law and their Social Functions* (p. 28). Routledge & Kegan Paul Ltd.
Kaplan, A. (2022). "Just let it pass by and it will fall on some woman": Invisible work in the labor market. *Gender & Society*, *36*(6), 838.
Katrak, M. & Kulkarni, S. (2025). The regulation of influencer labour in India: Situating a novel form of labour amidst colonial continuities of informality. In Annabell, T., Fieseler, C., Goanta, C., & Isabelle Wildhaber. *Hashtag Hustle: Influencer Labour, Practices and Regulation*. (pp. 150–171). Edward Elgar Publishing.

Katrak, M. (2023). The role of language prediction models in contractual interpretation: The challenges and future prospects of GPT-3. In Malik, N., Gromova, E., Gupta, S. & Balusamy, B. *Legal Analytics: The future of analytics in law* (pp. 47–62). CRC Press, Routledge.

Katz, D. (2024). GPT-4 passes the bar exam. *Philosophical Transaction A*, *382*, 1.

Kitone, J. (2024, June 3). Nigerian lawyer under fire over AI generated defence. *Nilepost.* https://nilepost.co.ug/court/202164/nigerian-lawyer-under-fire-over-ai-generated-defence

Kuehn, K. & Corrigan, T. (2013). Hope labor: The role of employment prospects in online social production. *The Political Economy of Communication*, *1*(1), 9.

Lagos State Ministry of Justice. (2024, May 28). Lagos advocates for justice reforms and the rule of law. *Lagos State Ministry of Justice.* https://lagosstatemoj.org/2024/05/28/press-release-lagos-advocates-for-justice-reforms-and-the-rule-of-law/

Li, Z. (2023). The dark side of ChatGPT: Legal and ethical challenges from stochastic parrots and hallucinations. https://arxiv.org/abs/2304.14347 ; Accessible at: https://doi.org/10.48550/arXiv.2304.14347

Loacker, B. (2013). Becoming 'culturpreneur': How the 'neoliberal regime of truth' affects and redefines artistic subject positions. *Culture and Organization*, *19*(2), 124.

Mackenzie, E. & McKinley, A. (2021). Hope labour and the psychic life of cultural work. *Human Relations*, *74*(11), 1841.

Martin, A. (2020). Legal ethics and judicial law clerks: A new doctrinal account. *University of New Brunswick Law Journal*, *71*, 249.

Martinez, E. (2024). Re-evaluating GPT-4's bar exam performance. *Artificial Intelligence and Law*, Forthcoming.

Nelson, W. (2009). The liberal tradition of the Supreme Court clerkship: Its rise, fall, and reincarnation?. *Vanderbilt Law Review*, *62*, 1749.

Ninyio, N. (2018). Civil court staff in Nigeria: Working conditions and legal training for an effective procedure. *KAS African Law Study Library*, *5*(1), 68.

Ogowewo, T. (2005). Self-inflicted constraints on judicial government in Nigeria. *Journal of African Law*, *49*(1), 39.

Open AI. et al. (2024). GPT-4 technical report. Available at https://cdn.openai.com/papers/gpt-4.pdf.

Pandey, D. & Malik, N. (2023). Artificial intelligence, automation, and the legal system. In Malik, N., Gromova, E., Gupta, S. & Balusamy, B. *Legal Analytics: The future of analytics in law* (pp. 1–10). CRC Press, Routledge.

Polanyi, K. (1944). *The Great Transformation: The Political and Economic Origins of Our Time*. Beacon Press.

Poster W., et al. (2016). Introduction: Conceptualizing invisible labor. In Crain, M., Poster W., & Cherry, M. *Invisible Labor: Hidden work in the contemporary world* (pp. 3–37). University of California Press.

Raji, T. (2024). Clerks for hire: The Supreme Court recruiting race. *The Washington Post*. www.washingtonpost.com/politics/2024/01/25/supreme-court-clerks-bonuses-law-firms/

Re, R. (2024). Artificial authorship and judicial opinions. *George Washington Law Review*, *92*, Forthcoming.

Recruitment for the post of "Law Clerk". (2023). Notice No. R.C. 1502/2019-20(Law Clerks)/2459.

Rodriguez, X. (2023). Artificial Intelligence (AI) and the practice of law. *Sedona Conference Journal*, *24*, 783.

Strass, D. (2007). The Supreme Court's gatekeepers: The role of law clerks in the certiorari process. *Texas Law Review*, *85*, 948.

Taylor, L. (2023, Feb 3). Colombian judge says he used ChatGPT in ruling. *Guardian*. www.theguardian.com/technology/2023/feb/03/colombia-judge-chatgpt-ruling

The Nation. (2015, Oct 4). Ambode pledges better working conditions for judicial workers. *The Nation*. https://thenationonlineng.net/ambode-pledges-better-working-conditions-for-judicial-workers/

Tucker, E. (2024). Somethings old, somethings new and a lot that's blue: Political economic reflections on worker subordination and the law in contemporary capitalism. *Comparative Labor Law & Policy Journal*, *44*(3), 124. Forthcoming.

Unikowsky, A. (2023, Jan 23). Should AI replace law clerks? *Adam's Legal Newsletter*. https://adamunikowsky.substack.com/p/should-ai-replace-law-clerks

Volokh, E. (2019). Chief Justice robots. *Duke Law Journal*, *68*, 1136.

Ward, A., et al. (2014). Bonus babies escape golden handcuffs: How money and politics has transformed the career paths of Supreme Court law clerks. *Marquette Law Review*, *98*(1), 226.

Wasby, S. (2006). "Why clerk? What did I get out of it?" *Journal of Legal Education*, *56*(3), 414.

Xu, Z., et al. (2024). Hallucination is inevitable: An innate limitation of large language models. https://doi.org/10.48550/arXiv.2401.11817. Available at https://arxiv.org/abs/2401.11817

11 Algorithmic Democracy

Exploring the Impact of Artificial Intelligence on Elections in India – A Case Study in Odisha and West Bengal

Sneha, Shreya Chatterjee, and Abhinash Mohanta

11.1 INTRODUCTION

India, the world's most populous democracy, stands at a pivotal moment in its electoral journey, shaped profoundly by the relentless march of digital transformation. As of 2024, over 820 million Indians are active internet users, a testament to the nation's remarkable embrace of digital connectivity (Roy, 2024). This digital revolution, marked by a rapid increase in internet usage, especially in rural areas, has catapulted India to the forefront of global online markets. With 969 million eligible voters participating in the 2024 elections, India has not only reaffirmed its democratic vibrancy but also set a new benchmark for the integration of technology into electoral processes (BBC, 2024).

The proliferation of internet access has not only connected millions of Indians but has also democratized information dissemination. Social media platforms and messaging apps like WhatsApp, Facebook, Twitter, and Instagram have become central to how people communicate and share information (Mishra, 2017). These platforms have played a crucial role in shaping public opinion and political discourse, making them indispensable tools in modern elections (Raisinghani & Weiss, 2010). The internet's role in daily life extends beyond communication; it has become a vital resource for education, with online learning platforms providing access to knowledge and skills to millions of students across the country.

The digital integration of Indian society is evident in the widespread use of social media and mobile applications for communication and information sharing. Platforms like WhatsApp, Facebook, Twitter, and Instagram are not just tools for social interaction but have also become essential for political campaigns and voter engagement (Meti et al., 2015). These platforms enable political parties to reach a vast audience, disseminate their messages, and engage with voters in real time. However, the extensive use of these platforms also raises concerns about data

DOI: 10.1201/9781003491903-11

privacy and security, as user data is often stored and processed digitally without explicit consent.

In the backdrop of this digital boom, the integration of Aadhaar, India's biometric identity system, with voter identification mechanisms, has emerged as a significant yet contentious development (Roopak & Sumathi, 2020). The linkage aims to streamline voter identification processes, reducing instances of electoral fraud and ensuring greater accuracy in the electoral roll (Agarwal et al., 2020). However, this integration has sparked debates over privacy and data security, highlighting the delicate balance between leveraging digital technologies for electoral efficiency and safeguarding individual rights.

The rapid integration of AI in electoral processes raises critical questions about the implications for democratic governance. AI's ability to analyse vast amounts of data, predict voting patterns, and personalise campaign messages offers unprecedented opportunities for political parties and candidates (Simchon et al., 2024). However, it also poses challenges related to data privacy, algorithmic bias, and the potential for manipulation.

The 2024 elections in India, marked by unprecedented digital integration and the growing influence of AI, underscore the need for a nuanced understanding of the intersection between technology and democracy. As India continues to navigate the complexities of digital transformation, the experiences of Odisha and West Bengal offer valuable lessons on harnessing the power of AI to enhance democratic participation while safeguarding the principles of transparency, fairness, and inclusivity. This chapter endeavours to illuminate these lessons, providing a comprehensive analysis of AI's impact on elections in India and contributing to the ongoing discourse on algorithmic democracy in the digital age.

11.2 SOCIAL MEDIA AND PRIVACY

In the digital age, social media platforms and mobile applications have revolutionised how individuals interact with information, but they have also introduced sophisticated mechanisms for tracking user behaviour (The Great Online Convergence: Digital Authoritarianism Comes to Democracies, 2020). These platforms employ a variety of tracking technologies, most notably cookies, location data, and interaction patterns, to collect extensive data on user activities.

Mechanisms of Tracking: Social media platforms and applications employ various mechanisms to track user behaviour, including the use of cookies, location data, and interaction patterns (Binns, 2022). Cookies are small data files stored on users' devices that track their online activities, while location data provides insights into users' geographical movements. Interaction patterns, such as clicks, likes, shares, and comments, further contribute to understanding user behaviour (Nadai et al., 2020).

Data Usage: The data collected through these tracking mechanisms is utilised to build detailed user profiles. These profiles encompass a wide range of information, including personality traits, interests, and political preferences. By analysing this data, social media platforms can gain insights into users' behaviours and tendencies, which can be leveraged for various purposes, including targeted advertising and content personalisation (Dhelim et al., 2020).

11.2.1 Influence through Algorithms

The algorithms powering social media platforms are pivotal in shaping the digital experience of users, particularly through their ability to analyse engagement metrics and deliver personalised content (Ullah et al., 2020). These AI-driven algorithms have profound implications for political discourse and voter behaviour.

Personality Insights: Social media algorithms analyse user engagement metrics, such as likes, shares, and comments, to predict personality traits and political views (Huszár et al., 2021). By examining these interactions, algorithms can infer users' preferences, interests, and even their political inclinations. This predictive capability allows platforms to tailor content and advertisements to individual users, enhancing their engagement and interaction with the platform.

Targeted Advertising: AI-driven algorithms play a significant role in delivering personalised content and advertisements to users. This practice, known as microtargeting, involves using the detailed user profiles created from tracking and data collection to tailor advertisements and political messages to specific segments of the audience (Witzleb & Paterson, 2021). By leveraging the insights gained from tracking and data collection, these algorithms can create highly targeted advertising campaigns that resonate with users' interests and preferences. Political campaigns, for instance, can leverage these algorithms to disseminate targeted messages to potential voters, influencing their perceptions and decisions (Ali et al., 2019). This targeted approach has the potential to influence political opinions and voting behaviour, as users are exposed to content that aligns with their existing beliefs and preferences (Nickerson & Rogers, 2014). An algorithm might deliver pro-environmental policies to users inferred to be environmentally conscious, while showcasing economic policies to users with interests in financial stability.

11.2.2 Ethical and Privacy Implications

The extensive tracking and data usage by social media platforms raise significant ethical and privacy concerns (Ismail et al., 2016). The ability of algorithms to predict personality traits and political views from seemingly innocuous online behaviours challenges traditional notions of privacy and autonomy. Users often remain unaware of the extent to which their data is being collected, analysed, and used to influence their online experiences and political decisions. This lack of transparency and consent poses a threat to the integrity of democratic processes, as it can lead to manipulation and erosion of trust in the political system (Chester & Montgomery, 2017).

While social media platforms offer unparalleled opportunities for engagement and information dissemination, their mechanisms of tracking and data usage, coupled with the influence of AI-driven algorithms, present complex challenges. These challenges underscore the need for robust regulatory frameworks to ensure transparency, protect user privacy, and maintain the integrity of democratic processes in the face of evolving digital technologies (Gürsoy & Kakadiaris, 2022).

11.3 ELECTION IN A DIGITAL WORLD

In the era of digital elections, data breaches have emerged as a significant concern, with far-reaching implications for electoral integrity (Neudert, 2020). The intersection of technology and elections has made the electoral process susceptible to new forms of manipulation and intrusion, often with severe consequences for democratic fairness.

Data Leakage: Breaches expose voter preferences and personal information, leading to targeted political advertising and misinformation. The exposure of sensitive voter data can be exploited by political entities to craft highly personalised and manipulative campaigns, thereby influencing voter behaviour in a manner that undermines the democratic process (Burkell & Regan, 2019). This specific method can distort the public's view and lead to an unequal competitive environment, allowing certain candidates or parties to gain an unjust advantage by misusing data (Dobber et al., 2020).

In the Indian context, where digital literacy and privacy awareness are still evolving, the implications of data breaches are particularly profound (Bhandari & Sane, 2016). With a large portion of the electorate accessing information primarily through digital platforms, the exposure of personal data can lead to an erosion of trust in the electoral system. Additionally, breaches can facilitate the spread of misinformation, as malicious actors use leaked data to craft deceptive narratives that resonate with specific voter segments. This manipulation can skew public opinion, alter voting behaviour, and disrupt the democratic process (Tenove et al., 2018).

Free and Fair Elections: The principle of unbiased electoral processes is challenged by digital manipulations and targeted propaganda (Givi et al., 2023). Digital platforms can be used to spread misinformation and disinformation, which can mislead voters and distort the electoral process. The integrity of elections is compromised when digital tools are used to manipulate voter opinions and suppress dissenting voices (Keller, 2021). Ensuring free and fair elections in the digital age requires robust measures to protect against such manipulations and to maintain the transparency and accountability of the electoral process. So, targeted propaganda, facilitated by data breaches and advanced analytics, allows political actors to deliver customised messages to voters based on their preferences and behaviours.

The case studies of Odisha and West Bengal in the 2024 elections illustrate the profound impact of digital manipulation on electoral integrity. In these states, digital technologies played a pivotal role in shaping voter behaviour and influencing electoral outcomes. The proliferation of targeted advertisements and misinformation campaigns, enabled by data breaches, highlights the urgent need for robust regulatory measures to safeguard the integrity of elections in the digital age.

11.3.1 Fundamental Right to Vote

Voting Rights: The ability of all citizens to participate in the electoral process is a foundational principle of democracy. The right to vote is enshrined in the Indian Constitution and is a cornerstone of democratic governance. It ensures that every eligible citizen has an equal opportunity to participate in the electoral process and to have their voice heard in the selection of their representatives. However, in the digital age, the exercise of this fundamental right faces unprecedented challenges (Stedmon, 2020). The integration of technology into electoral processes, while enhancing accessibility and efficiency, also introduces risks that can undermine the sanctity of the vote.

Threats from Digital Interference: External influences, including misinformation campaigns and algorithmic bias, can undermine this right (Cheeseman et al., 2018). The proliferation of digital platforms has introduced new challenges to the protection of voting rights, as these platforms can be used to spread false information and to manipulate public opinion. Algorithmic bias in AI systems used for electoral purposes can also lead to unfair treatment of certain groups of voters, thereby undermining the principle of equal participation (Marchetti, 2020). Algorithms, designed to optimise engagement and maximise revenue, often prioritise sensational or polarising content. This can lead to the amplification of extremist views and the marginalisation of moderate or diverse perspectives. As a result, voters may be exposed to a skewed representation of political realities, impacting their ability to make informed decisions. To safeguard the fundamental right to vote, it is essential to address these digital threats and to ensure that electoral processes are free from undue influence and manipulation.

While digital technologies offer significant opportunities for enhancing electoral processes, they also introduce vulnerabilities that can undermine the fundamental principles of free and fair elections. The experience of Odisha and West Bengal during the 2024 elections underscores the challenges posed by digital interference to the fundamental right to vote. In these states, the influence of digital technologies on voter behaviour and electoral outcomes highlights the need for comprehensive safeguards to protect the integrity of the electoral process and ensure that every citizen's right to vote is upheld in a fair and transparent manner.

11.4 DIGITAL WORLD AND CHALLENGES TO ELECTORAL INTEGRITY IN INDIA

The Model Code of Conduct (MCC), guided by Article 324 of the Indian Constitution, plays a crucial role in ensuring fair and impartial elections (Model Code of Conduct, 2024). This article empowers the Election Commission of India (ECI) to regulate the conduct of elections and enforce adherence to the MCC. While traditionally focused on physical campaign activities, the MCC has been extended to encompass the digital realm, reflecting the evolving nature of electoral campaigns in the digital age (Singh, 2021).

Digital violations of the MCC have become a pressing concern, particularly with the proliferation of fake news, misinformation, and online abuse (Tapsell, 2020). Instances of fake news, such as false claims about candidates or manipulated information regarding electoral procedures, undermine the democratic process by misleading voters and eroding trust in the electoral system (Lee, 2019). Misinformation campaigns, often orchestrated through social media, can create confusion and influence voter perceptions, distorting the electoral discourse.

Online abuse, including targeted harassment and defamation of political opponents, also violates the MCC. Such digital misconduct not only contravenes the principles of fair campaigning but also contributes to a toxic electoral environment. The challenge for the ECI is to adapt traditional regulatory measures to effectively address these digital violations, ensuring that the MCC remains relevant in the context of modern electoral campaigns.

11.4.1 Role of Digital Platforms

Digital platforms have become integral to political campaigns, offering unprecedented reach and engagement opportunities. However, their use also raises ethical and regulatory challenges, particularly with the integration of AI technologies. The use of AI-generated content, deepfakes, and targeted ads can significantly affect voter perception and behaviour (How could deepfakes impact the 2020 U.S. elections?, 2019). Deepfakes, which involve the creation of hyper-realistic fake videos, can be used to spread disinformation or discredit political opponents (Diakopoulos & Johnson, 2020). Political parties increasingly rely on digital platforms for campaign strategies, leveraging social media, websites, and mobile apps to connect with voters. These platforms enable parties to disseminate their messages quickly and broadly, engaging with constituents through targeted advertisements and personalised content. However, this digital engagement often blurs ethical lines, as parties exploit user data and algorithmic biases to influence voter behaviour.

For example, during the 2024 elections in Odisha and West Bengal, political campaigns extensively utilised social media for targeted messaging. Campaigns tailored their content to specific voter segments, using data analytics to refine their strategies. While this approach enhances campaign effectiveness, it raises concerns about the ethical implications of data usage and the potential for manipulation.

11.4.2 Legislative Framework

The legal framework governing elections in India, including digital campaigning, is primarily outlined in the Representation of the People Act, 1951 (McMillan, 2012). Section 126 of this act is particularly relevant in the context of digital elections. Section 126 of the Representation of the People Act, 1951, governs election campaigning, including regulations on digital campaigning. This section prohibits electioneering through public meetings, processions, or any other form of public display 48 hours before the conclusion of polling. Recent case law (*Monu Upadhay v. State of Madhya Pradesh 2023*) case have highlighted the challenges of ensuring fair elections in the digital age. This case underscored the need for stringent regulations and vigilant monitoring of digital platforms to prevent the misuse of technology in influencing voter behaviour.

11.4.3 Emerging Issues

The digital transformation of electoral processes has introduced emerging issues that challenge traditional notions of electoral integrity and fairness (Neudert, 2020). The issue of deepfakes and AI-generated content has emerged as a major worry in the realm of digital elections. Instances related to AI-generated videos depicting well-known political figures from history, like Muthuvel Karunanidhi in India, underscore how technology can be exploited for disseminating false information and influencing voter opinions (Bali, 2024). These artificially created videos closely resemble authentic footage, enabling the fabrication of misleading stories and undermining confidence in political discussions.

Automated phone calls, also known as robo calls, have become a controversial topic, especially before elections. During the silent period preceding elections in Odisha and West Bengal in 2024, the use of robo calls violated electoral conduct regulations by trying to sway voters at a crucial juncture. These automated communications frequently spread political propaganda or false information, disturbing the quiet time designed to enable voters to make independent choices without outside influence.

11.5 EMPIRICAL VIEW AND REPORT

The survey conducted to understand perceptions regarding the use of artificial intelligence (AI) in India's electoral processes, focusing on the states of Odisha and West Bengal. The questionnaire assessed public awareness, beliefs, and concerns about AI's role in enhancing or compromising electoral integrity, particularly during the silent period before voting. Responses were collected using a snowball sampling method, offering insights into the awareness and opinions on AI's impact on fairness, privacy, engagement, and accountability in elections.

11.5.1 Overview of Respondent Demographics

The survey involved 100 respondents, with a regional distribution of 55% from Odisha and 45% from West Bengal. The age breakdown included 30% of participants aged 18–25 years, 40% aged 26–40 years, 20% aged 41–60 years, and 10% above 60 years. The gender composition was 60% male and 40% female. Regarding education, 35% had undergraduate degrees, 45% were graduates, 15% postgraduates, and 5% had other educational backgrounds.

11.5.2 Awareness and Understanding of AI in Elections

The survey revealed that 78% of respondents were aware of the use of AI in elections, while 22% were unaware. Of those aware, 65% had a basic understanding of AI applications, 15% had an advanced understanding, and 20% had no understanding. Social media was the primary source of information for 45% of respondents, followed by news outlets (30%), educational institutions (15%), and other sources (10%).

11.5.3 Perceptions on AI's Impact on Electoral Fairness

Regarding AI's impact on electoral fairness, 52% of respondents believed AI could enhance fairness, 28% disagreed, and 20% were neutral. However, 60% expressed concerns that AI might compromise electoral fairness, with 25% not concerned and 15% undecided. Common concerns included targeted advertising (70%), manipulation of voter preferences (55%), and the spread of misinformation (50%).

11.5.4 Privacy Concerns Related to AI in Elections

Data privacy emerged as a significant concern, with 55% of respondents very concerned, 30% somewhat concerned, and 15% not concerned. Only 35% believed that current data protection measures were adequate, while 50% disagreed and 15% were unsure. The types of data feared to be compromised included personal data (65%), voting preferences (55%), and demographic information (50%).

11.5.5 Influence of AI on Voter Engagement

The belief that AI could increase voter engagement was held by 48% of respondents, while 32% disagreed and 20% were neutral. Conversely, 45% believed that AI could reduce voter agency, with 35% disagreeing and 20% neutral. Perceived tactics of influence included algorithmic content delivery (60%), AI-generated messaging (50%), and interactive campaign tools (40%).

11.5.6 Accountability and Transparency Concerns

A significant majority (62%) felt that AI systems used in elections lacked transparency, 25% disagreed, and 13% were neutral. Regarding accountability, 50% believed AI systems were not accountable, 35% thought they were, and 15% were unsure. There was a strong demand for regulatory measures, with 70% strongly agreeing, 20% agreeing, and 10% disagreeing.

11.5.7 Specific Observations from Odisha and West Bengal

In Odisha, 80% of respondents were aware of AI in elections, 55% perceived a positive impact, 65% had concerns about fairness, 60% were worried about privacy, and 50% acknowledged AI's influence on voter engagement. In West Bengal, 75% were aware, 50% perceived a positive impact, 60% had fairness concerns, 55% were worried about privacy, and 45% noted AI's influence on engagement.

The findings indicate a mixed perception of AI's role in India's electoral processes. While there is a general awareness and recognition of AI's potential to enhance fairness, engagement, and accountability, significant concerns remain regarding privacy, transparency, and the potential for misuse. The majority of respondents advocate for stricter regulatory measures to ensure the responsible use of AI in elections. The regional differences in perceptions also suggest that localised approaches may be necessary to address specific concerns and enhance public trust in AI-driven electoral processes.

11.6 CHALLENGES TO DEMOCRATIC PROCESS AND POLICY RECOMMENDATIONS

The findings of this survey highlight the complex challenges posed by the use of AI in electoral processes. The integration of AI into electoral processes has revolutionised how elections are conducted, particularly in the context of digital democracy. However, this technological transformation brings forth a set of significant challenges that threaten the core principles of democratic governance. These challenges, which include privacy concerns, algorithmic bias, and transparency issues, necessitate comprehensive policy interventions to safeguard the integrity of elections in India.

Privacy Concerns: One of the primary challenges is the inadequate protection of voter data, underscored by public concerns about privacy breaches. AI systems in electoral contexts often rely on extensive data collection to enhance campaign strategies and voter targeting. This includes the aggregation of personal information, voting patterns, and demographic data, which, without robust data protection frameworks, can be susceptible to misuse (Rubinstein, 2014).

The survey highlights that a significant portion of respondents are apprehensive about how their personal data is handled. The current regulatory environment lacks stringent measures to safeguard against unauthorised access and exploitation of voter information. As a result, there is a heightened risk of data being used to manipulate voter preferences or for other malicious activities, undermining the integrity of the electoral process.

Algorithmic Bias: AI algorithms, central to modern electioneering, are not free from biases, which can skew electoral fairness. These biases often stem from the data on which the algorithms are trained or the inherent design of the algorithms. For instance, if the training data reflects historical biases or is not representative of the entire electorate, the AI system might perpetuate these biases, leading to unfair advantages for certain political entities (Pessach & Shmueli, 2020).

Respondents from the survey expressed concerns about the potential for AI to introduce or reinforce biases in voter engagement and campaign strategies. This could result in disproportionate attention to certain voter demographics while neglecting others, thereby impacting the fairness of the election. In states like Odisha and West Bengal, where socio-economic and cultural diversity is significant, the risk of algorithmic bias affecting electoral outcomes is particularly pronounced.

Transparency Issues: A significant challenge in the use of AI in elections is the lack of transparency. The operational mechanisms of AI systems used in campaigns, including how they process data and make decisions, are often opaque. This lack of clarity undermines public trust and makes it difficult for voters and regulators to understand or challenge the influence of AI on electoral processes (Juneja, 2024).

Survey results indicate a substantial demand for transparency in how AI is deployed in elections. Voters are concerned about the unseen mechanisms that drive AI-driven campaign tactics and the lack of accountability from those who implement these technologies. Without transparent practices, the potential for AI to be used in manipulative ways remains unchecked, raising questions about the legitimacy of the electoral process.

11.6.1 Policy Recommendations

Addressing these obstacles and strengthening the democratic process against the threats presented by AI and digital technologies requires a comprehensive policy approach (Protecting Democratic Elections through Safeguarding Information Integrity, 2024). The recommendations below delineate crucial areas for action to improve regulatory structures, guarantee transparency, and raise public consciousness.

Regulatory Frameworks: To address the challenges posed by AI in elections, it is essential to establish robust regulatory frameworks that safeguard against AI manipulation. These regulations should include stringent data protection laws to prevent the misuse of personal information and ensure the security of voter data (Deepak et al., 2023). Additionally, there should be clear guidelines on the ethical use of AI in electoral processes, including the development and deployment of unbiased algorithms.

Transparency and Accountability: Ensuring transparency and accountability in the use of AI in political campaigns is crucial for maintaining public trust. Clear guidelines should be established for the disclosure of AI usage in electoral processes, including the sources of data and the decision-making criteria of AI algorithms (Sanderson et al., 2022). Independent monitoring bodies should be empowered to oversee the implementation of these guidelines and conduct regular audits to ensure compliance.

Public Awareness: Increasing voter awareness about the digital influences and data privacy issues associated with AI in elections is vital. Public education campaigns should be launched to inform voters about how their data is used and the potential impacts of AI on electoral fairness. These campaigns should also emphasise the importance of data privacy and provide practical tips for protecting personal information. Engaging civil society organisations and leveraging media platforms can help amplify these messages and reach a broader audience.

By addressing these difficulties and putting into practice the suggested strategies, it is feasible to utilise the advantages of AI in electoral processes while ensuring the honesty and impartiality of democratic procedures.

11.7 CONCLUSION

The examination of the effects of AI on elections in Odisha and West Bengal indicates a strong impact on electoral procedures, encompassing both positive and negative elements. AI is acknowledged for its potential to improve electoral fairness, efficiency, and voter involvement; however, concerns about privacy, transparency, and accountability remain prevalent. The research reflects a high level of respondent awareness regarding AI's role in elections with varying levels of comprehension. While many believe that AI can enhance electoral fairness, a significant portion express worries about potential biases and manipulation of voter preferences. Privacy issues emerge as particularly prominent, with most respondents expressing concern about the adequacy of existing data protection measures. The influence of AI on voter engagement is viewed as two-sided—some see it as a tool for increased participation while others fear it may diminish voter agency. Transparency and accountability in AI systems during elections are major points of concern which has led to demands for regulatory measures to ensure ethical use by stakeholders. This study underscores the necessity for balanced integration of AI into electoral processes to safeguard democratic integrity.

Balancing the integration of technology with the preservation of democratic principles is crucial in the context of AI's growing role in elections. The study highlights the importance of safeguarding democratic values while embracing technological advancements. Ensuring transparency in AI algorithms used in electoral processes is essential to build public trust and maintain the integrity of elections. This involves clearly defining the use of AI at various stages, such as voter registration, candidate selection, and result tallying, and making the decision-making processes and data sources transparent to the public. Ethical considerations must be prioritised in the design and implementation of AI systems to prevent biases and ensure fairness. Regular audits and independent reviews can help identify and rectify any flaws in AI systems, further enhancing their credibility. Public participation and education are vital to fostering a better understanding of AI's role in elections and addressing concerns about its impact. Informing the public about the benefits, risks, and safety measures associated with AI technology through public information efforts, meetings, and training programs can build trust and encourage informed engagement.

Ensuring the security and privacy of data is crucial in the era of AI, requiring strong measures to safeguard voting information from unauthorized access or alteration. By implementing robust data privacy regulations, encryption, secure data storage, and regular vulnerability assessments, the reliability of voting data can be maintained. It is also important to promote inclusivity and accessibility in AI-powered election systems to avoid marginalization and enable all groups to participate in the electoral process. This includes offering support for multiple languages, assistance for individuals with disabilities, and alternative voting methods for those who are unable or unwilling to utilize AI systems. Establishing independent monitoring and governance mechanisms to supervise the use of AI in elections can ensure compliance with ethical standards and legal obligations. Collaboration with experts, civil society organizations, and scholars can aid in developing comprehensive review systems that are effective.

In summary, the ethical and accountable application of AI in elections, along with openness, involvement from the public, safeguarding data, inclusiveness, and impartial oversight can support democratic principles and cultivate trust in the voting process. Embracing new technologies while confronting related difficulties is crucial to guarantee that AI advances the honesty and credibility of elections. Through these measures, stakeholders can collaborate to preserve the integrity of polls and uphold equitable and open elections in an age defined by AI.

REFERENCES

Agarwal, S., Haider, A., Jamwal, A., Dev, P., & Chandel, R. (2020, July 1). Biometric based secured remote electronic voting system. https://doi.org/10.1109/icsss49621.2020.9202212

Ali, M., Sapieżyński, P., Korolova, A., Mislove, A., & Rieke, A. (2019, January 1). Ad delivery algorithms: The hidden arbiters of political messaging. https://doi.org/10.48550/arxiv.1912.04255

Bali, M. (2024, May 29). Deepfakes take just minutes to make with artificial intelligence. Here's how Indian political parties use them against opponents. ABC News. www.abc.net.au/news/2024-05-30/how-ai-is-disrupting-india-election-campaign/103899138

BBC. India elections 2024: When were they, who could vote and why do they matter? (2024, June 4). www.bbc.com/news/world-asia-india-68678594

Bhandari, V., & Sane, R. (November 2016). Towards a privacy framework for India in the age of the internet. Working Paper No. 179, NIPFP Working Paper Series, Available at SSRN: https://ssrn.com/abstract=2892368 or http://dx.doi.org/10.2139/ssrn.2892368

Binns, R. (2022, January 1). Tracking on the web, mobile and the internet-of-things. arXiv:2201.10831. Accessible at: https://doi.org/10.48550/arXiv.2201.1083

Burkell, J., & Regan, P. M. (2019, December 31). Voter preferences, voter manipulation, voter analytics: Policy options for less surveillance and more autonomy. *Internet Policy Review*, 8(4). https://doi.org/10.14763/2019.4.1438

Cheeseman, N., Lynch, G., & Willis, J. (2018, June 8). Digital dilemmas: The unintended consequences of election technology. *Democratization*. doi:10.1080/13510347.2018.1470165

Chester, J., & Montgomery, K. (2017). The role of digital marketing in political campaigns. *Internet Policy Review*, 6(4). https://doi.org/10.14763/2017.4.773

Deepak, P., Simoes, S., & MacCárthaigh, M. (2023, August 1). AI and core electoral processes: Mapping the horizons. https://doi.org/10.1002/aaai.12105. Available at https://onlinelibrary.wiley.com/doi/full/10.1002/aaai.12105

Dhelim, S., Aung, N., & Ning, H. (2020Mining user interest based on personality-aware hybrid filtering in social networks. Knowledge-based systems, 206, 106227, Article 106227, Accessible at: https://doi.org/10.1016/j.knosys.2020.106227

Diakopoulos, N., & Johnson, D. (2020). Anticipating and addressing the ethical implications of deepfakes in the context of elections. *New Media & Society*, *23*(7), 2072-2098. https://doi.org/10.1177/1461444820925811 (Original work published 2021)

Dobber, T., Metoui, N., Trilling, D., Helberger, N., & Vreese, C. D. (2020, July 25). Do (microtargeted) deepfakes have real effects on political attitudes? *The International Journal of Press/Politics*, *26*(1), 69–91. https://doi.org/10.1177/1940161220944364

Givi, G. M., Delabays, R., Jacquemet, M., & Jacquod, P. (2023, January 1). On the robustness of democratic electoral processes to computational propaganda. *Scientific Reports, 14*, 193. Accessible at: https://doi.org/10.48550/arXiv.2308.11569

Gürsoy, F., & Kakadiaris, I. A. (2022, January 1). System cards for AI-based decision-making for public policy. Available at https://arxiv.org/abs/2203.04754

Huszár, F., Ktena, S. I., O'Brien, C. C., Belli, L., Schlaikjer, A., & Hardt, M. (2021, December 21). Algorithmic amplification of politics on Twitter. https://doi.org/10.1073/pnas.2025334119

Ismail, M. I. B., Rahman, M. A., & Azad, S. (2016, July 1). Exploiting privacy-policy and -management features on social networks: A user's perspective. *International Conference on Computer and Communication Engineering (ICCCE)*, 66–71, doi: 10.1109/ICCCE.2016.27. Available at https://ieeexplore.ieee.org/document/7808285

Juneja, P. (2024, April 29). Artificial intelligence for electoral management. 978-91-7671-764-6 (PDF). https://doi.org/10.31752/idea.2024.31

Keller, C. I. (2021). Don't shoot the message: Regulating disinformation beyond content. Direito Público, ISSN 2236-1766, Instituto Brasiliense de Direito Público – IDP, Brasília DF, *18*(99), 486–515. www.portaldeperiodicos.idp.edu.br/direitopublico/article/view/6057

Lee, T. (2019, July 1). The global rise of "fake news" and the threat to democratic elections in the USA. . *Public Administration and Policy, 22*(1), 15–24. https://doi.org/10.1108/PAP-04-2019-0008

Marchetti, G. (2020, July). The role of algorithms in the crisis of democracy. *Athens Journal of Mediterranean Studies*, *6*(3), 179–214. Accessible at: www.athensjournals.gr/mediterranean/2020-6-3-2-Marchetti.pdf

McMillan, A. (2012, June 1). The Election Commission of India and the Regulation and Administration of Electoral Politics. https://doi.org/10.1089/elj.2011.0134

Meti, V., Khandoba, P. K., & Guru, M. C. (2015, January 1). Social media for political mobilization in India: A study. *Journal of Mass Communication and Journalism*, *5*(9). DOI: 10.4172/2165-7912.1000275. Accessible at: www.hilarispublisher.com/open-access/social-media-for-political-mobilization-in-india-a-study-2165-7912-1000275.pdf

Mishra, K. D. (2017, April 19). Social media revolution – The new digital frontiers of journalism. *5*(1), 610–620. 10.24297/jah.v5i1.6068. Available at : https://journals.indexcopernicus.com/search/article?articleId=2244706

Model Code of Conduct. (2024, January 1). www.eci.gov.in/mcc

Nadai, M. D., Lepri, B., & Oliver, N. (2020, January 1). Understanding individual behaviour: From virtual to physical patterns. 24th European Conference on Artificial Intelligence - ECAI 2020 Santiago de Compostela, Spain. Accessible at: https://doi.org/10.3233/faia200455

Neudert, L. (2020, September 10). Hurdles and pathways to regulatory innovation in digital political campaigning. https://doi.org/10.1111/1467-923x.12915

Nickerson, D. W., & Rogers, T. (2014, May 1). Political Campaigns and Big Data. *Journal of Economic Perspectives, 28*(2), 51–74. Available at: www.aeaweb.org/articles?id=10.1257/jep.28.2.51

Pessach, D., & Shmueli, E. (2020, January 1). Algorithmic fairness. https://arxiv.org/abs/2001.09784

Protecting Democratic Elections through Safeguarding Information Integrity. (2024, January 30). https://doi.org/10.31752/idea.2024.1

Raisinghani, M. S., & Weiss, R. (2010, January 1). The impact of the internet on politics: The "Net Effect" on political campaigns and elections. *Journal of Global Information Technology Management*, *13*(1), 1–4. https://doi.org/10.1080/1097198X.2010.10856506

Roopak, T., & Sumathi, R. (2020, March 1). Electronic voting based on virtual ID of aadhar using blockchain technology. *2nd International Conference on Innovative Mechanisms for Industry Applications (ICIMIA)*, Bangalore, India. 71–75. Doi: 10.1109/ICIMIA48430.2020.9074942

Roy, A. (2024, March 10). How India is using the Internet. *The Economic Times*. https://economictimes.indiatimes.com/tech/technology/how-india-is-using-theinternet/articleshow/108354854.cms?from=mdr

Rubinstein, I. (2014, January 1). Voter privacy in the age of big data. *Wisconsin Law Review*, 861. Available at SSRN: https://ssrn.com/abstract=2447956 or http://dx.doi.org/10.2139/ssrn.2447956

Sanderson, C., Lu, Q., Douglas, D., Xu, X., Zhu, L., & Whittle, J. (2022, December 17). Towards implementing responsible AI, Cornad Sanderson, Qinghua Lu, David Douglas, Xiwei Xu, Liming Zhu, Jon Whittle, IEEE International Conference on Big Data, 2022, https://doi.org/10.1109/BigData55660.2022.10021121. Available at https://arxiv.org/abs/2205.04358

Simchon, A., Edwards, M., & Lewandowsky, S. (2024, February). The persuasive effects of political microtargeting in the age of generative AI. , *PNAS Nexus*, *3*(2). pgae035, https://doi.org/10.1093/pnasnexus/pgae035

Singh, M. N. (2021, June 1). Election commission, electoral democracy and constitutionalization of elections in India. *67*(2). https://doi.org/10.1177/00195561211022579

Stedmon, N. (2020, January 1). The impact of cyber security threats on the 2020 US elections, Nicholas Stedmon, https://doi.org/10.48550/arXiv.2012.08968. Available at https://arxiv.org/abs/2012.08968

Tapsell, R. (2020, November 9). Social media and elections in Southeast Asia: The emergence of subversive, underground campaigning. *Asian Studies Review*, *45*(1), 117–134. https://doi.org/10.1080/10357823.2020.1841093

Tenove, C., Buffie, J., McKay, S., & Moscrop, D. (2018, January 1). Digital threats to democratic elections: How foreign actors use digital techniques to undermine democracy. *Research Report*. Centre for the Study of Democratic Institutions, University of British Columbia. Available at SSRN: https://ssrn.com/abstract=3235819

The Great Online Convergence: Digital Authoritarianism Comes to Democracies. Seva Gunitsky. (2020, February 19). https://warontherocks.com/2020/02/the-great-online-convergence-digital-authoritarianism-comes-to-democracies/

Ullah, I., Boreli, R., & Kanhere, S. S. (2020, September 16). Privacy in targeted advertising: A survey. *TechRxiv* . DOI: 10.36227/techrxiv.12952073.v1

Witzleb, N., & Paterson, M. (2021). Micro-targeting in political campaigns: Political promise and democratic risk. . In: Kohl U, Eisler J, eds. *Data-Driven Personalisation in Markets, Politics and Law,* 223–240. Cambridge University Press..

KEY TERMS AND DEFINITIONS

1 **Digital Democracy:** Refers to the use of digital technologies and the internet to enhance citizen participation and engagement in democratic processes, including online voting, e-petitions, and digital platforms for political discourse.

2 **Electoral Automation:** Encompasses the use of technology to automate various aspects of the electoral process, such as electronic voter registration, electronic voting machines, and automated vote counting, aiming to improve efficiency, accuracy, and transparency.

3 **Democratic Governance:** A system of governance characterized by citizen participation, accountability, transparency, and the rule of law, where citizens have the right to participate in decision-making processes that affect their lives.

4 **AI-driven Elections:** Refers to the increasing integration of artificial intelligence in various stages of the electoral process, including voter profiling, targeted campaigning, misinformation detection, and potentially even aspects of decision-making, raising concerns about fairness, transparency, and democratic values.

12 Justice in the Digital Age
Popular Culture and the Rise of AI-Powered Legal Decision-Making

Gagandeep Kaur

12.1 INTRODUCTION

AI and automation have led to the advent of automated legal systems that aid or substitutes for human decision-making in the courts and the legal system. This covers quite a few different systems, from AI-enabled legal research tools and predictive analytics of case law to AI-based contract drafting and even AI-based dispute resolution systems (Surden, 2019). Even though the development of these kinds of technology has been largely motivated by efficiency, accuracy, and accessibility, the acceptability of these technologies is more crucial. Popular culture is one of the biggest influences on public perception and acceptance of automated legal systems. Movies, television shows, books, and online content have for some time now delved into what the implications of AI are within the legal field and justice systems, typically depicting them as either ultimate problem solvers or dystopian vehicles that suppress human autonomy. Whether imagined in Philip K. Dick's Minority Report or contemporary British TV series such as Black Mirror, the portrayal of automated justice in science fiction has shaped people's perceptions of the AI's role within the law. Legal processes that are automated of these types are no better (or worse) than their human counterparts; these portrayals can only serve to bolster scepticism or introduce unjustified optimism concerning the reliability and ethics of these processes. This research paper analyses the acceptability of automated legal advice systems from a popular culture perspective and studied the relationship between fictional and real-world media representations and public perceptions.

This chapter has also explored the concepts like "How does popular culture inform public views of AI-driven legal systems?" and "What moral, legal, and societal challenges does automate legal decision-making raise?" and "How do real-world AI applications in law measure up to their fictional counterparts?" In addressing these questions, this study seeks to reconcile the disconnect between what the public perceives regarding these systems and the reality of their technological underpinnings, as well as identify the potential opportunities that can be exploited through advances in legal automation along with the dangers associated with this shift. This manuscript has analysed if cultural narratives serve as an impediment to or as an impetus for the broader uptake of AI in law. This means that policymakers, legal practitioners, and technologists need to understand better the reasons behind popular

 DOI: 10.1201/9781003491903-12

attitudes towards AI in law. Public pushback against AI in legal delivery often stems from misconceptions circulated through the media, despite systems offering obvious benefits on cost, speed, and access grounds (Calo, 2019). On the other hand, a utopian blind faith in AI could result in ethical malaise and systemic biases in legal automated decision-making (Mittelstadt et al., n.d.).

12.2 TRACING THE FOOTPRINTS: GLIMPSE OF CHRONOLOGICAL EVOLUTION OF LEGAL AUTOMATION

Since then, legalised automated mechanisms have grown explosively along different avenues and achieved exponential success along the processes, which caused the complexity of legal frames to grow tremendously over the processes over the years. The mechanisation of legal processes has been the subject of heated debate for centuries. However, the notion of automating legal decision-making emerged in the legal realm in the second half of the 20th century. Early developments, such as the creation of legal databases and computer-assisted legal research, were useful but didn't change the game; however, in the past year or so, the evolution of artificial intelligence (AI) and machine learning has enabled more sophisticated applications (e.g., contract automation, predictive legal analytics, and AI-assisted judicial decision-making) (Ashley, 2017).

The move to electronic databases, rather than paper copies of relevant case law and statutes, massively changed the landscape of legal research and eventually made finding applicable case law easy and advocates and lawyers accessible to all. Expert systems strongly propelled the transition of the legal process by mimicking human reasoning and applying legal norms to specific cases. By the dawn of the 21st century, these AI-based tools would become integral to the practice of law, used for everything from reviewing documents to assessing risk. More recently, with courts and legal institutions adopting AI more widely, discussions around the acceptability, fairness, and accountability of automated legal systems have also increased (Susskind, 2019).

From early 1980 to now, the forward step for each technological evolution was the legal automation. These represent milestones along the way from basic computer-assisted legal research toward sophisticated AI-based decision support systems.

1. Pre-Digital Era: Roots of Legal Standardisation (Before the 1970s)
   The pre-digitised world of legal automation concerned standardising legal texts and codifying rules. The rise of codified legislation in the 19th century, such as the Napoleonic Code, laid the groundwork for more organised approaches to legal interpretation. Back then, lawyers did manual legal research by using physical case law reporters, compilations of statutes, and legal encyclopaedias. There were no computational tools, and therefore, legal decision-making was entirely human-centred: courts and law firms invested a lot of time and resources in case research and precedent analysis (Leith, 2010).

2 The Development of Computer-Assisted Research: Special Relevance to the Legal World (1970s–1980s)
The rise of digital legal databases in the 1970s revolutionized legal research. Breakthrough tools like LexisNexis and Westlaw brought instant access to enormous volumes of legal data, revolutionizing outdated manual research methods. Litigators used databases with keyword-based search features that provided quicker access to statutes, case law and secondary sources. While not yet powered by AI, these systems greatly cut down the time and effort needed to do legal research (Hutchinson, 2002).
Simultaneously, the first legal expert systems were being developed. Inspired by advances in AI, these systems attempted to emulate human reasoning by applying legal rules to particular facts. The early rule-based expert systems, for example, the British Nationality Act system, showed that automated legal reasoning could be achieved; however, it was always constrained by a definitional and inflexible rule base (Bench-Capon, 1991).

3 The Development of Expert Systems and AI with Special Relevance to Legal Analysis (1990s–2010s)
The generations of expert systems have matured since the 1990s by adding AI capabilities to allow for improved legal reasoning. Most systems built for purposes such as tax law, contract analysis, and compliance rely on decision trees and logic-based reasoning to assess legal scenarios (Rissland et al., n.d.). One notable early use case comes from the Internal Revenue Service (USA), which is using AI to assist with tax audits and compliance assessments (Tax Policy Center Organisation, n.d.).
At the same time, progress in natural language processing (NLP) technology has enabled a better reading of legal texts. Applications driven by AI, like IBM Watson and the first generation of ML algorithms, have demonstrated the ability of AI to process, comprehend, and translate complex legal language. This would pave the way for future advancements in predictive legal analysis and automated legal document creation (Surden, 2019).

4 AI-Powered Legal Research and Predictive Analytics (2010s–Present)
By the 2010s, AI had been widely integrated into legal practice, most visibly in the review of key documents and with data analysis. Using AI, ROSS Intelligence (and similar tools powered by IBM Watson) allowed lawyers to submit legal questions in conversational language and receive AI-generated answers, accompanied by relevant existing case law. Machine learning algorithms have also become more adept at predicting case outcomes, analysing past court decisions, and helping lawyers assess the likelihood of winning a case (Katz, 2013).
In this era, AI was also used extensively in predictive policing and the criminal justice system. Predictive tools such as COMPAS (Correctional Offender Management Profiling for Alternative Sanctions) have been used to assess the risk of recidivism in criminal defendants. However, such systems have not gone without controversy as questions regarding algorithmic bias and opacity in AI-assisted legal rulings loom over these movements (Angwin et al., 2016).

5 Automation of Contract Drafting and AI in Judicial Processes (2020s–Present) Over the last few years, AI's role in legal automation, namely in contract drafting and dispute resolution, has been growing. Tools such as Kira Systems (a Canadian company) and LawGeex (Israel) will automatically review contracts using machine learning to highlight compliance or risk, cutting down the time taken to negotiate contracts by a huge percentage (Apple Tech., 2023). Automated legal assistants, like DoNotPay (An American Company), which has been called the world's first robot lawyer, are AI-powered chatbots that help users navigate legal issues from small claims to traffic violations to consumer rights (Barton, 2023).

The integration of AI identifiers into judicial processes has gained momentum as well. Some courts tried to use AI-friendly sentencing suggestions, and other courts paid attention to the role of virtual courts that run automated legal reasoning systems. Yet while such advances offer the promise of new efficiency and access to justice, they raise serious ethical and legal challenges related to due process, responsibility, and human oversight (Sreelatha & Choudhary, 2023).

12.3 CHALLENGES IN LEGAL AUTOMATION: AN ANALYSIS

The incorporation of legal automation into judicial and legal systems poses numerous issues that require meticulous attention. A major concern is the absence of transparency and accountability in AI-driven legal decision-making, as intricate algorithms frequently operate as "black boxes" with minimal elucidation. Moreover, bias in automated systems is a significant issue, since AI models trained on previous legal data may reinforce systematic inequality. Data privacy and security problems emerge due to the sensitive nature of legal information handled by these technologies. The lack of standardised regulations for legal automation generates confusion about its ethical and legal ramifications. Opposition from legal practitioners, stemming from apprehensions regarding job displacement and the dependability of AI in complex legal analyses, further hinders acceptance. Confronting these difficulties necessitates strong legislative frameworks, ethical AI research, and a balanced strategy that incorporates automation while preserving human oversight to guarantee justice, accuracy, and accountability within the legal system (Contissa et al., 2024).

Below is a chart describing several typical difficulties encountered by legal automation systems. The table includes the name of the problem, a brief description of it, and possible examples of its occurrence (Table 12.1).

In addition to the above challenges mentioned in the above table, much of the rollout of legal automation has struggled to overcome issues of ethics, legitimacy, or basic trust. The practical dilemmas surrounding the use of generative AI to address ethical, legal, and social implications are multiple, one of the most pressing being the issue of algorithmic bias, in which AI models trained on historical legal data may reproduce systemic injustices. Transparency and accountability issues, too: Too many AI-driven decisions that have gone through the automation sausage machine allow little or no room for explanation or justification. So it is understandable that the convulsive keeping operation of rule-of-law-based regulatory frameworks has

TABLE 12.1
Challenges in legal automation

Legal challenge with legal automation	Nature of the challenge	Need for policy and compliance
Data Privacy and Security	Legal automation systems must manage highly sensitive information. Breaches or mishandling of data can result in severe privacy violations and legal penalties.	Compliance with GDPR and HIPAA requirements - Secure handling of client data in automated contract reviews
Complexity of Legal Language	Legal texts are often ambiguous, nuanced, and context dependent. Automation systems may struggle to interpret complex language accurately	- Ambiguity in contractual clauses - Nuances in case law interpretations
Ethical Considerations	Automated legal systems risk embedding or amplifying biases present in training data, potentially leading to unfair outcomes or discriminatory practices.	- AI-based sentencing recommendations with inherent biases - Automated legal advice that does not consider ethical implications
Intellectual Property Rights	The use of copyrighted legal texts and proprietary databases to train automation tools may infringe on intellectual property rights.	- Use of case law databases without proper licensing - Training AI models on proprietary legal documents without consent
Regulatory compliance	Legal automation tools must comply with existing laws and adapt to new regulations, which can vary significantly by jurisdiction	- Automated legal advice platforms facing scrutiny over the unauthorized practice of law - Systems that need to adapt to changes in regulatory standards
Accountability and liability	Errors or misinterpretations made by automated systems can have significant legal and financial repercussions, raising questions about responsibility	- Faulty legal document analysis leading to contractual disputes - Incorrect legal advice causing client losses or litigation
Integration with human judgment	Balancing the efficiency of automation with the need for human expertise is challenging, especially when decisions have significant legal ramifications	- Hybrid systems where AI conducts preliminary analysis but a human lawyer finalizes decisions - Automated contract analysis needing expert review

been challenged to keep things on the level with convulsive technological advances, resulting in heavy grey areas in legal and ethical terms in the regulated domains of business today (Binns, 2018a). As AI continues to transform the legal field, its future will ultimately be determined by how well it balances efficiency with equity. Legal automation perceived credibility human collaboration: It can help legal automation gain significant acceptance and make people credible by solving issues such as transparency of AI and regulatory safeguards (Brynjolfsson & McAfee, 2017).

12.3 GLIMPSE OF POPULAR CULTURAL TREND TOWARDS LEGAL AUTOMATION

Popular culture has long served as a mirror, reflecting technology's changing place in society. Automation and its effect on law and the courts also appear in literature, film, television, and digital media, and these together reflect and shape public understandings of justice and fairness as well as the role of technology in making decisions about the law. Over the years, they have transitioned from speculative fiction to more sophisticated analyses of the role of AI and automation in the practice of law.

Fictional representations of automated legal systems tend to oscillate between utopian and dystopic extremes. Popular conception, however, envisions AI as a tool to achieve efficiency, reduce corruption, and increase access to justice. On the other hand, it raises issues of bias, accountability, and the risk of rendering human judgement obsolete in legal enforcement (Calo, 2015). They are emerging in the context of deeper social anxiety about whether technology will undermine these—and other—foundational human rights and moral precepts (Balkin, 2009).

12.3.1 Legal AI in Literature: Historical Speculative Fiction and Modern Representations

The idea of machines replacing human judgement in courtrooms is one of those through lines in literature that run for decades. The speculative-fiction frame of the early days tends to "speculate" that legal automation is still some way out; it's in the world of the future.

1. Early Speculative Fiction (1900s–1950s)

   One of the early literary treatments of legal automation can be seen in E.M. Forster's The Machine Stops (1909). Although not about legal AI, it imagined a world in which every human action was directed by a self-sufficient system that regulated human interaction. Particular concerns are technological determinism and the dangers of over-reliance on technology (Forster, 1909).

   In I, Robot (1950), Isaac Asimov introduced the "Three Laws of Robotics," which also involved law, as robots could obey humans' activities' commands but could discard the orders if they might cause harm (Asimov, 1950). Asimov's stories probed how such automated reasoning could not only serve but also subvert justice and how the fault lines of legal culpability might thread into the limitations of AI-driven decisions.

2 Modern Literature and Legal AI (1980s–Present)
In some instances, newer literature foregrounded contingencies with AI and the law. The corporations in William Gibson's Neuromancer (1984) were powered by AI long before they were powered by algorithms (the novel anticipated a world where algorithmic entities could shape laws and corporate governance, for example) (Gibson, 1984). Neal Stephenson's Snow Crash (1992) envisioned a future of AIs running a private legal system and invited implicit questions of privatisation of justice as well as computational legal enforcement (Stephenson, 1992).

Legal automation makes increasingly realistic appearances in speculative fiction today. Novels like Malka Older's Infomocracy (2016) imagine governance structures manned by algorithms, suggesting the possible efficiency of an automated legal system but also calling out the tendential manipulability of such systems (Older, 2016). As AI technologies become more embedded within our legal institutions, issues of fairness, transparency, and accountability become more critical.

12.3.2 Film and Television: The Legal "Robot" as Judge, Jury, and Enforcer

Film and TV have been key in shaping public opinion of automated legal systems. Often, these imagined scenarios are more dramatized to highlight the ethical and moral dilemmas the replacement of human judges, lawyers, and law enforcement with AI would raise.

1 Early Cinematic Representations (1950s–1980s)
Automated justice is a cinematic trope that dates back to (the world of) early science fiction films, usually with dystopian overtones. In Metropolis (1927), Fritz Lang imagined a mechanised society in which decisions were made by authoritarian figures, predicting later visions of machine-controlled legal systems (Lang, 1927).

The cyborg law enforcer of RoboCop (1987) embodied the union between technology and justice. Through the film, they critically examined an automated law enforcement technology, showcasing how interests by corporations would undermine AI law and cause biased policing (Verhoeven, 1987).

2 The Emergence of AI Judges and Legal Automation (1990s–Present)
Modern movies and TV shows show more and more AI-enabled legal systems, depicting them as efficient and dangerous. The 2002 movie Minority Report, inspired by Philip K. Dick's short story, popularised the concept of "predictive policing"—preventing crimes before they were committed using AI predictions (Spielberg, 2002). The idea (though fictional) parallels aspects of modern predictive policing programs and poses risks of due process violations and algorithmic bias.

Legal automation has also been scrutinised in television shows such as Black Mirror (2011–2019). Then there's the episode Metalhead (2017), in which self-operating robotic enforcers had replaced human law enforcement—fears of AI because AI lacks morality. Other episodes, like Nosedive (2016), hinted at how AI-society credit systems could dictate criminal penalties—a rather easy extrapolation, one which is now being tested in the real world in the form of AI-assisted judgements in criminal cases (Brooker).

12.3.3 The Influence of Popular Culture on Public Perception of Legal AI

Popular culture has a huge influence on how people view AI in the legal system and lawyers in general. Some narratives focus on efficiency and objectivity, while others warn of dangers such as bias, loss of human control, and ethical dilemmas. Such representations stoked ongoing debates on whether AI had a place in legislative processes at all, and if so, what safeguards would meet the bar (or law) of justice and transparency (Gasser, 2016).

The intersection of legal automation and popular culture is only going to become more topical as AI technology develops. Pondering how invented stories influence attitudes in the world is of use to legal scholars and people in government who want to figure out how this certain kind of technology may influence social facts as we navigate the field of AI as it floats into this specific human institution.

12.4 CASE STUDIES: SPECIAL RELEVANCE TO POPULAR CULTURE

The portrayal of automated legal systems in fiction transcends mere fantasy; it explores a complex interplay of societal aspirations, anxieties, and ethical dilemmas regarding AI and the law. Popular culture has consistently examined the ramifications of technology-infused justice systems across film, literature, television, and digital media. These depictions do not simply construct narratives but actively influence politics by shaping public perception, stimulating policy.

Our critical reading of examples from popular culture, of this genre of justice-porn, can upturn patterns, from the utopian fictions, up and down the spectrum, of frictionless, incorruptible, AI-powered justice to dystopic warnings from the academy about the dangers of mechanising justice. These kinds of cultural representations often suggest a tension between efficiency and fairness, automation and human judgement, and justice and bias. While some works offer the fantasy of an AI that can even the playing field by making the system more objective and accessible, others expose the fragility of ceding too much trust to algorithms, the danger of wrongful convictions and ethical mucking about, and the disappearance of human oversight. Unlike most cultural objects studied within legal fields, representations provide insight into the ways that they shape public understandings, shape legal conversations, and even at times redirect technological advancement towards real-life legal systems.

12.4.1 Robot (2004) and the Law of Robotics

One of the most well-known examples of legal automation in pop culture can be found in the 2004 movie I, Robot, which was inspired by one of Isaac Asimov's most celebrated works, The Three Laws of robotics. Based on the movie, the story takes place in a future world where robots are subject to a legal system that prioritises the protection of humans. For readers who haven't seen it, in that universe, robots employ three fundamental ethical laws: a robot never injures a human; must obey human orders, except where such orders would conflict with the first law; and a robot must protect its existence so long as such protection does not conflict with the first two laws (Asimov, 1950).

These are "laws" that highlight the conflict between doing something we know to be ethical versus doing something that has been automated and argue for the removal of humans as legal authorities in favour of having robots run a robot legal system. After these laws are violated, the law becomes an important tool in levelling accusations of murder against a robot, which raises the potential for machines to make decisions that we would consider legal in the future. In the 21st century, the concept of "robot justice" may be at odds with the traditional concepts of the rule of law and the traditional courts, but just how are they to adapt to rapidly changing this new technology?

12.4.2 Minority Report (2002) and Predictive Justice

Another seminal case study is the 2002 film Minority Report, produced by Steven Spielberg, warning against a futuristic criminal justice regime founded on predictive technologies. In the film, a specialised police unit called "PreCrime" arrests people for crimes they haven't yet committed—this is thanks to the visions of three "precogs" (humans with the ability to see future crimes). This model of preemptive basis, AI legal systems, operates, very literally, on the presumption of guilt before the crime is committed (Spielberg, 2002).

The film goes into the ethical consequences of this idea: Is it fair to charge an individual with a crime they haven't even committed yet? Is it fair to punish someone for a crime they haven't committed but will, according to predictive algorithms? Data-driven storylines pave the way for Bayesian law and, if we're not careful, flawed algorithmic decision-making that could make a bad neighbourhood mean a bad neighbour, dooming you to a life behind bars—indefinitely.

Predictive justice algorithms—those that predict who is likely to commit a crime—are already controversial in real life as AI creeps into more and more of the criminal justice process, including sentencing, parole, and even risk assessments.

12.4.3 RoboCop (1987) and Legal Authority of AI Enforcement

In RoboCop, the main protagonist is a police officer named Alex Murphy who was turned into a cyborg. RoboCop is built with a strict code of justice but often finds its machine-based decision-making process doing battle with moral quandaries. The underlying theme here is who has real authority in law enforcement, human users or AI systems that must comply with specific laws and procedures without empathy or discretion?

As the film notes, automation of law enforcement has led to dystopias where the element of "human" judgement disappears. RoboCop's programming clashes with human emotions, and his strict adherence to the legal code ultimately results in a loss of individual liberty. This raises serious questions about the automation of not only the legal decision-making process but also the enforcement of laws—a step that would rob the justice system of its human-centric face (Verhoeven, 1987).

12.5 PUBLIC PERCEPTION AND ETHICAL CONCERNS

With the growing use of automated systems in legal systems, one of the significant ethical concerns involves a fear that these automated systems might fully take over human judgement. This is no longer science fiction, and many people are scared when machines decide critical matters of the law—that automation could strip the rulings of empathy and context." Legal systems traditionally depend on human judges who take into account not only the law but also the specific context of every case. However, automated legal systems are not always able to consider these nuances, which prevents them from always being efficient and consistent.

Public perception tends to be sceptical, with many seeing automated systems as infallible or not having the intuition and ethical reasoners that human judges do. There are scenarios where representing human experiences is crucial (family law, criminal sentencing, civil rights violations), and the issue of feature starving is even more pronounced (Susskind R., 2013).

12.5.1 Algorithmic Bias and Discrimination

Ethical implications of the Automated systems—algorithmic bias Numerous machine learning algorithms are trained on historical data that reflects social inequities and therefore may have biases. As a result, these biases can become unintentionally embedded in the decision-making of legal machine-automating bodies, thereby repeating, and in some cases aggravating discrimination. Take the criminal justice system, for instance; predictive policing algorithms, for instance, have been shown disproportionately to target minority communities because those algorithms are trained on past arrest data, which can be racially biased. Risk assessment tools applied in the context of sentencing can accurately reproduce racial or socioeconomic biases and have adverse impacts on marginalised communities.

As a result, algorithmic transparency and fairness have emerged as the focus of much discussion regarding legal automation. That is why, as many legal scholars and ethicists agree, automated systems must be closely scrutinised to ensure they are free of bias and uphold society's values of fairness and equality (Angwin et al., 2016). Most of the public opinion towards these technologies is heavily influenced by whether they have been raised to be aware of these biases, resulting in distrust of their capability to make objective autonomous decisions.

12.5.2 Accountability and Liability

But you have automated systems making decisions in the domain of law, and accountability is in the foreground. Who is responsible when an automatic legal system makes a mistake? Who is responsible for it: the developers of the software, users of the technology, or the AI itself? This question gets particularly tricky when the law automates and leads to severe harm, such as wrongful imprisonment or unjust contracts.

The "black box" nature of many AI systems means understanding all the dimensions of an AI's decision-making processes can be hard, which complicates matters of liability. This lack of transparency can make it difficult to pinpoint where things go wrong when a system breaks down. The regulations around the scope of legal automation may be expanding, yet this is a long way from what would be needed to offer sound legal accountability in an ethical and responsible automated system (Calo R., The Case for a Federal Robotics Commission, 2014).

12.5.3 Loss of Human Agency and Autonomy

But more worrying from a human ethics standpoint is the degradation of human judgement and agency in legal affairs. When these systems are deployed across different areas of society, they might create something where people can have their legal challenges addressed pretty much with minimal agency. Being governed by a ruling made by a machine, particularly one that a human might not fully understand, can undercut a person's agency.

And there are alarm bells about the loss of privacy and the increase of surveillance in embedded automated systems. As AI continues to integrate more fully into the fabric of the law, the risk is that with the systems not designed with optimal privacy protections, personal data will be utilised, misused, or abused in a way that has truly massive implications (Brynjolfsson & McAfee, 2014). The days when algorithms constantly watch us and follow us around are already here, and what we lose is individual freedom, which is terrifying.

12.5.4 The Balance Between Efficiency and Justice

Automated systems may prioritise efficiency in a way that is almost immediately visible to users, such as eliminating the backlogs of cases and speeding up processes in courts, but there remains a fear that this efficiency would be at the expense of justice. Automated legal decisions could sacrifice fairness for speed, with disastrous results (Lefebvre & Maclure, 2022). The risk is an overreliance on models that seem very efficient indeed and forsake the slow but noble work of careful deliberation here.

In an ideal legal system, justice must not be constraint by time, even if it is costly. However, with automated legal systems becoming increasingly common, it may also be a temptation to trade careful consideration of the facts and their context for expediency. This tension is central to a leading debate about what automation looks like in the legal domain.

12.5.5 Public Trust and Perception of Legitimacy

The legitimacy of the legal system is based on trust, and with automated systems on the rise, the question of maintaining public trust in those systems is a question. If members of the public view automated legal systems as unfair, biased, or too complex to comprehend, they may also lose faith in the system of justice more generally.

Automated systems should be (properly) designed to be transparent, accountable, and human values aligned to enable public trust. The legitimacy of AI in law will depend on regular audits, ethical reviews, and public discourse to be based on ethical autonomy (Susskind R., 2013).

12.6 LEGAL AND POLICY CONSIDERATIONS: AN EXHAUSTIVE ANALYSIS

The increase of automated labour legal systems in the legal market introduces pressing legal and policy challenges. These systems, while potentially improving efficiency and reducing human error, also introduce particular risks to privacy, fairness, and access to justice. Data science has a lot to offer about the law but also has a lot of challenges: new laws will have to be implemented; existing laws and frameworks will have to be adapted; new regulations will have to be developed, and a lot more. So we are going to talk about the key legal and policy considerations that need to be taken into account to responsibly and ethically deploy automated systems.

12.6.1 Regulatory Frameworks for Legal Automation

Well-designed regulatory systems must be established to ensure that these automated systems function correctly and that the rights of individuals are protected when automated decisions are made about them. We must re-engineer our present legal system, which was predicated on human decision-making, to incorporate that AI and algorithms also have a much larger role. Currently, there is no regulation on automated legal technologies; without governance, systems of law and logistic processes can misalign and corrupt.

The EU's General Data Protection Regulation (GDPR) set rules about AI across sectors, for example, but the regulation's provisions on automated decision-making and profiling have minimal scope for the practice of law (European Union, 2016). Similarly, the United States lacks a comprehensive federal framework regarding AI-based legal tools and has instead pursued regulation through sector-specific efforts like the 2022 proposal for an AI Bill of Rights (White & Case LLP, 2024). There is also no ubiquitous framework for legal automation in India (Maheshwari & CO, 2024).

This raises important questions about how the transparency of these automated systems should be regulated and how those affected by automated decisions regarding the law should know how those decisions were made. We need to set benchmarks for explainable governance, and as we learn more about how AIs operate, we should translate that information into intelligible rationale for stakeholders directly affected by the AI and lawyers who deploy them. Legal automation systems also need to be transparent and accountable; that is, human beings must be able to make decisions so that they not only work efficiently but also make sense and withstand human scrutiny (Susskind, 2013).

12.6.2 Data Privacy and Security

The first legal issue related to automated legal systems is personal data protection. These systems often rely on vast amounts of data, including sensitive personal and financial information, to make legal decisions or predictions. Utilising automatic tools to process such confidential data is inherently vulnerable to infrastructure-level data leaks or unauthorised access.

However, the laws of data privacy, like the General Data Protection Regulation (GDPR) in Europe, the California Consumer Privacy Act (CCPA) in the US, and the Data and Digital Personal Data Protection Act in India, are binding on the legal system. They ensure that no one should be able to misuse or exploit any form of personal data. These laws were not, however, devised with the complexities of AI and automated decision-making systems in mind. AI technologies will only further cover sensitive information that the policymakers never imagined (Zarsky, 2015).

Policymakers will now need to balance these laws with the new complexities introduced by automated systems, all while being careful to not intrude on individuals' rights to privacy. That is creating clear rules around things like how invisible AI systems will store, access, and process people's data and who is responsible if this information is used to do harm.

12.6.3 Responsible and Liable Automated Decision-Making

The most significant dilemma in automated legal systems is about accountability, like who is responsible when an AI system errs or commits acts of bias. Traditional legal frameworks assess culpability against human actors such as judges, lawyers, and corporate entities. But as automated systems take decision-making roles, liability becomes harder and harder to pin down.

If a legal system run on AI comes to a wrong conclusion that causes harm to someone, who should take responsibility—the developers of the system, the people who use it, or the AI itself? Adding another layer to this debate is the fact that many AI systems operate in a "black box" manner, making "decisions" in ways that only humans cannot understand or interpret, often making it very difficult to come to a consensus for our morality.

Policymakers must develop frameworks for ensuring that AI systems are held to the same standards of accountability that we apply to human decision-makers, and they must do so on the basis of the first principles of AI in society (Susskind R., 2013). That includes requiring AI developers to keep comprehensive logbooks documenting their algorithms' decision-making processes and providing individuals impacted by errors with the opportunity to take even legal action.

12.7 FUTURE PROSPECTS AND ACCEPTABILITY

The technology is advancing rapidly, and its use in the legal sphere will inevitably grow. Though the explosive promise of enhancing efficiency and access to legal services is great, the sustained viability of such systems will rest upon the fidelity with which they address the basilar challenges and concerns that underpin the discussion above. In this instance, these two divisions lead to an exploration of the future of automated legal systems and their acceptance in individual legal practices and greater society.

However, AI and ML will continue to play a pivotal role in the development of automated legal systems. When these technologies proudly cross the finish line, AI itself will be capable of doing sophisticated legal work. Existing applications such as contract review, legal research, and document automation are baby steps that will ultimately become fully automated legal services (Susskind, 2019). For example, ROSS Intelligence and Lex Machina provide AI-powered legal analytics to predict case outcomes and accelerate legal research with machine learning (Ariwala, 2024).

In the coming several decades, AI systems are expected to take on ever more complex aspects of legal work, anything from the predictive modelling of outcomes to automated legal advice to, in some instances, autonomous decision-making (Surden, 2019). Further parallel advances may reduce the length and cost of legal institutions while making outcome-by-outcome outputs more precise and consistent. Platforms such as DoNotPay, which provide rudimentary forms of automatic legal support to consumers, are already threatening traditional service providers (Daso, 2021).

But as AI gets more developed, regulation will be very important to ensure that these systems function properly and are principled and reasonable. Lawyers, legislators, and technology developers need to work together to make sure that AI-powered tools used in law are subject to important legal standards, including fairness, accountability, and transparency (Brynjolfsson & McAfee, 2014). Striking that balance between seeing the vast potential for AI and also maintaining human judgement will be critical for the legal profession.

12.7.1 Public and Professional Acceptance

A key obstacle to the large-scale adoption of automated legal systems is acceptability. Public and legal professionals will need to trust these systems to handle legal matters fairly and justly. The extent to which the general practitioner community will be able to trust AI-driven legal tools will primarily depend upon system transparency and explainability (Susskind R., 2019). Transparent AI systems with interpretation and appeals (e.g., decision review) are better accepted by users.

Especially in spaces where human IQ is critical, professionals may be slow to embrace it. The legal establishment may push back against AIs to avoid the risk of unemployment and loss of control of the legal process. But AI isn't replacing lawyers; it's working with and for them, allowing them to spend their time on the complicated legal work that requires a human touch and critical thinking (Bloomberg, 2024). As these tools are integrated more routinely into their professional workflows, they will become more accustomed to using AI-backed legal systems (Remus & Levy, 2016).

12.7.2 Ethical and Social Considerations in Acceptability

And there are critical conversations to be had about the ethical and societal concerns informing any agreement with automated legal systems. Timeliness of AI and Decision-Making: Of all the issues of using AI in decision-making, timeliness is arguably one of the most important points to discuss; it is one of many challenges, but others include issues of bias and fairness and human rights protection that can be found in the literature. AI systems based on biased datasets can unintentionally end up reinforcing loaded biases themselves, creating a divergence in what they produce and public discourse, ultimately harming trust in their fairness. For fairness, we will need wider representative training data, more frequent audits, and oversight mechanisms to recognise and counter algorithmic bias (Binns, 2018b).

The application of such technologies in the justice system must also give pause, especially in the context of human judgement becoming alienated from certain processes, particularly those that affect core rights and freedoms. AI lacks empathy, moral reasoning, and contextual sensitivity, all of which are necessary for weighing in on criminal sentencing and family law disputes. Legal scholars argue that AI increases efficiency but is an adjunct, not a substitute, for human judgement in critical legal decisions (Calo, 2019).

12.7.3 Potential for Global Implementation and Impact

Although this chapter will focus on developed environments and automated legal systems, these technologies can play an important role in developing environments. Overall, AI-powered legal tools have the potential to revolutionise the legal industry in various ways, particularly in developing countries with limited access to legal resources. For example, using AI-powered chatbots and document automation tools could enable people to represent themselves in legal systems more effectively (TechStaunch Team, 2024).

Despite this promise, implementation worldwide is fraught with challenges, including differences in technological infrastructure, data access, and differences in legal traditions. Policymakers should also ensure that prescribed measures can be adapted to local circumstances and are in line with cultural and legal practices. Until that time, the international community will need to cooperate in developing global standards for legal automation for its fair and ethical implementation that traverses national borders (Brynjolfsson & McAfee, 2014).

The prospects of automated systems of law are bright, yet hiccups lie ahead. This will significantly evolve the capacity of AI and will contribute to seamless legal services, accessible to many. However achieving that success will require acceptance among the public and the professional community alike, as well as the resolution of ethical, legal, and social issues. For automated legal systems to be widely accepted, they should be transparent, fair, and accountable, and humans should still need to be involved in high-level and critical matters of the law. As the legal profession evolves with generative AI, the world is going to witness the rise of AI-powered legal systems.

12.8 CONCLUSION

The question of when automated legal systems might plunge into the real world is not a question of technology; it is a question of trust, justice, and our shared stake in fairness. As we stand at the crossroads of technological advancement, we must step back and ask the critical question, how do we want the future of law to look? Do we allow machines that efficiency and law are all too human to face, or do we wrest these systems and allow us to make them work for us, preserving what makes justice the right kind of justice?

The idea of automated legal systems is an enticing one. It can break down barriers, bring legal services to the vast majority who find them beyond reach, and help the millions who have long been excluded from the justice system, however, with this promise comes the charge to ensure that those systems are not only efficient but also fair and humane. Going forward, it is of utmost importance to contend with the ethical challenges they pose and demand that technology be built responsibly with full accountability. Because the law is not just a set of rules; it is our shared principles, our community, and our ability to make fair decisions.

The road to acceptance may be long ahead, however with each inch gained, there lies the opportunity to reshape the landscape of legal truth in an ever-evolving world. The systems we create is going to be the world we live in tomorrow; we must guarantee they reflect the highest principles of fairness, equality, and kindness. Therefore, it is always significant to make sure that legal automation must ensure principles of natural justice. After all, it is not the machines that judicial system trust; it is the people who create and steer them. The only thing to do is make the future of law, however automated, a shining light of justice for all.

REFERENCES

Angwin, J., Larson, J., Mattu, S., & Kirchner, L. (2016, May 23). *Machine bias: There's software used across the country to predict future criminals. And it's biased against blacks.* Retrieved from Pro Publica: www.propublica.org/article/machine-bias-risk-assessments-in-criminal-sentencing

Apple Tech. (2023, April 6). *Role of AI in legaltech and its impact on the legal industry.* Retrieved from Appletech soft: www.appletechsoft.com/role-of-ai-in-legaltech-and-its-impact-on-the-legal-industry/

Ariwala, P. (2024, Sept). *The AI frontier in law: 12 innovative AI tools for law firms.* Retrieved from Maruti Techlabs: https://marutitech.com/top-12-legal-ai-tools/

Ashley, K. D. (2017). *Artificial intelligence and legal analytics: New tools for law practice in the digital age.* Cambridge University Press. https://doi.org/10.1017/9781316761380

Asimov, I. (1950). *I, Robot.* Gnome Press.

Balkin, J. M. (2009). The future of free expression in a digital age. *Pepperdine Law Review, 36*(2), 427–444. Retrieved from https://digitalcommons.pepperdine.edu/plr/vol36/iss2/9/

Barton, B. H. (2023). The future of American legal tech. In *Legal Tech and the Future of Civil Justice.* Cambridge University Press. Retrieved from www.cambridge.org/core/books/legal-tech-and-the-future-of-civil-justice/future-of-american-legal-tech/33EA5F398CD139FBB95C1124A413B6EB

Bench-Capon, T. (1991). *Knowledge-Based Systems and Legal Applications.* Academic Press. https://doi.org/10.1016/C2009-0-21602-3

Binns, R. (2018a). *AI Surveillance and Privacy: A Global Perspective.* Springer.

Binns, R. (2018b). Fairness in machine learning: Lessons from political philosophy. *Conference on Fairness, Accountability, and Transparency.* https://doi.org/10.48550/arXiv.1712.03586

Bloomberg. (2024, May 23). *How is AI Changing the Legal Profession?* Retrieved from Bloomberg Law: https://pro.bloomberglaw.com/insights/technology/how-is-ai-changing-the-legal-profession/#how-technology-is-changing-the-legal-field

Brynjolfsson, E., & McAfee, A. (2014). *The Second Machine Age: Work, Progress, and Prosperity in a Time of Brilliant Technologies.* W.W. Norton & Company.

Brynjolfsson, E., & McAfee, A. (2017). *Machine, Platform, Crowd: Harnessing Our Digital Future.* W.W. Norton & Company.

Calo, R. (2014). *The Case for a Federal Robotics Commission.* Brookings Institution Center for Technology Innovation. Retrieved from https://papers.ssrn.com/sol3/papers.cfm?abstract_id=2529151

Calo, R. (2015). Robotics and the lessons of cyberlaw. *California Law Review, 103*(3), 513–563. https://dx.doi.org/10.2139/ssrn.2402972

Calo, R. (2019). Artificial intelligence policy: A primer and roadmap. *UC Davis Law Review, 51.* https://papers.ssrn.com/sol3/papers.cfm?abstract_id=3015350

Contissa, G., Laukyte, M., Sartor, G., Schebesta, H., Masutti, A., Lanzi, P., & Marti, P. (2024). Liability and automation: Issues and challenges for socio-technical systems. *Information & Communications Technology Law*, 1–25.

Daso, F. (2021, Oct. 31). *DoNotPay, A Consumer Robotic Process Automation Startup, Encodes Consumer Rights Into Society's Operating System.* Retrieved from Forbes: www.forbes.com/sites/frederickdaso/2021/10/31/donotpay-a-consumer-robotic-process-automation-startup-encodes-consumer-rights-into-societys-operating-system/

European Union. (2016). General Data Protection Regulation (GDPR), Regulation (EU) 2016/679. Retrieved from https://eur-lex.europa.eu/legal-content/EN/TXT/?uri=CELEX%3A32016R0679

Forster, E. M. (1909). *The Machine Stops.* Archibald Constable.

Gasser, U. (2016). Recoding privacy law: Reflections on the future relationship among law, technology, and Privacy. *Harvard Law Review, 130*(2). Retrieved from https://harvardlawreview.org/forum/vol-130/recoding-privacy-law-reflections-on-the-future-relationship-among-law-technology-and-privacy/

Gibson, w. (1984). *Neuromancer.* Ace Books.

Hutchinson, T. C. (2002). *Researching and Writing in Law.* Thomson Reuters.

Katz, D. M. (2013). Quantitative legal prediction—or—How I learned to stop worrying and start preparing for the data driven future of the legal services industry. *Emory Law Journal, 62*, 910–966.

Lang, F. (Director). (1927). *Metropolis* [Motion Picture].

Lefebvre, H., & Maclure, J. (2022, November 16). *AI's fairness problem: understanding wrongful discrimination in the context of automated decision-making*. Retrieved from https://link.springer.com/article/10.1007/s43681-022-00233-w

Leith, P. (2010). The rise and fall of the legal expert system. *European Journal of Law and Technology, 1*(1). https://doi.org/10.1080/13600869.2016.1232465

Maheshwari & CO. (2024, December 28). *The Growing Impact of AI in India.* Retrieved from: www.maheshwariandco.com/blog/artificial-intelligence-in-india/#:~:text=Current%20Indian%20law%20lacks%20comprehensive,risk%20across%20the%20AI%20ecosystem.

Older, M. (2016). *Infomocracy.* Tor Books.

Remus, D., & Levy, F. (2016). Can robots be lawyers? Computers, lawyers, and the practice of law. Available at SSRN: https://ssrn.com/abstract=2701092 or http://dx.doi.org/10.2139/ssrn.2701092

Spielberg, S. (Director). (2002). *Minority Report* [Motion Picture].

Sreelatha, A., & Choudhary, G. (2023, Sept.). *Exploring the use of AI in legal decision making: Benefits and ethical implications.* Retrieved from Woxen University: https://woxsen.edu.in/research/white-papers/exploring-the-use-of-ai-in-legal-decision-making-benefits-and-ethical-implications/#:~:text=Transparency%20in%20AI%20systems%20allows,use%20of%20rule%2Dbased%20systems.

Stephenson, N. (1992). *Snow Crash.* Bantam Books.

Surden, H. (June 28, 2019). Artificial intelligence and law: An overview. *Georgia State University Law Review, 35*(4), 19–22. Retrieved from https://download.ssrn.com/19/06/28/ssrn_id3411869_code709715.pdf?response-content-disposition=inline&X-Amz-Security-Token=IQoJb3JpZ2luX2VjEIT%2F%2F%2F%2F%2F%2F%2F%2F%2F%2FwEaCXVzLWVhc3QtMSJHMEUCIAt5%2FsNBKc0WgopkEGz7sGGSr5nod5shB2ma6dzAt0RuAiEAjgxn3Y9bVVm

Susskind, R. (2013). *Tomorrow's Lawyers an Introduction to Your Future.* Oxford University Press.

Susskind, R. (2019). *Online Courts and the Future of Justice.* Oxford University Press.

TechStaunch Team. (2024, November 18). *How AI Chatbots Are Changing Legal Research for Lawyers.* Retrieved from https://techstaunch.com/blogs/ai-chatbots-for-legal-research

Verhoeven, P. (Director). (1987). *RoboCop* [Motion Picture].

White & Case LLP. (2024, December 18). *AI Watch: Global regulatory tracker – United States.* Retrieved from www.whitecase.com/insight-our-thinking/ai-watch-global-regulatory-tracker-united-states#:~:text=As%20noted%20above%2C%20there%20is,or%20deployers%20of%20AI%20systems.

Zarsky, T. (2015). The trouble with algorithmic decisions: An analytic road map to examine efficiency and fairness in automated and opaque decision making. *Science, Technology, & Human Values, 41*(1), 118–132. https://doi.org/10.1177/0162243915605575

13 The Intersection of Artificial Intelligence and Procedural Laws

Reimagining Justice in the Digital Era

Jasdeep Singh and Riya Chugh

13.1 INTRODUCTION

Procedural laws are the foundation of the judicial system, ensuring justice is delivered with precision and fairness. These laws, such as the Code of Civil Procedure (CPC) and the Code of Criminal Procedure (CrPC), regulate the judicial process, but their efficiency is increasingly questioned due to delays and backlogs. As technology evolves, especially with the rise of artificial intelligence (AI), there is a growing need for procedural reforms that integrate AI into legal practices.

Globally, AI has been used to enhance judicial efficiency, such as predictive justice in China and automated legal research in the U.S. However, in India, AI's integration into the legal system is still in its early stages. While AI holds potential to streamline procedures and improve accuracy, its adoption must be carefully managed, addressing issues like evidence admissibility, algorithmic fairness, and data privacy.[1]

Adapting procedural laws to AI requires thoughtful amendments and ethical guidelines to ensure fairness and transparency. For instance, revising the Indian Evidence Act to include AI-generated evidence could be a crucial step. The integration of AI should be guided by principles of justice, ensuring that technological progress does not compromise the integrity of the judicial system.[2]

13.2 CURRENT PROCEDURAL LAWS: AN OVERVIEW

Procedural laws are the bedrock upon which the edifice of justice rests. These laws ensure that the substantive rights and obligations of individuals are enforced in a manner that is fair, equitable, and systematic. In the Indian context, the CPC, the CrPC, and the Indian Evidence Act form the triad of procedural frameworks that govern judicial processes. While these laws have withstood the test of time and continue to serve as the cornerstone of justice delivery, they also face significant challenges, particularly in the rapidly evolving digital age.

 DOI: 10.1201/9781003491903-13

13.2.1 Importance of Procedural Laws in Ensuring Justice

The role of procedural laws is indispensable in maintaining the integrity and efficiency of the justice delivery system. The CPC, for instance, outlines the procedures to be followed in civil litigation, ensuring consistency and fairness in resolving disputes. Similarly, the CrPC governs the conduct of criminal proceedings, from investigation to trial and sentencing, ensuring that due process is followed at every stage. The Indian Evidence Act, on the other hand, provides a comprehensive framework for determining the admissibility and relevance of evidence, ensuring that trials are conducted based on reliable and credible information.

These laws are not merely procedural formalities; they are instruments of justice. They uphold the principles of natural justice, such as audi alteram partem (the right to be heard) and nemo judex in causa sua (no one should be a judge in their own cause). By providing a structured process, they ensure that justice is not only done but is also seen to be done. However, the effectiveness of these laws largely depends on their adaptability to societal changes and technological advancements.

13.2.2 Challenges Posed by the Rigidity of Procedural Frameworks

Despite their importance, procedural laws in India often exhibit a rigidity that undermines their effectiveness in the modern context. Many provisions in the CPC, CrPC, and the Indian Evidence Act were conceptualized during colonial times and have not been sufficiently updated to address the complexities of the 21st century. This rigidity manifests in various forms, including procedural delays, outdated practices, and resistance to technological integration.

One of the most glaring issues is the procedural delays that plague the Indian judicial system. The insistence on adhering to procedural technicalities often results in protracted litigation, denying parties timely access to justice. For instance, procedural requirements such as the issuance of summons, service of notices, and compliance with evidentiary rules can take months, if not years, to complete. Such delays not only frustrate litigants but also erode public confidence in the judiciary.

Another significant challenge is the lack of flexibility in accommodating technological advancements. While the world is moving towards digitalization, many procedural provisions remain rooted in archaic practices. For instance, the CrPC mandates the recording of evidence in a written format, which is not only time-consuming but also fails to leverage the potential of digital tools such as video recordings and transcription software. Similarly, the Indian Evidence Act lacks comprehensive provisions for the admissibility of electronic evidence, leading to inconsistencies and uncertainties in its interpretation.

13.2.3 Case Studies Showcasing Procedural Delays and Inefficiencies

The rigidity and inefficiencies of procedural laws are best illustrated through real-world case studies. One such example is the infamous Ayodhya dispute,[3] which spanned over seven decades before being resolved by the Supreme Court in 2019. The case underwent multiple rounds of litigation, appeals, and reviews, highlighting the procedural labyrinth that litigants often have to navigate. Delays in issuing summons, procedural objections, and the sheer volume of evidence contributed to the prolonged duration of the case.

Another pertinent example is the 2G spectrum case,[4] where procedural delays in recording evidence and examining witnesses significantly hampered the progress of the trial. The case, which involved allegations of corruption in the allocation of telecom licenses, took nearly a decade to reach its conclusion. During this period, procedural inefficiencies not only delayed justice but also allowed public trust in the judiciary to wane.

In the realm of criminal law, the Nirbhaya gang rape case[5] serves as a stark reminder of the delays inherent in the Indian judicial system. Despite being a case of national outrage, the trial and subsequent appeals took over seven years to culminate in the execution of the convicts. The procedural requirements for filing appeals, reviews, and mercy petitions significantly contributed to the delay, causing immense anguish to the victims' families and raising questions about the efficiency of the judicial process.

While procedural laws have played a pivotal role in maintaining the sanctity of the Indian judicial system, their rigidity and inefficiencies cannot be overlooked. The challenges posed by procedural delays, outdated practices, and resistance to technological integration underscore the need for urgent reforms. By embracing technology, simplifying procedures, and prioritizing substantive justice, the Indian legal system can transform its procedural frameworks to meet the demands of the digital age. The journey to reform may be fraught with challenges, but it is a necessary step towards ensuring that justice remains accessible, efficient, and equitable.

13.3 TECHNOLOGICAL ADVANCEMENTS AND THEIR IMPACT ON LEGAL SYSTEMS

The legal landscape has historically been characterized by its adherence to precedent, traditional practices, and manual processes. However, the advent of technology, particularly AI, has begun to redefine this domain, presenting new paradigms for justice delivery. AI-driven tools have made significant inroads into legal systems worldwide, promising efficiency, precision, and accessibility. This chapter explores the integration of AI into legal frameworks, its applications across jurisdictions, and the transformative benefits it offers.

13.3.1 Overview of AI-Driven Tools in Legal Systems

AI in the legal domain leverages machine learning algorithms, natural language processing (NLP), and data analytics to perform tasks that traditionally required human intervention. These tools have emerged as indispensable allies for legal practitioners, judiciary members, and litigants alike.

One prominent application of AI is **predictive justice**, where algorithms analyze past judgments, case histories, and legal precedents to predict the outcome of ongoing or future cases. This approach not only aids lawyers in formulating strategies but also assists judges in understanding trends, ensuring consistency in decisions. Predictive tools such as ROSS Intelligence and Lex Machina have been instrumental in revolutionizing legal research, providing insights at unprecedented speeds.

Another significant AI application is **automated documentation**. Tools like Casetext and Contract Express facilitate the creation, review, and management of legal documents with remarkable accuracy and efficiency. By automating routine tasks such as drafting contracts, summarizing case files, or flagging inconsistencies in agreements, these tools enable legal professionals to focus on more substantive aspects of their work.

AI-powered **eDiscovery systems** are transforming the labor-intensive process of sifting through voluminous data for relevant evidence. Using advanced search capabilities, these systems can quickly identify critical documents, emails, or other digital evidence, reducing the time and cost traditionally associated with discovery. For instance, companies like Everlaw and Relativity have set benchmarks in this area, providing robust tools for managing complex litigation data.

13.3.2 Global Examples of AI Integration in Legal Systems

The integration of AI into legal systems has been a global phenomenon, with diverse jurisdictions adopting innovative approaches tailored to their unique contexts.

In **China**, AI has been seamlessly integrated into the judiciary through the establishment of internet courts and AI judges. These courts, operational in cities like Hangzhou, Beijing, and Guangzhou, use AI to mediate disputes, particularly those arising from e-commerce and digital contracts. The AI judges, equipped with NLP capabilities, interact with litigants, analyze evidence, and draft verdicts. Such initiatives have significantly reduced case backlogs, demonstrating the transformative potential of AI in streamlining judicial processes.[6]

The **United States** has witnessed a surge in the adoption of AI tools for eDiscovery and legal analytics. Law firms and corporations use platforms like Logikcull and Nextpoint to manage litigation data, ensuring compliance with discovery obligations while minimizing human error. Additionally, AI-driven tools like LegalMation generate responses to lawsuits, creating a new standard for efficiency in legal proceedings.[7]

In **European nations**, AI integration has focused on regulatory compliance and dispute resolution. The European Union's initiative to establish ethical guidelines for AI underscores its commitment to balancing technological innovation with human rights considerations. Countries like Estonia have introduced AI-based small claims courts, where disputes involving minor monetary claims are resolved expeditiously.[8]

Even in **developing countries**, AI is making strides. For instance, in India, AI-based initiatives like SUPACE (Supreme Court Portal for Assistance in Court Efficiency) aim to assist judges by providing research inputs and case summaries. While still in its nascent stages, such tools reflect the growing recognition of AI's role in addressing systemic inefficiencies in the legal system.

13.3.3 Potential Benefits of AI in Legal Systems

The integration of AI into legal systems offers numerous benefits that address longstanding challenges of speed, cost, and accuracy.[9]

1 **Enhanced Speed in Decision-Making**: One of the most significant advantages of AI-driven tools is their ability to process vast amounts of data in record time. Predictive justice systems, for instance, can analyze thousands of precedents and legal documents within seconds, providing judges and lawyers with actionable insights. This efficiency is particularly valuable in jurisdictions plagued by case backlogs, enabling faster resolution of disputes.
2 **Cost Reduction for Stakeholders**: Legal services have often been criticized for their prohibitive costs, which deter many individuals from seeking justice. By automating routine tasks such as document review and evidence analysis, AI tools reduce the reliance on extensive human resources, thereby lowering costs for clients. Moreover, cost-effective AI solutions democratize access to legal assistance, bridging the gap between privileged and underprivileged litigants.
3 **Improved Accuracy and Consistency**: Human decision-making in legal contexts is susceptible to biases, fatigue, and inconsistencies. AI systems, driven by data and algorithms, offer a more objective approach to analyzing evidence and predicting case outcomes. For instance, algorithms trained on extensive datasets can identify patterns of judicial bias, ensuring that judgments adhere more closely to legal principles.
4 **Accessibility and Inclusivity**: AI-powered tools like chatbots and virtual assistants are making legal information accessible to a broader audience. Platforms such as DoNotPay offer free legal advice and assistance, empowering individuals who may otherwise lack the means to hire professional legal counsel. This inclusivity strengthens the justice delivery system, making it more equitable and user-friendly.
5 **Reduction in Procedural Delays**: Procedural inefficiencies, such as delays in document filing or evidence submission, have long plagued legal systems. AI tools streamline these processes, enabling real-time updates and efficient case management. For instance, automated case filing systems can instantly validate documents, flagging errors or omissions that might otherwise result in costly delays.

13.3.4 Challenges and Ethical Considerations

While the benefits of AI in legal systems are undeniable, it is essential to address the accompanying challenges and ethical concerns. The reliance on data-driven algorithms raises questions about transparency, accountability, and potential biases embedded in the systems. Furthermore, the role of AI in decision-making must be carefully delineated to ensure that it complements, rather than supplants, human judgment.

For example, a 2023 study published in *ArXiv* highlights the challenges of adapting modern AI models to the Indian legal context, particularly in terms of linguistic diversity and jurisdictional complexities (ArXiv, 2023). Such challenges underscore the need for robust regulatory frameworks that balance innovation with ethical safeguards.

As nations continue to experiment with AI integration, the legal profession must embrace this change with caution and adaptability, ensuring that technology serves as a tool for empowerment rather than exclusion. With the right balance, AI can pave the way for a more efficient, equitable, and accessible legal system, redefining jurisprudence in the digital age.

13.4 GAPS IN EXISTING PROCEDURAL LAWS

Procedural laws form the backbone of any legal system, ensuring that justice is not only done but is seen to be done. The Indian legal framework, encompassing the Code of Civil Procedure (CPC), the Code of Criminal Procedure (CrPC), and the Indian Evidence Act, has provided a robust foundation for justice delivery. However, these laws, largely shaped by colonial legacies and incremental amendments, often struggle to meet the dynamic needs of a rapidly evolving society. This chapter examines the gaps in procedural laws that impede justice delivery and explores how these limitations can be addressed in the context of modern challenges.

13.4.1 Inflexibility in Addressing Contemporary Issues

One of the most significant limitations of existing procedural laws is their rigidity. The CPC and CrPC, codified in the 19th and 20th centuries, were designed to address the socioeconomic realities of their time. While subsequent amendments have sought to modernize these laws, they often fall short of addressing the complexities of contemporary disputes, particularly those involving technology, commerce, and cross-border issues.

For instance, e-commerce disputes and cybercrimes frequently encounter procedural hurdles, such as jurisdictional ambiguities and outdated evidentiary requirements. The Indian Evidence Act, 1872, although amended to accommodate electronic evidence, still lacks the nuanced provisions required to handle the complexities of digital forensics and data privacy. These gaps often result in delays and inconsistent judgments, undermining the credibility of the legal system.

13.4.2 Procedural Delays and Case Backlogs

Procedural delays remain one of the most visible gaps in the Indian legal system. The CPC, with its extensive provisions for adjournments, interim reliefs, and appeals, often becomes a tool for litigants to prolong disputes. Similarly, the CrPC's elaborate pre-trial and trial procedures contribute to the pendency of cases. As of 2023, over 40 million cases were pending across Indian courts, a testament to the inefficiencies inherent in the procedural framework (Supreme Court of India, 2023).

The issue is further compounded by the absence of stringent timelines for the completion of cases. While the Commercial Courts Act, 2015 introduced strict deadlines for resolving commercial disputes, such measures are yet to be uniformly applied across other areas of law. This lack of procedural discipline creates an environment where justice is often delayed, eroding public trust in the judiciary.

13.4.3 Inaccessibility for Marginalized Communities

Another critical gap in procedural laws is their failure to ensure equitable access to justice for marginalized communities. The procedural framework often assumes a level playing field, ignoring the socio-economic disparities that hinder access to legal remedies.

For instance, the complex language and structure of the CPC and CrPC can be intimidating for individuals with limited literacy. Additionally, procedural requirements such as filing fees, documentation, and travel to distant courts disproportionately affect underprivileged litigants. Despite provisions for legal aid under the Legal Services Authorities Act, 1987, many remain unaware of their rights or face bureaucratic hurdles in accessing assistance.

13.4.4 Inadequate Provisions for Alternative Dispute Resolution

While the Arbitration and Conciliation Act, 1996, and subsequent amendments have sought to promote alternative dispute resolution (ADR) mechanisms, procedural laws still lack a comprehensive framework for integrating ADR into the mainstream justice system. The CPC's provisions for mediation and arbitration are often underutilized due to the absence of standardized procedures and trained professionals.

For example, court-annexed mediation centers, though present in several states, face challenges such as inadequate infrastructure, lack of awareness among litigants, and resistance from lawyers who perceive ADR as a threat to their practice. This gap not only limits the potential of ADR in reducing case backlogs but also denies litigants a quicker and less adversarial means of resolving disputes.

13.4.5 Lack of Technological Integration

The procedural laws have been slow to embrace technological advancements that could streamline judicial processes. While initiatives like eCourts and virtual hearings gained momentum during the COVID-19 pandemic, their implementation remains uneven and fraught with challenges.

For instance, electronic filing of cases (e-filing) and virtual hearings have been criticized for being inaccessible to individuals in rural areas or those lacking digital literacy. Additionally, procedural laws do not provide clear guidelines for the admissibility and authenticity of electronic records in such settings, creating uncertainty for litigants and lawyers alike.

13.4.6 Case Studies Highlighting Procedural Gaps

1. **Arnesh Kumar v. State of Bihar, (2014):**[10] This landmark case highlighted the misuse of procedural provisions related to arrests under Section 498A of the IPC. The Supreme Court emphasized the need for stricter procedural safeguards to prevent arbitrary arrests, underscoring the inadequacies in existing laws that allow for misuse.
2. **Hussainara Khatoon v. State of Bihar, (1979):**[11] This case brought to light the plight of undertrial prisoners languishing in jails due to procedural delays. The Supreme Court's directives for expediting trials and ensuring bail for undertrials underscored the systemic gaps in the criminal justice system.
3. **Sahara India Real Estate Corporation Ltd. v. SEBI, (2012):**[12] The case illustrated how procedural delays and multiple appeals can be exploited to evade accountability. The Supreme Court's intervention highlighted the need for streamlining procedures to prevent such misuse.

13.4.7 Recommendations for Bridging the Gaps

To address these gaps, procedural laws must evolve to reflect the realities of a modern, diverse, and technologically driven society.

1. **Simplification and Modernization**: The language and structure of procedural laws should be simplified to ensure accessibility for all litigants. Additionally, amendments should focus on incorporating provisions for handling technology-driven disputes, such as those involving blockchain, cryptocurrency, and AI.
2. **Strict Timelines and Accountability**: Uniform timelines for case resolution should be introduced across all areas of law, with provisions for penalizing noncompliance. Judicial accountability mechanisms can further ensure adherence to procedural discipline.
3. **Enhanced Access for Marginalized Communities**: Legal awareness campaigns and streamlined legal aid processes can bridge the gap for underprivileged litigants. Special provisions, such as mobile courts and localized filing mechanisms, can further enhance accessibility.
4. **Institutionalizing ADR Mechanisms**: Comprehensive guidelines and infrastructure for ADR must be integrated into procedural laws. Training programs for mediators, arbitrators, and lawyers can ensure the effective utilization of these mechanisms.
5. **Leveraging Technology**: Procedural laws should mandate the use of technology in judicial processes, with clear guidelines for its implementation. Investments in digital infrastructure, along with capacity-building initiatives, can ensure that technological integration is both effective and inclusive.

The gaps in existing procedural laws are not merely academic concerns but have real-world implications for justice delivery. By addressing these limitations through thoughtful reforms, the legal system can become more responsive, efficient, and inclusive. While the challenges are formidable, they also present an opportunity to reimagine procedural laws as dynamic tools for justice in the 21st century.

13.5 COMPARATIVE ANALYSIS: LESSONS FROM OTHER JURISDICTIONS

Global legal systems have been undergoing significant transformations due to advancements in technology and AI. While some countries have been pioneers in integrating AI into their procedural frameworks, others are still exploring ways to balance technological benefits with judicial integrity. This section offers a comparative analysis of procedural innovations in the United States, the European Union, and China, focusing on their lessons for India.

13.5.1 United States: eDiscovery and Its Impact on Procedural Rules

The United States has been a forerunner in leveraging technology in legal procedures, particularly through electronic discovery (eDiscovery). eDiscovery refers to the process by which electronic data is identified, collected, and produced for litigation purposes. Governed by the Federal Rules of Civil Procedure (FRCP), eDiscovery has transformed pre-trial processes, enabling parties to handle vast amounts of data efficiently[13].

13.5.1.1 Impact on Procedural Rules

The inclusion of eDiscovery in procedural rules has necessitated significant amendments to the FRCP. For instance, Rule 26 outlines the obligation of parties to disclose electronically stored information (ESI) relevant to their case. Similarly, Rule 34 allows for the production of ESI in response to discovery requests, ensuring that digital evidence is treated on par with physical documents. These rules have been instrumental in streamlining litigation, reducing delays, and promoting transparency.

However, eDiscovery also presents challenges. The costs associated with processing and analyzing ESI can be prohibitive, particularly for smaller law firms and litigants. Additionally, the sheer volume of data often leads to disputes over relevance, privilege, and admissibility. Despite these challenges, eDiscovery has proven invaluable in ensuring that the judicial system keeps pace with technological advancements.

13.5.1.2 Lessons for India

India can draw several insights from the U.S. experience with eDiscovery. While the Indian Evidence Act, 1872, recognizes electronic records, its provisions remain rudimentary compared to the comprehensive framework established under the FRCP. Integrating clear guidelines for the identification, preservation, and disclosure of ESI could significantly enhance India's procedural laws, especially in commercial disputes and cybercrime cases.

13.5.2 European Union: GDPR and Its Intersection with AI in Legal Systems

The European Union (EU) has been a global leader in regulating data protection and privacy, with the General Data Protection Regulation (GDPR) serving as a cornerstone of its framework. Enforced in 2018, the GDPR imposes stringent obligations on entities handling personal data, including legal systems.[14]

13.5.2.1 Impact on AI in Legal Systems

The GDPR has significant implications for AI-driven tools in legal systems. Articles 22 and 35 of the regulation mandate human oversight in automated decision-making processes and require impact assessments for high-risk AI applications. These provisions ensure that AI tools used in judicial procedures adhere to principles of fairness, transparency, and accountability.

Moreover, the GDPR's emphasis on data minimization and purpose limitation has influenced how AI systems are designed and deployed in legal contexts. For instance, predictive justice tools in the EU are required to anonymize personal data to comply with privacy norms. This careful integration of AI with data protection laws sets a benchmark for balancing technological innovation with individual rights.

13.5.2.2 Lessons for India

India, with its recently enacted Digital Personal Data Protection Act, 2023, can benefit from the EU's approach to regulating AI in legal systems. By incorporating provisions that mandate transparency and accountability in AI-driven judicial tools, India can ensure that its legal system remains ethical and inclusive. Additionally, introducing guidelines for data protection impact assessments could prevent misuse and build public trust in AI-enabled legal procedures.

13.5.3 China: AI Courts and Procedural Innovations

China has emerged as a global leader in integrating AI into its judiciary, exemplified by the establishment of AI courts. Since 2017, China has launched internet courts in Hangzhou, Beijing, and Guangzhou to handle disputes related to e-commerce, intellectual property, and online fraud. These courts leverage AI tools, blockchain technology, and online platforms to streamline judicial processes.[15]

13.5.3.1 Key Features of AI Courts

1. **Virtual Hearings**: AI courts in China conduct virtual hearings, allowing litigants to participate remotely. These hearings are facilitated by AI-powered systems that manage scheduling, documentation, and evidence presentation.
2. **AI Judges**: One of the most innovative aspects of Chinese AI courts is the use of AI judges for preliminary dispute resolution. These virtual judges, equipped with natural language processing capabilities, provide litigants with legal advice and recommend settlements.

3 **Blockchain Integration**: To address concerns of tampering and fraud, AI courts rely on blockchain technology for evidence preservation. Blockchain ensures that digital evidence is immutable and easily verifiable, enhancing the credibility of judicial outcomes.

13.5.3.2 Impact on Procedural Efficiency

AI courts in China have significantly reduced the time and cost associated with litigation. According to official reports, the Hangzhou Internet Court resolves cases in an average of 38 days, compared to the national average of 80 days (Supreme People's Court of China, 2020). This efficiency has been particularly beneficial in cases involving small claims, where prolonged delays often deter litigants.

13.5.3.3 Lessons for India

India's judicial system, plagued by procedural delays and case backlogs, can learn from China's integration of AI in courts. Establishing specialized tribunals for technology-related disputes, equipped with AI tools for evidence management and case tracking, could significantly enhance procedural efficiency. However, India must also consider ethical concerns, such as bias in AI algorithms and the need for human oversight, to ensure that justice remains fair and impartial.

13.5.4 Insights for India from Global Examples

The comparative analysis of the United States, the European Union, and China offers several actionable insights for India:

1 **Comprehensive E-Discovery Framework**: Drawing from the U.S., India should develop a robust framework for eDiscovery, addressing issues of cost, accessibility, and admissibility of ESI. This framework could be integrated into the CPC and CrPC through amendments.

2 **Regulating AI with Privacy Safeguards**: Inspired by the EU's GDPR, India should enforce strict guidelines for AI applications in the judiciary, ensuring that data privacy and human oversight remain paramount. This approach would not only protect individual rights but also enhance public confidence in AI-driven systems.

3 **Specialized AI Courts**: Following China's example, India could establish AI-enabled courts for handling specific categories of disputes, such as cybercrime, intellectual property, and e-commerce. These courts could leverage blockchain for evidence preservation and AI tools for preliminary dispute resolution.

4 **Capacity Building and Training**: To implement these innovations effectively, India must invest in training judges, lawyers, and court staff in the use of AI and digital tools. Partnerships with global institutions could facilitate knowledge exchange and capacity building.

The experiences of the United States, the European Union, and China demonstrate that technological advancements, when carefully integrated into procedural frameworks, can revolutionize legal systems. While each jurisdiction offers unique lessons, the underlying message is clear: embracing innovation is no longer a choice but a necessity for modern judiciaries. For India, the challenge lies in adapting these global best practices to its socio-legal context, ensuring that technological progress is accompanied by ethical safeguards and inclusivity. By doing so, India can transform its procedural laws into dynamic instruments of justice in the digital age.

13.6 KEY AREAS FOR REFORM IN PROCEDURAL LAWS

As the judiciary embraces technology, particularly AI, procedural laws must evolve to sustain fairness, efficiency, and accessibility. While AI holds promise in transforming the legal landscape, its integration also presents challenges related to accountability, transparency, and fairness. This section examines the critical areas requiring reform in procedural laws, focusing on the Indian Evidence Act, procedural timelines, algorithmic accountability, and safeguards to ensure procedural fairness.[16]

13.6.1 Amendments Required in the Indian Evidence Act

The Indian Evidence Act, 1872, remains the cornerstone of evidentiary rules in India. However, being a product of its time, it does not adequately address the challenges posed by digital and AI-generated evidence.

13.6.1.1 Inclusion of AI-Generated Evidence

AI tools are increasingly used to generate evidence, such as facial recognition data and predictive analyses. These technologies, while revolutionary, raise concerns about bias and reliability. Sections 3 and 65B of the Indian Evidence Act require amendments to explicitly include AI-generated evidence, with clear protocols for verifying algorithmic accuracy and input integrity. Such provisions would establish credibility and reduce ambiguity in admitting AI-driven data in courtrooms.

13.6.1.2 Authentication Standards

The current guidelines under Section 65B for authenticating electronic records are insufficient for AI-generated data. Amendments should introduce robust mechanisms like independent audits of AI tools, traceability of data sources, and blockchain-based systems to ensure tamper-proof records. These reforms would bolster trust in the authenticity and reliability of AI-generated evidence.

13.6.1.3 Global Lessons

The European Union's General Data Protection Regulation (GDPR) provides an excellent example by emphasizing transparency and accountability in data use. India could adopt similar safeguards to ensure AI-generated evidence upholds privacy and fairness standards.

13.6.2 Revisions to Procedural Timelines to Accommodate AI-Based Analysis

Delays in evidence collection and presentation remain significant contributors to judicial inefficiency in India. AI has the potential to expedite these processes, but procedural timelines must be recalibrated to integrate AI-driven analysis effectively.

13.6.2.1 Accelerating Evidence Processing

AI tools like natural language processing (NLP) and predictive coding can analyze vast datasets swiftly, identifying relevant information in minutes rather than weeks. Procedural codes, such as the Code of Civil Procedure (CPC) and Code of Criminal Procedure (CrPC), should incorporate flexible timelines that harness AI capabilities, reducing delays while maintaining procedural integrity.

13.6.2.2 Avoiding Unnecessary Delays

While AI can streamline timelines, system malfunctions or biases could lead to setbacks. Reforms must include contingency plans, such as provisions for human review in cases of technical failures, ensuring timelines balance speed with accuracy.

13.6.2.3 Case Studies and Global Practices

The U.S. Federal Rules of Civil Procedure (FRCP) demonstrate how eDiscovery tools have successfully streamlined pre-trial processes. India can adapt similar practices to suit its unique judicial context, ensuring procedural efficiency without compromising fairness.

13.6.3 Frameworks for Algorithmic Accountability and Transparency

The "black box" nature of AI systems, which obscures the decision-making process, poses a significant challenge to public trust in judicial outcomes.

13.6.3.1 Establishing Accountability Standards

Procedural reforms must mandate regular audits of AI tools, focusing on parameters such as algorithmic fairness, data quality, and output accuracy. Independent regulatory bodies could oversee these audits to maintain impartiality and ensure compliance with ethical standards.

13.6.3.2 Transparency Measures

To foster trust, developers should disclose critical information about their algorithms, including training datasets and decision-making criteria. For instance, an AI tool used in sentencing decisions should provide clear explanations of its recommendations, enabling judges to make informed choices.

13.6.3.3 Inspiration from Global Frameworks

China's AI courts, which emphasize transparency through open hearings and accessible rulings, offer a valuable model. India can adapt such practices to ensure openness and accountability in AI-driven legal processes.

13.6.4 Safeguards to Ensure AI Does Not Undermine Procedural Fairness

While AI can enhance procedural efficiency, it also poses risks, such as algorithmic bias, unequal access to technology, and over-reliance on automated systems.

1. **Mitigating Algorithmic Bias**
   Bias in AI often stems from skewed training data. Procedural laws should mandate rigorous predeployment testing and continuous monitoring of AI systems to ensure fairness over time.
2. **Ensuring Access to Technology**
   Reforms must address technological disparities by ensuring AI tools are accessible to all litigants, particularly marginalized communities. Free legal aid services could incorporate AI tools to empower underprivileged individuals in navigating complex legal processes.
3. **Balancing Automation with Human Oversight**
   AI should serve as a tool, not a substitute for human judgment. Procedural laws must emphasize the role of judges and legal practitioners in overseeing AI-driven decisions, preserving the nuanced understanding required for complex cases.
4. **Ethical Considerations**
   Ethical guidelines, prioritizing transparency, accountability, and fairness, should be central to AI integration in legal systems. Mandatory training for legal professionals on the responsible use of AI could ensure adherence to these principles.

The integration of AI into procedural laws offers immense potential to revolutionize the judiciary by enhancing efficiency and accuracy. However, these advancements must be balanced with robust safeguards to preserve fairness, accountability, and transparency. By drawing on global best practices and tailoring reforms to India's unique challenges, the legal system can harness AI as a tool for justice, ensuring it serves society equitably and effectively.

13.7 KEY AREAS FOR REFORM IN PROCEDURAL LAWS

As technology transforms the judicial landscape, procedural laws must adapt to maintain fairness, efficiency, and accessibility. Integrating AI into the legal framework offers immense opportunities but also demands amendments to address challenges like accountability, transparency, and fairness. This section explores key areas for reform in procedural laws, with a focus on the Indian Evidence Act, procedural timelines, algorithmic accountability, and safeguards for procedural fairness.

13.7.1 Amendments Required in the Indian Evidence Act

The Indian Evidence Act, 1872, forms the backbone of evidentiary standards in India. However, being a predigital era legislation, it lacks provisions to tackle modern challenges, such as the admissibility and authenticity of AI-generated evidence.

13.7.1.1 Inclusion of AI-Generated Evidence

AI systems increasingly generate evidence, such as facial recognition data, predictive analytics, and digital forensics. While these advancements improve accuracy and efficiency, they also raise questions about reliability and potential biases. Amending Sections 3 and 65B of the Indian Evidence Act could clarify the admissibility criteria for AI-generated evidence. Clear guidelines should also ensure the integrity of AI algorithms and data inputs.

13.7.1.2 Authentication Standards

The Act currently provides limited guidance for authenticating electronic records under Section 65B. These provisions are inadequate for AI-generated data. Proposed reforms could mandate robust verification mechanisms, such as independent audits of AI systems and traceable data sources. Employing blockchain technology to create tamper-proof records could also enhance evidentiary credibility in judicial proceedings.

13.7.1.3 Global Lessons

The European Union's General Data Protection Regulation (GDPR) highlights transparency and accountability in data usage. Adopting similar practices could help ensure that AI-generated evidence complies with stringent privacy and fairness standards.

13.7.2 Revisions to Procedural Timelines to Accommodate AI-Based Analysis

Delays in evidence collection, analysis, and presentation are significant contributors to judicial backlogs in India. AI has the potential to expedite these processes, but procedural timelines must be recalibrated to incorporate AI-based analysis effectively.

13.7.2.1 Accelerating Evidence Processing

AI tools, such as natural language processing (NLP) and predictive coding, can process large datasets in minutes. However, procedural rules often mandate manual reviews, which are time-consuming and redundant. Reforms to the Code of Civil Procedure (CPC) and Code of Criminal Procedure (CrPC) could introduce flexible timelines, leveraging AI for faster evidence processing.

13.7.2.2 Avoiding Unnecessary Delays

While AI can speed up processes, over-reliance may lead to delays during technical malfunctions. Procedural reforms should incorporate contingency plans, such as human review mechanisms, to mitigate risks. Balancing speed with accuracy is crucial to ensure justice is neither rushed nor compromised.

13.7.2.3 Global Practices

The U.S. Federal Rules of Civil Procedure (FRCP) streamline pretrial processes through eDiscovery, demonstrating how timelines can adapt to technological advancements. India could adopt similar practices while tailoring them to its judicial framework.

13.7.3 Frameworks for Algorithmic Accountability and Transparency

The opacity of algorithms, commonly referred to as the "black box" problem, poses significant challenges in integrating AI into judicial systems. Transparency and accountability are critical for public trust in AI-driven legal outcomes.

13.7.3.1 Establishing Accountability Standards

Procedural reforms should include regular audits of AI tools to ensure they are fair, unbiased, and reliable. Independent regulatory bodies could conduct these audits, focusing on parameters such as data quality, algorithm design, and output accuracy.

13.7.3.2 Transparency Measures

Transparency is key to fostering trust in AI systems. Laws should require developers to disclose algorithmic details, including training data and decision-making criteria. For instance, an AI tool used in sentencing must explain how it arrived at its recommendation, enabling informed judicial decisions.

13.7.3.3 Global Inspiration

China's AI courts, which prioritize transparency through open hearings and accessible rulings, provide valuable lessons. India could adopt similar measures, emphasizing openness and public scrutiny.

13.7.4 Safeguards to Ensure AI Does Not Undermine Procedural Fairness

Although AI enhances procedural efficiency, it also poses risks to fairness, including algorithmic bias, unequal access to technology, and over-reliance on automated systems.

- **Mitigating Algorithmic Bias**
  Bias often arises from skewed training data or flawed design. Reforms must mandate rigorous testing of AI systems to detect and eliminate biases. Continuous monitoring mechanisms should also be implemented to ensure long-term fairness.
- **Ensuring Access to Technology**
  Marginalized communities often lack access to digital tools, exacerbating inequalities. Procedural reforms should ensure AI technologies are accessible to all litigants, regardless of socio-economic background. For example, free legal aid services could incorporate AI to assist underprivileged individuals.
- **Balancing Automation with Human Oversight**
  AI systems should complement, not replace, human judgment. Judges and legal practitioners must retain final decision-making authority, ensuring technology serves as a tool rather than a substitute for nuanced legal reasoning.
- **Ethical Considerations**
  Ethics must underpin AI integration. Procedural reforms should introduce ethical guidelines emphasizing fairness, transparency, and accountability. Training programs for judges and lawyers can equip them to navigate AI-driven legal processes responsibly.

Integrating AI into procedural laws can significantly enhance judicial efficiency, accuracy, and accessibility. However, these advancements require comprehensive reforms addressing AI-generated evidence, algorithmic accountability, and procedural fairness. By learning from global best practices and tailoring reforms to India's unique legal context, the judicial system can ensure technology serves justice while maintaining fairness and equality.

13.8 POLICY RECOMMENDATIONS AND ROADMAP

The rapid evolution of AI has the potential to revolutionize India's legal system by addressing issues like case backlogs and inefficiencies. However, its integration must prioritize fairness, transparency, and accountability. Below is a concise roadmap for AI's responsible adoption in the legal domain[17].

- **Drafting AI-Specific Procedural Laws**
  Existing laws like the Indian Evidence Act and procedural codes must be updated to accommodate AI's complexities, such as algorithmic biases and AI-generated evidence. Clear guidelines should regulate AI evidence admissibility and system audits for fairness, ensuring AI operates within a structured legal framework.
- **Establishing Regulatory Authorities**
  Dedicated regulatory bodies should oversee AI's use in legal processes, ensuring compliance with ethical and legal standards. These authorities could certify AI tools, monitor fairness, and facilitate public input, mirroring models like the EU's AI oversight framework.
- **Training Legal Professionals**
  Judges and lawyers must be trained to leverage AI tools effectively while understanding their limitations. National training programs can include workshops and continuing legal education to prepare legal professionals for a tech-driven judiciary.
- **Testing Through Pilot Programs**
  Pilot projects in areas like contract law can assess AI tools' practicality, enabling policymakers to address challenges and refine integration strategies.

Through these steps, India can unlock AI's potential while safeguarding the principles of justice and equity

13.9 CONCLUSION

Procedural laws are the foundation of the judicial system, ensuring justice is delivered with precision and fairness. These laws, such as the CPC and the CrPC, regulate the judicial process, but their efficiency is increasingly questioned due to delays and backlogs. As technology evolves, especially with the rise of AI, there is a growing need for procedural reforms that integrate AI into legal practices.

Globally, AI has been used to enhance judicial efficiency, such as predictive justice in China and automated legal research in the U.S. However, in India, AI's integration into the legal system is still in its early stages. While AI holds potential to streamline procedures and improve accuracy, its adoption must be carefully managed, addressing issues like evidence admissibility, algorithmic fairness, and data privacy.

Adapting procedural laws to AI requires thoughtful amendments and ethical guidelines to ensure fairness and transparency. For instance, revising the Indian Evidence Act to include AI-generated evidence could be a crucial step. The integration of AI should be guided by principles of justice, ensuring that technological progress does not compromise the integrity of the judicial system.

NOTES

1 Reuters (2024). Illinois Supreme Court allows the use of AI tools in legal proceedings. *Reuters*. www.reuters.com/article/us-illinois-ai-court-idUSKBN1ZC2L8
2 ArXiv. (2023). General Data Protection Regulation (GDPR): Safeguarding personal data in the digital age. *ArXiv*. https://arxiv.org/abs/2309.05765
3 Supreme Court of India. (2019). *M. Siddiq (D) through LRs v. Mahant Suresh Das* (2019) 4 SCC 140.
4 Supreme Court of India. (2012). *Center for Public Interest Litigation v. Union of India* (2012) 3 SCC 1.
5 Supreme Court of India. (2017). *Vishal v. State of NCT of Delhi* (2017) 1 SCC 650.
6 Supreme People's Court of China. (2020). Annual Report on Internet Courts.
7 McMahon, P. (2023). eDiscovery: Transforming litigation in the digital era. *Harvard Law Review*.
8 European Commission. (2024). The GDPR's role in AI governance.
9 Reuters. (2024). Illinois top court says judges, lawyers can use AI with limits.
10 Supreme Court of India. (2014). *Arnesh Kumar v. State of Bihar* (2014) 8 SCC 273.
11 Supreme Court of India. (1979). *Hussainara Khatoon v. State of Bihar* (1979) 3 SCC 658.
12 Supreme Court of India. (2012). *Sahara India Real Estate Corporation Ltd. v. SEBI* (2012) 10 SCC 603.
13 U.S. Department of Justice. (2023). The use of artificial intelligence in legal research and litigation. U.S. Department of Justice.
14 European Union. (2018). General Data Protection Regulation (GDPR). European Union.
15 Zhao, Z., & Wei, J. (2023). AI-driven judicial systems: The evolution of courts in China. *Journal of Legal Technology*, 15(4), 223–245.
16 Patil, R. (2024). AI in Indian judiciary: Opportunities and challenges. *Indian Legal Review*, 32(1), 45–60.
17 Koh, M. (2023). The role of AI in modernizing legal systems. *Journal of Law and Technology*, 45(3), 78–89.

14 Utility and Efficiency of AI-Driven Legal System

Illustrations around the Globe

Bommuluri Bhavana Rao and Megha Patel

14.1 THE TERM "ARTIFICIAL INTELLIGENCE"

The technology known as "Artificial Intelligence (AI)," which is man-made and resembles human intelligence, makes the claim that it is capable of thinking like a person. AI is a science and a collection of computing tools that draw inspiration from how individuals learn, reason, and act as well as how they use their bodies, senses, and nervous systems[1].Without explicit programming, machine learning allows a machine to learn from data, enhance performance based on experiences, and make predictions[2]. It is believed to bridge the fields of computer science and statistics because it works with large amounts of data. How does it operate? When given historical data, the system analyses it and creates logical models that further forecast the results when given fresh data. Among its many applications are face recognition software, self-driving cars, social media recommendations from friends, and much more.

Artificial neural networks are the foundation of deep learning, a relatively new branch of machine learning. Its approach to learning from the data and how it does so are different from machine learning.[3] It has networks that can learn from unstructured or unlabelled data without supervision.

14.2 ARTIFICIAL INTELLIGENCE IN JUDICIAL SYSTEM

The first step in implementing AI's potential to transform the legal system is to follow the three guidelines established by Tania Sourdin in her paper, "Justice and Technological Innovation". These guidelines are as follows:

1 Supportive technology: As the name suggests, this level offers the individuals involved the majority of the help, guidance, or support. Many people are now able to learn about the justice system and locate justice services online thanks to helpful innovation, which has also fuelled the expansion of online legal services firms in recent years.

DOI: 10.1201/9781003491903-14

2 The second level of technology replaces the tasks and operations that were previously performed by people. It can be found in the modification of online court procedures to settle specific kinds of conflicts.
3 The last stage of disruptive technology results in the reformation of the methods of justice offered to the point where human decision-making is completely replaced.[4]

However, in the modern world, only first- and second-level technology is integrated into judicial changes. Some of the technical programs are designed to promote the growth and variety of conflict resolution choices rather of generating a single result based on conventional rational decision-making techniques.[5]

14.3 WORLD VIEW

Around the world, courts are being impacted differently by the wave of digital revolution. Some nations use more sophisticated strategies with practical implications in terms of legal assistance. For example, Singapore uses AI to transcribe court proceedings in real time, and Estonia uses a robot judge to decide small claims (replacement technology).To assess a person's risk assessment, the US uses COMPAS (Correctional Offender Management Profiling for Alternative Sanctions), whereas the UK uses HART (Harm Assessment Risk Tool).

In the Netherlands, an advanced ADR application called Rechtwitjerz uses AI to help a couple through the divorce or separation procedure.[6] AI is being used as a supporting technology in several nations; for example, China, Mexico, and Russia employ it to approve pensions and provide legal advice. In Argentina and Colombia, AI is utilised to detect urgent instances in a matter of minutes, whereas in Austria, it is employed for complex document management. AI is used by Malaysia to assist with sentencing judgements. The legal system is changing significantly as a result of various nations' adoption of diverse AI integration strategies.

14.4 REAL WORLD EXAMPLES OF AI IN LEGAL SERVICE

1 **Baker McKenzie:** The international law firm Baker McKenzie uses AI technologies to expedite contract analysis and due diligence. These tools have improved accuracy while drastically cutting down on the amount of time needed for these operations.
2 **JP Morgan:** JP Morgan examines commercial credit agreements using its Contract Intelligence (COIN) software. COIN can save about 360,000 hours a year by processing thousands of documents in a matter of seconds.
3 **Clifford:** Chance uses AI to manage regulatory compliance and risk analysis, ensuring adherence to complex global regulations.

14.5 KEY APPLICATIONS OF AI IN LEGAL SERVICES

AI is being applied in a number of legal practice domains, providing creative answers to age-old problems.

1 **Document Review and Management:** For attorneys, reviewing documents is one of the most time-consuming activities, especially when it comes to litigation and due diligence procedures. Natural language processing (NLP) is a technique used by AI technologies to evaluate documents, extract pertinent data, and spot trends.
Example: Millions of documents can be sorted through by eDiscovery platforms in a fraction of the time required by a human team.

2 **Contract Analysis and Drafting:** The foundation of many legal partnerships is a contract. By spotting discrepancies, making recommendations for enhancements, and guaranteeing adherence to legal requirements, AI systems can generate, evaluate, and analyse contracts more quickly.
Example: AI is used by platforms such as Luminance to expedite contract evaluation, cutting down on time by as much as 80%

3 **Legal Research:** Conventional legal research entails examining a great deal of statutes, rules, and case law. By providing accurate, relevant results based on particular searches, AI-powered solutions improve this process.
Example: IBM Watson-powered ROSS Intelligence offers specialised legal research insights.

4 **Predictive Analytics:** Legal teams can better plan by using AI's ability to forecast case outcomes based on past evidence.
Example: An AI tool called Premonition forecasts court decisions and case results using analytics.

5 **Chatbots and Virtual Assistant:** AI chatbots help clients with preliminary chores, respond to frequently asked questions, and offer rudimentary legal guidance. This lessens the workload for legal practitioners and enhances accessibility.
Example: An AI-powered chatbot called DoNotPay assists consumers with small legal matters including parking ticket contests.

6 **Compliance Management:** By automating compliance checks and identifying possible hazards, AI solutions assist businesses in staying current with rapidly evolving rules.
Example: AI is used by regulatory compliance platforms to keep an eye on international regulations and guarantee that industry standards are being followed.

14.6 BENEFITS OF AI IN LEGAL SERVICE

AI in legal services has many important benefits and is changing how law firms function and interact with their clients.

1 **Increased Efficiency:** Lawyers can concentrate on more valuable duties like client advice and legal strategy development by using AI to automate monotonous activities.
2 **Enhanced Accuracy:** In legal research and document review, human mistake is a frequent problem. AI reduces these mistakes by producing dependable and consistent outcomes.
3 **Cost Reduction:** By automating processes that would otherwise need a large amount of people, AI lowers operating expenses. Clients can now afford legal services as a result.
4 **Improved Accessibility:** Small firms and individuals who might not be able to afford traditional legal representation can now get legal services thanks to AI tools.
5 **Scalability:** The workload of law companies rises with their size. AI systems can easily grow to accommodate increased workloads.

14.7 AI AND INDIAN JUDICIARY

India is also experimenting with AI as the rest of the globe adjusts to this new idea. Indian courts seek to speed dispute settlement, automate repetitive operations, and streamline case administration by utilising AI algorithms and data analytics. The Indian courts' dedication to utilising technology for the good of the legal system and the people it serves is demonstrated by their adoption of AI. India has started a number of initiatives to achieve its goal of expediting the delivery of justice.

14.7.1 E-Court Project of Government of India

The Supreme Court of India's e-committee created the "National Policy and Action Plan for Implementation of Information and Communication Technology (ICT) in the Indian Judiciary – 2005" in order to increase judicial productivity both qualitatively and quantitatively. This led to the creation of the E-court project.[7]

Phase 1, which was introduced in 2007, was the first stage of the subordinate courts' digitisation. For the convenience of litigants and solicitors, District and Taluka Courts were computerised through the installation of hardware, LAN, and Case Information Software (CIS). Judicial officers and court employees received training on how to use the case information software, and the District Court officially opened its website.

Phase 2, which was introduced in 2015, is important to litigants, solicitors, and other interested parties. This involved the addition of hardware with a (1+3) system to the courts that had already been covered during phase 1, as well as the establishment of new, uncovered courts with a (2+6) hardware installation system.

Phase 3: The vision calls for a legal system that is easily accessible from anywhere in the world and that enhances accessibility, effectiveness, and equity for everyone looking for justice.

14.7.2 AI in Courts

AI has been welcomed into Indian courts' operations and decision-making procedures. They are aware of how AI technology can improve the administration of justice in terms of effectiveness, precision, and accessibility.

"Supreme Court Portal for Assistance in Court's Efficiency" is what AI PORTAL SUPACE stands for. This platform, which was introduced in April 2021, facilitates the judge's legal research. Its sole purpose is to process facts and provide them to judges seeking input for a judgement; it is not intended to render judgements.

"Supreme Court Vidhik Anuvaad Software," or SUVAS for short, is specialised open-source judicial software used to translate court rulings into vernacular languages and vice versa.

The Supreme Court committee has considered using AI to track cases, particularly those from the past, in addition to assisting with legal research and translating court papers.

14.7.3 AI in Criminal Justice System

The criminal justice system has changed as a result of the digital culture, particularly in the areas of crime prevention, criminal detection, criminal investigation, and prosecution. This has changed the face of law enforcement. From law enforcement to case administration, risk assessment, and sentencing, AI technologies can improve many facets of the legal system. AI has gained popularity in criminology due of its predictive capabilities.

In addition to predicting which criminals are most likely to commit new crimes, AI risk assessment algorithms like HART (Harm Assessment Risk Tool), which is integrated into the UK Criminal Justice System, also help with appropriate supervision for defendants when needed. Predictive analytics and AI are also used by the Indian Criminal Justice System to identify possible offenders, predict criminal behaviour, and notify authorities. This helps identify high-risk locations for targeted patrols .Facial recognition software driven by AI has increased the speed and precision of suspect identification.[8]

Additionally, AI is used as a tool to evaluate court rulings and assist in finding precedents, which helps to streamline case administration and analysis inside CJS. Statutes, precedents, and any other pertinent document for legal research can all be analysed with the aid of algorithms like the NLP algorithm. As was previously indicated, it is also used in nations like Malaysia to assist in sentence judgements.

As a result, AI has significantly altered how CJS operates in the modern world. To guarantee that justice is served without reinforcing prejudices or impairing human judgement, as well as in accordance with ethical principles like accountability, transparency, and privacy, its implementation must be carried out under close supervision.

14.8 LEGAL FRAMEWORK TO REGULATE AI

Global and Indian Perspective: Concerns over AI's effects on the economy, society, and human rights have grown as a result of its development and application. A legal framework to control AI's research, use, and use is becoming more and more necessary as technology becomes more widespread.

Global perspective: A new voluntary framework for creating AI products safely has been launched by a global consortium of data scientists and AI specialists. Among the 25,000 members of the World Ethical Data Foundation (WEDF) are employees of tech behemoths like Samsung, Google, and Meta. When beginning an AI project, developers can take into account the 84 questions in the framework. But as the use of AI grows, there is an increasing need for specific laws to regulate it, get rid of innate or learnt prejudice, and deal with ethical issues when applying it.

Algorithmic effect assessment and the eradication of algorithmic biases are the focus of white papers, recommendations, and policies in countries like the UK, USA, and EU.

Recently, the AI Act was amended by the European Parliament. With the exception of law enforcement, with judicial approval, the amendment would forbid the use of AI technology in biometric surveillance. It would also require generative AI systems, such as ChatGPT, to reveal information created by AI.

As AI continues to revolutionise industries and society, the legal framework for its regulation is a critical issue on a worldwide scale. Globally speaking, a number of institutions and countries have started working to create rules and policies for the responsible development and application of AI. By placing a strong emphasis on responsibility, transparency, and data protection, the General Data Protection Regulation (GDPR) of the European Union establishes a standard for AI regulation. Transparency, accountability, and human-centered values are among the guidelines responsible for AI development and application that the Organisation for Economic Co-operation and Development (OECD) has established.

A framework for the ethical development of AI has also been developed by the Institute of Electrical and Electronics Engineers (IEEE), with an emphasis on accountability, transparency, and human well-being. Additionally, the UN has started a campaign to advance AI for social good, highlighting the necessity of responsible AI development and application that respects human rights and dignity.

14.9 INDIAN PERSPECTIVE

India does not currently have any legislation specifically governing AI. The executive agency for AI-related strategies is the Ministry of Electronics and Information Technology (MEITY), which has established committees to propose an AI policy framework. Safety and reliability, equality, inclusivity and nondiscrimination, privacy and security, openness, responsibility, and the preservation and upholding of positive human values are among the seven responsible AI principles that the Niti Ayog has established.

The Constitution requires the Supreme Court and other courts to uphold fundamental rights, such as the right to privacy. The legal foundation for AI regulation in India is currently developing. With an emphasis on ethics, accountability, and transparency, the National Strategy for Artificial Intelligence (NSAI) highlights the necessity of responsible AI development and implementation. The 2019 Draft

Personal Data Protection Bill seeks to control the gathering, storing, and processing of personal information, including information utilised by AI systems. The necessity of accountability, openness, and data protection is emphasised throughout the measure. Guidelines for the responsible development, application, and use of AI are part of the AI governance framework that the Ministry of Electronics and Information Technology (MeitY) has also recommended. In order to oversee and implement data protection regulations, especially those pertaining to AI, the Indian government has also suggested creating a Data Protection Authority. Nonetheless, India currently lacks comprehensive legislation specifically addressing AI, and the laws and regulations that do exist are frequently insufficient to handle the complexity of AI.

Furthermore, MEITY has introduced the Digital Personal Data Protection Bill; however, it has not yet been formally enacted. People will be able to ask questions about the data that is gathered from them by both public and private organisations, as well as the procedures used to process and preserve it, if this measure is passed into law. Guidelines for the responsible development, application, and use of AI are part of the AI governance framework that the Ministry of Electronics and Information Technology (MeitY) has recommended. To oversee and implement data protection regulations, especially those pertaining to AI, the Indian government has suggested creating a Data Protection Authority.

The legal framework for AI regulation in India confronts a number of difficulties, such as the need to strike a balance between regulation and job displacement and skills gaps, tackling bias and discrimination in AI systems, and guaranteeing transparency and accountability. Furthermore, the question of culpability in AI-related incidents as well as the requirement for ongoing AI system monitoring and assessment must be addressed by the Indian legal system. The Indian government has made great strides in regulating AI in spite of these obstacles, and more changes to the legal environment are anticipated in the years to come.

Establishing a strong legal framework that supports responsible AI development and deployment while simultaneously defending human rights and dignity is crucial as AI continues to revolutionise businesses and societies.

14.10 CHALLENGES AND CONCERNS

A number of issues and obstacles are also brought up by the incorporation of AI in legislation, which require attention. One of the main worries is that lawyers and other legal professionals may lose their careers as AI-powered tools and platforms automate repetitive tasks. Concerns have also been raised regarding bias in AI systems, which have the potential to reinforce racial and socioeconomic prejudices already in place, producing unjust results and sustaining inequity. Furthermore, it may be challenging to comprehend how AI-powered tools get their results because to the opaqueness and inability to explain AI decision-making processes, which can be problematic in high-stakes judicial proceedings. Furthermore, relying too much on AI-powered tools may lead to a dependence on technology and a decline in lawyers' analytical and critical thinking abilities. Because AI-powered technologies need access to vast volumes of sensitive data, which might be subject to cyberattacks and data breaches, there are also worries over data security and privacy. Furthermore, uneven and untrustworthy outcomes may arise from the creation and application of AI-powered legal instruments lacking standardisation and oversight. Lastly, there are worries that AI-powered solutions will worsen already-existing power disparities in the judicial system by giving preference to those who can afford cutting-edge resources and technology. In order to guarantee that the use of AI in law is responsible, moral, and advantageous for all parties involved, it will be imperative to address these issues and concerns.

14.10.1 Can AI Really Replace Judges?

This question is worth 64 dollars. If the AI will become so powerful and useful that it will start rendering decisions in court and replace the judges. Even nevertheless, it is undeniably true that judges, being human themselves, frequently bring preconceived notions with them that influence their choices. AI is here to save the day; it can administer justice consistently and without bias. However, a judge contributes much more to society than just rendering a decision. A judge has a wide range of effects on society[9].

Judges and AI can be used as a supplementary technology, not as a substitute. Judges can benefit from the many characteristics that AI offers, such as the ability to decide on penalty or sentencing, bail issues, etc.

14.10.2 Implications of AI on the Legal Profession

It is anticipated that the use of AI in law will have a significant impact on the legal industry, changing how solicitors practise, communicate with clients, and provide legal services. The move towards a more hybrid model of legal practice, where attorneys collaborate with AI-powered tools and platforms to provide legal services, is among the most important ramifications. To effectively work with AI systems, lawyers will need to acquire new abilities including data analysis, technical literacy, and a comprehension of AI algorithms. AI will also free up lawyers to concentrate on higher-value work like strategic decision-making, intricate problem-solving, and client counselling that calls for human judgement, creativity, and empathy.

AI will also alter how solicitors communicate with their clients; chatbots and virtual assistants driven by AI will offer round-the-clock assistance and make it easier for clients to obtain legal information and services. AI will also upend established legal firm business models. AI-powered tools and platforms will allow nontraditional and new firms to enter the market, boosting competition and spurring innovation. Important ethical questions will also be brought up by the use of AI, such as making sure that AI systems are impartial, transparent, and accountable and that attorneys are aware of their possible drawbacks. In order to be relevant and competitive in the market, attorneys will ultimately need to adjust to new technology, business models, and working methods, which will need a fundamental change of the legal profession.

14.11 CONCLUSION

There is no denying AI's increasing impact on the legal field. AI technology is changing how solicitors operate, communicate with clients, and provide legal services as it develops and advances. AI offers the legal industry many benefits, such as greater productivity, accuracy, and efficiency, but it also brings up significant issues and ramifications that need to be considered.

Lawyers must be prepared to learn new skills, adjust to new technology, and reconsider conventional law firm business structures in order to fully profit from AI. This calls for a comprehensive overhaul of the legal industry, one that is fuelled by creativity, teamwork, and a dedication to quality.

In the end, how law and technology interact will determine the direction of the legal profession. It will be crucial for solicitors to keep ahead of the curve as AI develops, adopting new innovations and technology that help progress their practice, improve client results, and propel corporate success.

To sum up, the increasing impact of AI on the legal industry offers a singular chance for solicitors to reinvent their practice, rethink their role, and transform the provision of legal services. Lawyers can build a better, more sustainable future for themselves, their clients, and the legal industry overall by embracing AI and all of its advantages.

NOTES

1 B.J. Grosz, C. Russ, A. Eric, H.A. Mackworth, T. Mitchell, D. Mulligan, Y. Shoham, Artificial intelligence and life in 2030, 1 September 2016.
2 Artificial Intelligence vs. Machine Learning vs. Deep Learning: What's the difference? Built In. Available at: Artificial Intelligence vs. Machine Learning vs. Deep Learning | Built In
3 What is Deep Learning? | IBM.
4 The impact of artificial intelligence on Justice Systems – Biodiritto.
5 The impact of artificial intelligence on Justice Systems – Biodiritto.
6 Responsible-AI-in-the-Indian-Justice-System-A-Strategy-Paper.pdf
7 eCourts Mission Mode Project | Department of Justice | India.
8 AI and Indian Criminal Justice System – iPleaders.
9 The impact of artificial intelligence on Justice Systems – Biodiritto.

REFERENCES

Collins H. Artifictional intelligence: Against humanity's surrender to computers. John Wiley & Sons, 2018.

Copeland J. Artificial intelligence: A philosophical introduction. John Wiley & Sons, 1993.

Ghanghash MS. *Artificial intelligence in administration of justice in India: Challenges and opportunities*, 2022; 178–187, https://doi.org/10.55662/book.2022CCRS.008. Available at https://books.thelawbrigade.com/cyber-crime-regulations-and-security-contemporary-issues-and-challenges/artificial-intelligence-in-administration-of-justice-in-india-challenges-and-opportunities

Jain P. Artificial Intelligence for sustainable and effective justice delivery in India. *OIDA International Journal of Sustainable Development*, 2018;11(06):63–70. lawjournals.net/assets/archives/2024/vol6issue1/webster.com/dictionary/artificial intelligence

Mirza Aslam B. Role of artificial intelligence in legal education and legal profession. *Legal Service India E-Journal.*

Rajaraman V. John McCarthy—Father of artificial intelligence. *Resonance*, 2014;19:198–207.

Rowena R. Legal and human rights issues of AI: Gaps, challenges and vulnerabilities. *Journal of Responsible Technology*, 2020;4: 100005, ISSN 2666-6596. https://doi.org/10.1016/j.jrt.2020.100005

Samuel B, Abhijit S. The impacts of artificial intelligence on research in the legal profession. *International Journal of Law and Society*, 2022;5(1):53–65.

Sean S, Zeeve R. Artificial intelligence: Application today and implications tomorrow. *Duke Law & Technology Review*, 2017;16:85–99.

Shivani. Artificial intelligence in legal profession. *Supremo Amicus*, 18. ISSN 2456-9704, Available at https://supremoamicus.org/wp-content/uploads/2020/06/A1v18-99v18.pdf

Teresa R. Legal challenges of artificial intelligence: Modelling the disruptive features of emerging technologies and assessing the possible legal impact. *Uniform Law Review*, 2019;24(2):302–314.

Index

Made in the USA
Las Vegas, NV
19 September 2026

4742ace5-1490-4615-b77c-9d60c477538aR01